# ON YOUR FEET

# ON YOUR FEET

## Criminal Law Practice
in the Parish Courts in Jamaica

Nadine C. Atkinson-Flowers

The **C**aribbean Law
PUBLISHING COMPANY

Kingston • Miami

First published in Jamaica, 2021 by
The Caribbean Law Publishing Company
*An imprint of* Ian Randle Publishers
16 Herb McKenley Drive
Box 686
Kingston 6
www.ianrandlepublishers.com

**NATIONAL LIBRARY OF JAMAICA CATALOGUING-IN-PUBLICATION DATA**

Name: Atkinson-Flowers, Nadine C., author.
Title: On your feet : criminal law practice in the Parish Courts of Jamaica /
    Nadine C. Atkinson-Flowers.
Description: Kingston : Caribbean Law Publishing Company, 2021. | Includes
    index.
Identifiers: ISBN 9789768167958 (pbk) | ISBN 9789769628335 (e-bk)
Subjects: LCSH: Courts – Jamaica. | Criminal courts – Jamaica. | Criminal
    procedure (Law) – Jamaica. | Procedure (Law) – Jamaica.
Classification: DDC  347.02504 – dc23.

Cover and Book Design by The Caribbean Law Publishing Company
Printed and Bound in the United States of America

# Contents

# List of Figures and Tables

# Table of Cases

# Table of Statutes

# List of Secondary Legislation

# Acronyms and Abbreviations

The following are some of the most common acronyms used in the Parish Courts. These notations often appear in the endorsement of files, the court sheet and the records of police officers in the court. Notably too, as files are dealt with in the court by the Clerk of the Courts such acronyms are of great value as they can be written on the case files and used when one is on one's feet. This helps to save time and capture key details as the Parish Court's pace is often quite hectic.

| | |
|---|---|
| Absent …………………………………… .Abs | Legal Aid Assignment……………………… .LAA |
| Accused ………………………… ..A/Acc/ A^ | Mention. ……………………………………… M |
| Arresting Officer ……………………… ...AO | Next Court Date …………………………… NCD |
| Assault Occasioning Bodily Harm ……… … Ass. OBH | No Case Submission ……………………… NCS |
| Bail Extended ……………………………… ...BE | Not Before Court . ………………………… NBC |
| Bail Offer………………………………… B/O | Own Surety ………………………………… .O/S |
| Bench Warrant to Issue ………………… .BWI | Parish Court Judge/Judge |
| Bound Over…………………………… .. BO |   of the Parish Court ……………… ..J/PCJ/JPC |
| Causing Death by Dangerous Driving ……… . CDDD | Part Heard Committal Proceedings ……… ..PHCP |
| Committal Proceedings …………… .. CP/ Comm. Proc. | Part Heard Hearing .. …………………… PHH |
| Complainant. ………………………… C/Compl | Part Heard Trial ………………………… PHT |
| Court . ……………………………… Ct/C | Present.. …………………………… Pres/P |
| Custody ………………………………… .C | Question and Answer…………………… Q&A |
| Defendant ……………………………… .D | Remanded in Custody.. ………………… ...RIC/RC |
| Defendant Not Appearing ……………… DNA | Reissued …………………………………… .R |
| Driving Away Motor Vehicle | Reissued on Application . ……………… ..RIA |
|   Without Owner's Consent ………… . DAMVWOC | Same Bail Offer ………………………… SBO |
| Finger Print Order. …………………… FPO | Subpoena . ……………………………… .. Subp |
| Forensic Certificate .. …………………… ...FC | Subpoena Done ………………………… S/D |
| Government Forensic Laboratory …………… .GFL | Subpoena Investigating Officer ……………… . SIO |
| Hearing . ………………………………… .H | Subpoena Witness………………………… .SW/S/W |
| Identification Parade …………………… ID P | Summary .. ……………………………… .S |
| Identification of Body Witness. …………… .ID BW | Trial …………………………………… . T |
| Indictable.. ……………………………… ..I | Virtual Complainant. …………………… ...VC |
| Investigating Officer . ………………… IO | Witness. ………………………………… W |
| Investigating Officer Bound Over. …………… ...IOBO | Wounding With Intent .. ………………… WWI |
| Last Court Date ……………………… LCD | |

# Foreword

The efficient operation of the Parish Courts (formerly Resident Magistrate's Court) in Jamaica has had at its core the intersection of the functions and roles of all the stakeholders namely the Parish Court Judge, the Clerk of the Courts, the court staff including the Deputy Clerk of the Courts ("Deputy Clerk") and Assistant Clerk of the Clerk of Courts ("Assistant Clerk"), defence attorneys and the Police.

Clerks of Courts, defence attorneys and to a certain extent new members of the Parish Court Bench, up to this point, have largely gained their knowledge of the practical aspects of court practice from the institutional memories of more experienced court users and learning while doing, during the course of their work activities.

I recall clearly when I was a young graduate of the Norman Manley Law School in 1984 reporting shortly thereafter to the St James Parish Court, then St James Resident Magistrate's Court, on assignment as a newly minted Clerk of Courts. There was no official orientation session as there is presently. One was literally thrown into the deep-end to sink or swim. It was thought that this built character and grit, that is, if you survived. All one was armed with was the knowledge of the law derived from academia at the Law faculty and the Law School. There was no textbook, no manual or handbook that incorporated all of the material needed to guide you, practically speaking, in one place. It was a given that one had to rely on the generosity of the administrative staff, Deputy Clerk, other existing Clerks of Courts, very experienced Police Officers, defence counsel who did not hesitate to make their expertise and critically, their institutional memories, available to guide you at the beginning of this part of your professional journey. On the odd occasion, one also benefitted from the admonition from the Bench. It goes without saying, that variations of this may have been the experience of all other stakeholders coming into the system at the commencement of their careers depending on their entry level and core function.

It is quite clear that the purpose of this publication is to cure that deficit.

Experience has shown that the misapplication of the law, lack of knowledge, lack of understanding or the lack of proper execution of the practice by any stakeholder in the Parish Court may cause professional embarrassment which may, as a matter of law, cause a negative effect or unintended consequences. It cannot be denied, from the case law, that misapplication of the law and lack of sufficient appreciation of the practice/protocols has resulted in the allowance or dismissal of appeals depending on your perspective.

This book *On Your Feet: Criminal Law Practice in the Parish Court in Jamaica* provides an excellent guide and compendium of the intricacies and nuances attached to the duties of Clerk of Courts, Parish Court Judges, Deputy and Assistant Clerks, defence counsel, probation officers and the Police. I cannot recall having seen such a detailed and thorough collation of the criminal practice in this area which has effectively connected the dots between the law, practice and the procedure in many different areas in the Parish Court. I foresee that this work will become a highly valued and sought after training manual for all new stakeholders entering practice in their respective functions within the Parish Courts.

This publication spans all areas of the practice in the Parish Courts describing the roles, functions and responsibilities of court officers. It also outlines many sample forms in respect of different areas of the practice which have been helpfully exhibited. There is also the exposition of the law, likely court orders, definitions, offences, case law and legislation which are dealt with by Prosecutors and the Court on a regular basis. Within the context of the Parish Court scheme, we are wonderfully immersed in best practices, procedures and protocols relating to Committal Proceedings, file preparation, expert witnesses, the use of Section 31 of the Evidence Act and other statutory authorities to a name a few.

Not only is this a helpful guide to new counsel, judges and civil practitioners alike, but it may also enure to the benefit of members of the Police Force as it touches and concerns best practices, protocols and sample documents which are within their purview as they interface with court officers in bringing accused persons before the court.

It was with some nostalgia that I read the section on 'Courtesy Useful Words in the Courtroom.' Fortunately, I was well mentored by senior practitioners who made sure that I was *au fait* with these courtesy words and phrases. Having them helpfully reflected in this publication means that it is documented to the benefit of law students aspiring to be advocates as well as a reminder to all of the collegiality and professional courtesies that should obtain in the courtroom between all the parties.

When this book is made available in the public space, it is my view that the administration of justice will be the ultimate beneficiary as it will definitely enhance the capacity and knowledge base of new stakeholders as well as being a refresher for seasoned practitioners. It will place each stakeholder in the best position to enhance each other's contribution through the maintenance of high professional standards in our respective core functions which by extension will be advantageous to the public that we all serve.

I have had the pleasure of working with the author, Mrs Nadine Atkinson-Flowers, when she was a colleague at both the Clerk of the Courts level and as Assistant Director of Public Prosecutions at the Office of the Director of Public Prosecutions. I am delighted to see reflected in this work her customary diligence, great work ethic, thoroughness, attention to detail and keen intellectual acuity. I salute this very professional and excellent effort and with best wishes I look forward in the future to Volume Two.

**Paula V. Llewellyn, CD, QC**
*Director of Public Prosecutions*

# Introduction

This book provides a guide for the duties of the Clerk of the Courts in the Parish Court and eases the transition into learning and mastering the intricacies of working in the courts. As it focuses on criminal practice and procedure, the Clerk of the Courts, deputy Clerks of the Courts, and assistant Clerks, and other members of the prosecuting arm, can refer readily to it.

Law students with an interest in criminal practice should also find this book useful.

This guide is equally invaluable to defence counsel, civil practitioners who have clients with criminal cases, and new practitioners unfamiliar with the procedures and practices in the Parish Court, as it condenses the court's functioning. Lastly, the Parish Court Judge can use this book as a ready reference as well.

Within this book, the statutes of significance are many and varied, but there are several that should be familiar to all practitioners. These include the Evidence Act, the Judicature (Parish Courts) Act, the Justices of the Peace Jurisdiction Act, the Bail Act, the Recognizance of Sureties Act, the Dangerous Drugs Act, the Road Traffic Act, Offences Against the Person Act and the Sexual Offences Act.

In *On Your Feet*, the use of the term Clerk may refer variously to the Clerk, deputy Clerk, or assistant Clerk who prosecutes matters before the Parish Court Judge. The book clearly sets out the statutory authority, the roles, responsibilities, and functions of these officers who are critical to the administration of justice in the Parish Court.

The practice in the island's Parish Courts tend to vary, sometimes slightly, other times significantly and so this publication seeks to bring together best practices.

# Chapter 1

# Jurisdiction and the Court Structure in the Parish Court

## Summary

The Parish Courts were called the Resident Magistrate Courts for over a century, under the then Judicature (Resident Magistrates) Act, and the judges of the Parish Court were called Resident Magistrates under the same Act. The Judicature (Resident Magistrates) (Amendment and Change of Name) Act renamed the courts to be the Parish Courts. It also renamed the Resident Magistrate, to be now known as the Judge of the Parish Court. The Parish Court has both civil and criminal jurisdiction and its legal officers are usually attorneys-at-law, licensed by the General Legal Council and entitled to practice law in Jamaica.

## Terms _____

Jurisdiction of the Parish Court

The Parish Court

The Chief Parish Court Judge

The Judge of the Parish Court

Clerk of the Courts

Other Court Staff

_____

For the purposes of this book, the terms 'Judge of the Parish Court' and 'Parish Court Judge' will be used interchangeably. The 'Court' refers to the Parish Court Judge while s/he is sitting. The 'court' refers to the general court machinery. The terms 'Clerk of the Courts' and 'Clerk' will be used interchangeably. The term 'attorney-at-law' and 'attorney' will be used interchangeably. The term 'defence attorney' and the 'defence' or 'defence counsel' will be used interchangeably to mean the 'attorney-at-law/attorney' representing an accused. The term 'accused' and 'defendant' will be used interchangeably to represent the accused. S/he will be used to represent he and she.

## Jurisdiction of the Parish Court

Section 267 of the Judicature (Parish Courts) Act (JPCA) says that for the purposes of the criminal law, the jurisdiction of every court shall extend to the parish for which the Court is appointed and one mile beyond the boundary line of the said parish.

## The Parish Court

The Interpretation Section of the JPCA states that a 'Judge of a Parish Court'[1] means the officer appointed as a Parish Court Judge. Accordingly, s/he is to be styled 'the Parish Court Judge for the parish of ——.'[2] It also states that 'Court' means the Court in which the Parish Court Judge sits in the exercise of the civil or criminal jurisdiction assigned.[3]

Importantly, the Parish Court Judge has both civil and criminal jurisdiction. The Parish Court Judge may hold a position of an acting Parish Court Judge for a parish or be appointed as a Parish Court Judge for a parish. In the Parish Courts in the Corporate Area, there are specific and separate criminal, civil, family, and traffic divisions of the Parish Court.[4] In the other parishes, there are no such separations and so the sitting Parish Court Judges may well hear criminal, civil, traffic, and criminal matters at specified times or on particular days.

Accordingly:

> In each of the fourteen parishes of the Island there shall be a Court, to be styled the Parish Court for the parish of, with so many stations as may from time to time be fixed by the Minister, which shall have and exercise the jurisdiction by this Act assigned to and conferred upon such Court.[5]

The term 'outstation' is often used for the courts that are located in other parts of a parish. Outstations handle both criminal and civil matters and may possibly only sit on particular days. A Parish Court Judge as well as a Clerk of the Courts travels to these outstations on the requisite days.[6]

Matters that have their genesis in Kingston or St Andrew are heard in the Corporate Area Parish Court (Criminal Division/Civil Division/Traffic/Family) where jurisdiction lies.[7] This is a direct result of the provision in the JPCA, which stipulates that for the purposes of the Act, the jurisdiction for Kingston and St Andrew 'shall extend over the entire Corporate Area.'[8] Therefore, if the allegation is that the incident occurred in either Kingston or St Andrew, then the Corporate Area Parish Court has jurisdiction over the case. Jurisdiction may, therefore, become problematic if the incident is alleged to have occurred in one parish and the matter is being tried in another.[9]

## Chief Judge of the Parish Courts[10]

This position was created by the JPCA as was the position of executive legal officer.[11] There is a full discussion on these posts in the chapter on the Parish Court Judge.

---

1. Section 2 of the Judicature (Parish Courts) Act. See too, *Eric Alexander v R* 81 WIR 401; also see how jurisdiction has been extended to the high seas per s. 19(6) Exclusive Economic Zone Act; s. 10 Maritime Areas Act; s. 21 Maritime Drug Trafficking (Suppression) Act.
2. Section 3 of the Judicature (Parish Courts) Act.
3. Section 2 of the Judicature (Parish Courts) Act.
4. In section 3 of the Judicature (Parish Courts) Act. There is also sheer volume in the area designated 'Corporate Area' and, as such, the area accounts for a significant portion of cases before the court in any given year.
5. Outstations include Linstead, Christiana and Claremont to name a few.
6. Section 3A of the Judicature (Parish Courts) Act.
7. Supra. See too, the Morant and Pedro Cays Act where section 3 states 'The Morant Cays and Pedro Cays shall, for all purposes other than taxation, be deemed to be within and form part of the parish of Kingston.'
8. Section 9(1) of the Criminal Justice (Administration) Act.
9. Section 13 of the Judicature (Parish Courts) Act.
10. Section 4A of the Judicature (Parish Courts) Act.
11. See Section 15A of the Judicature (Parish Courts) Act.

## Senior Parish Court Judge

In practice, the senior Parish Court Judge should have many years standing as an attorney-at-law and may have been recruited to the bench from the private or public bar. S/he may have also served in the capacity of Parish Court Judge for various parishes over the years. The senior Parish Court Judge is the de facto supervisor of the legal and administrative staff in the particular Parish Court.

Currently, the legal staff report to the senior Parish Court Judge (but see information in chapter on the Clerk's duties), and the administrative and ancillary officers report to the court administrator.

## Judge of the Parish Court[12]

The Parish Court Judge must have a minimum of seven years standing as an attorney-at-law, be a member of the Bar in Jamaica, England, or otherwise as specified in the JPCA and fulfils the other prerequisites of the Act.

The Parish Court Judge may initially act as a Parish Court Judge and as such his or her jurisdiction might be limited to a particular parish.

## Clerks of the Courts[13]

There is no minimum standing for an attorney-at-law to be appointed as a Clerk of the Courts. The Clerk of the Courts is the prosecuting officer in the court and, therefore, combines prosecutorial and administrative duties. Notably, the Clerk of the Courts is appointed by the Offices of the Service Commission, and the interview process to become a Clerk of the Courts involves the Chief Justice of Jamaica and other officers of the commission.

## Other Court Staff

### Deputy Clerks of the Courts[14]

Most parish courts have multiple deputy Clerks of the Courts, who have some legal training. They prosecute matters in the same manner as the Clerk of the Courts and also assume administrative duties.

### Court Administrator

The court administrator is not required to have a legal background, but some do and these officers operate the daily administrative aspects of the court such as the physical plant, infrastructure, and administrative staff.

### Assistant Clerks of the Courts[15]

The assistant Clerk of the Courts is also able to prosecute matters.

### Administrative and Ancillary Staff

The administrative and ancillary staff finish the complement of staff in the Parish Court.

---

12. Section 3 of the Judicature (Parish Courts) Act. Section 12(1)(b) of the Judicature (Parish Courts) Act states that a Parish Court Judge must have been an attorney-at-law for no less than seven years. Section 15 of the Judicature (Parish Courts) Act states that 'Every Parish Court Judge shall be *ex officio a Justice of the Peace for every parish in the Island.'*
13. Section 16 of the Judicature (Parish Courts) Act.
14. Sections 18, 21, 22, 23, 24 of the Judicature (Parish Courts) Act.
15. Section 20 of the Judicature (Parish Courts) Act.

# Chapter 2

# Scope of the Duties of the Clerk of the Courts

## Summary

The Clerk of the Courts is a crucial officer in the Parish Court system and has multiple responsibilities. The most crucial responsibility is to prosecute cases in the criminal jurisdiction of the Parish Courts. Section 289 of the Judicature (Parish Courts) Act (JPCA) indicates that:

> in trials for indictable offences and in summary offenses, prosecutions for such classes of offences as the Minister may from time to time direct, *the Clerk of the Courts shall* (emphasis added), excepting in cases where a barrister, advocate, or solicitor appears on behalf of the prosecution and cases in which the Director of Public Prosecutions or someone deputed by him conducts the prosecution, *be the officer to conduct the prosecutions* (emphasis added).

This is crucial when the Clerk of the Courts is faced with significant challenges to his role and functions; therefore, this must become his mantra.

At section 290 of the said Act, it states that:

> The Clerk of the Courts in addition to conducting the prosecution in summary cases for such classes of offenses...shall conduct any particular case irrespectively of the class of offence charged therein, which he may be required by the Minister or the Director of Public Prosecutions to prosecute.

Clerks of the Courts make crucial prosecutorial decisions regarding matters before the court. The importance of this position cannot be overstated. The Clerk of the Courts is usually referred to as 'the Clerk' despite the fact that the proper title is styled 'the Clerk of the Courts'.

## Terms _____

Jurisdiction

Qualifications

Custodian of the Records

Specific Statutory Duties

Duties Regarding Bail

Notes of Evidence to the Court of Appeal

Immunities of the Clerk of the Courts

Broad Administrative Duties

Historical Matters for the Clerk of the Courts

Effecting the Orders of the Judge of the Parish Court

The Future of the Clerk of the Courts

_____

## Jurisdiction

The JPCA indicates that the Clerk of the Courts is 'styled the Clerk of the Courts of the parish of ———.'[1] The Clerk of the Courts is also an ex-officio Justice of the Peace for the parish in which s/he is appointed, or is acting by virtue of the said section. As such, the Clerk of the Courts can witness signatures and sign documents relevant to the court's proper administration.

## Qualifications

The Clerk of the Courts is a qualified attorney-at-law.[2] There is, however, no requirement for a minimum number of years at the Jamaican Bar unlike the position of a Parish Court Judge. As such, Clerks may be appointed immediately upon admission to the Jamaican Bar and may have no practical legal experience. The Clerk of the Courts is appointed for a parish and marshals evidence on behalf of the Crown, and also attends to many administrative matters in the court system. In court buildings with multiple courtrooms, a Clerk of the Courts is usually assigned to a particular courtroom, but is expected to assist in any court that has no Clerk of the Courts present on a particular day.

By virtue of section 17 of the JPCA, it is lawful for the Governor-General to periodically appoint additional Clerks for any parish. The Clerk of the Courts is a gazetted officer and, therefore, his or her acting and/or appointment information appears in the Jamaica Gazette.

## Custodian of the Records

The JPCA indicates that:

> The Records...shall be kept and preserved in the office of the Court...the Clerk of the Courts for the parish in which such place is situated, shall be the custodian thereof, and shall have the same authority to furnish copies of the same and to sign and certify the same under the seal of the court, as is by this Act conferred on him with regard to the records of the Parish Court; and the copies furnished as aforesaid and purporting to be signed and certified as aforesaid shall be admissible in evidence....[3]

This is a crucial function that runs the gamut of activities in a court, ranging from signing and certifying notes of evidence in a trial matter going on appeal to signing a myriad of other documentation that form part of the proper functioning of the court.

The Clerk of the Courts must ensure that a sound legal basis exists for all decisions made and, therefore, must critically appraise all documents before signing. Thus, the Clerk of the Courts should always have the requisite written supporting materials before signing any document such as court orders, court sheets, and case files.

For the most part, many documents, especially those that need to be signed, may be prepared by other court staff. It is always prudent for the Clerk of the Courts to ask questions and/or read the relevant Acts before appending a signature and the court's Seal if a document is unclear or the reason for a decision appears problematic.

---

1. Section 16 of the Judicature (Parish Courts) Act.
2. Section 19 of the Judicature (Parish Courts) Act speaks of the qualification of the Clerk of the Courts. The requirement is that s/he must be a member of the Bar of Jamaica or of England or of Northern Ireland or the Faculty of Advocates of Scotland, or a writer to the Signet, or a solicitor of the Supreme Court or of the Supreme Court of England, Scotland or Northern Ireland, or a law agent admitted to practice in Scotland.
3. Section 9 of the Judicature (Parish Courts) Act.

### The Court Seal

Any official court document that bears the signature of the Clerk of the Courts must carry the court's seal.[4] It is also commonly called the court stamp. Therefore, every summons as well as other process issuing out of the court shall be sealed or stamped.

## Specific Functions of the Clerk of the Courts

The legal functions of the Clerk of the Courts under section 16 of the JPCA are wide ranging and details the myriad of duties prescribed. It should be consulted regularly. Since the functions are so broad, it is useful to examine the ones that most commonly occur in some detail.

### Taking Information

Under section 16 of the JPCA, the taking of information is one of the core tasks of a Clerk of the Courts. When a police officer has arrested someone or a private prosecution has begun, the Clerk of the Courts must sign the relevant place on the number one information form that essentially begins the matter.[5] 'The document is often styled the 'number one information', 'the number one', or 'number ones' among criminal law practitioners. The police officer is required to complete all the relevant sections on the form for matters where the defendant was arrested or summoned. The court staff members who are so assigned complete the requisite sections of the number one information for private prosecutions. When a case file is submitted, the court staff will also give the number one information a chronological number.

If there are multiple offences, each has a number one information with the chronological number.

Victims or complainants in private prosecutions typically do not know the relevant offence's correct wording. Arresting or investigating officers (for arrestable/summoned offences) may also not know the specific wording for offences. Therefore, the Clerk of the Courts must ensure the correct wording on all offences or run the risk of the trial being a nullity. Under sections 9 and 10 respectively of the Justices of the Peace Jurisdiction Act, every information shall be for one offence only and, in all cases, the information shall be laid, 'within six calendar months from the time when the matter of such complaint or information respectively arose'.

It is, therefore, incumbent upon the Clerk of the Courts to ensure that the provision is explicitly adhered to in the information.

The Clerk of the Courts must check the dates on which the information was laid to ensure that s/he has the *locus standi* to sign it. Where such case files pre-date an appointment, a Clerk of the Courts who was so appointed and or acting at the time should be asked to sign.

### Administer Oaths

Persons who must swear to particular documents regarding matters before the Parish Court can do so before the Clerk of the Courts in his/her capacity of an ex-officio Justice of the Peace. These documents can include bail forms, copies of identification, *habeas corpus* documents, and even forms not related specifically to the court.

### Sign Summonses

A summons is a court document directed to the defendant in a private prosecution (matters brought to the court by the victim or complainant), when no arrest was initially made, or when the defendant may be

---

4. Section 11 of the Judicature (Parish Courts) Act.
5. See commencement of indictment, per section 287, Schedule E of the Judicature (Parish Courts) Act.

unaware that attendance in court is required. The summons thus constitutes notice. It is signed by the Clerk of the Courts and sent to the process office to be served on the defendant by the relevant court process service officers. For private prosecutions, it is the responsibility of the complainant to ensure the defendant is served.

**Figure 2.1     Sample of Summons**

---

**18**

**PETTY SESSIONS-FORM Y**

                                                    **Summons to Person Charged**

**JAMAICA SS.**

Parish of          Kingston          }

                                      }

To                 Tom Adams          }

                                      }

of the said parish


WHEREAS Information hath this day been laid before the undersigned, one of Her Majesty's Justices of the Peace in and for the said parish of    Kingston

that you    assaulted Mary Adams

on the   21st day of May

in the year of Our Lord two thousand and ----

at the said parish of      Kingston                    and within my jurisdiction


against the form of the Statute in such case made and provided and against the Peace or Our Sovereign Lady the Queen, her Crown and Dignity.

These are therefore, to require you,   in Her Majesty's name to be and appear on the

21st              day of              October

two thousand and ----                          at ten o'clock in the forenoon at the Court House at the Corporate Area Parish Court (Criminal Division) before such Justices of the Peace

for the said parish of              Kingston         as may then be there to answer to the said Complaint and to be further dealt with according to Law.

     Given under my hand this          21st                    day of      June


in the year of Our Lord two thousand and    ----

at the parish aforesaid

---

A summons must, therefore, be sent to the defendant, which puts him properly before the Parish Court. The summons thus compels the defendant to come to court on the date contained therein.[6]

## Service of Summons

The summons is to be personally or inmately served upon the defendant. Inmate service means that the summons is left with an adult of suitable age and discretion when personal service is impractical. The summons is to accompany the copy of the victim's statement (which would have been taken by a court officer such as an assistant Clerk) in a private prosecution. Notably, the copy summons is to be duly endorsed, as to whether service was personal or inmate. The copy summons is to be returned to court and placed on the relevant file and the court appropriately informed when the matter is called up in court. This is colloquially called the 'returns'. The Clerk must peruse the case file to ascertain that there are such 'returns' on the file to be able to properly advise the Parish Court Judge about service.

If the defendant does not appear, having been personally served, a warrant of disobedience of summons can be drawn for such a person.[7] If service was inmate, and the defendant does not appear, a new summons can be issued, and would, in effect, be called a 're-issued summons'.

For cases where the Crown is the complainant, a police officer will serve the summons on the defendant (such as the investigating or arresting officer or the police officers at the process service office).

## Specific Information on Subpoenas

When a matter is before the court, to ensure that required persons give evidence or information to the court, a subpoena can be sent to such a person to require their attendance.[8] When such a witness first attends on the court, he is usually bound over to attend court on a subsequent date that the matter will be before the court or on a particular date. Where such subpoenas are served and there is evidence of such service (i.e., the service information is written on the back of the copy subpoena) and the witness does not attend, the Judge of the Parish Court can issue and sign a warrant in disobedience of service of the subpoena for that person.[9]

This is a powerful tool that is available to the Court as the witness can actually be placed in custody for failing to attend if it proven that he was previously and properly served the subpoena. If the witness is so placed in custody, upon appearing before the Judge of the Parish Court, s/he can be admitted to bail in such terms as the Judge of the Parish Court deems fit.[10]

Witnesses, therefore, should know the importance of attending court when they have been subpoenaed, served, and subsequently bound over. Subpoenas can be issued and signed by the Clerk of the Courts for defence and prosecution witnesses. Indeed, it is not unusual to hear the Judge of the Parish Court ask the defence counsel if s/he wants subpoenas for witnesses.[11] Crucially, section 281 of the JPCA indicates that it shall be the duty of the Clerk of the Courts, with the assistance of the relevant officer of the Jamaica Constabulary Force (usually the investigating officer or the arresting officer), to procure the attendance of all necessary prosecution and defence witnesses.

---

6. See summons to the defendant upon an information or complaint per section 2, form 1, First Schedule of the Justices of the Peace Jurisdiction Act.
7. See warrant where the summons is disobeyed per section 3 of the Justices of the Peace Jurisdiction Act form 2 First schedule.
8. Such attendance can be secured by the court per the provisions of the Justices of the Peace Jurisdiction Act at sections 47 and by Forms 27 and 29.
9. Ibid.
10. Section 50 of the Justices of the Peace Jurisdiction Act.
11. Section 47 of the Justices of the Peace Jurisdiction Act.

**The Subpoena Duces Tecum**

One particular type of subpoena is the subpoena *duces tecum*, which is an instruction to a person or an entity to be present with an item in court or to have said item brought to court on the date in the subpoena. This wide-ranging power is conferred by section 48 of the Justices of the Peace Jurisdiction Act upon the Court in the person of the Judge of the Parish Court.[12] It is the Parish Court Judge who orders and signs the order for this particular subpoena.

The order is completed in duplicate by court staff for signature. It is then dispatched to the relevant police personnel for service. It is usually the investigator in the matter, another police officer, or the process office who will effect service accordingly and present the 'returns' as described above.

**Issue All Other Process or Proceedings Relating to Summary Proceedings or Indictable Offences**

Regarding indictable offences, section 29 of the Justices of the Peace Jurisdiction Act describes the information and gives the Judge of the Parish Court the power to order and sign a warrant to apprehend a defendant.[13] Under the same section, the summons to a person charged with an indictable offence is directed to the defendant. As such, it states:

> 'To *A.B.,* of                     (labourer) Whereas, you have this day been charged before the undersigned (one) of Her Majesty's Justices of the Peace....'[14]

**Admit to Bail Any Person on Recognizance**

When a person is admitted to bail by the Judge of the Parish Court, there are several documents the Clerk must sign during the bail processing. These include the notice to surety, which is the instruction and information to the person legally responsible for ensuring that the defendant honours all terms and conditions of the bail, including returning to court on every subsequent occasion.[15] The Clerk also signs the statutory declaration by surety.[16]

Significantly, if the defendant does not honour the bail conditions and absconds, a bench warrant may be ordered for his or her arrest. The Judge of the Parish Court may estreat the bonds at this time. The bonds are bail bonds – the monetary pledge of surety that the defendant will return to court until the case is disposed of. Regarding the surety, a Clerk must sign an accompanying warrant of *distingas* and *capias* so that the amount previously pledged as the bail sum can be disgorged from the surety and be paid into the court.

**Clerk of the Courts and Warrants**

Under section 16 of the JPCA, the Clerk does not have the authority to sign bench warrants. These are signed only by the Judge of the Parish Court for the apprehension of defendants or other such persons for whom a bench warrant is duly issued.

---

12. Section 48 of the Justices of the Peace Jurisdiction Act. This power is quite broadly construed and 'shall be deemed to include the power to summon and require a witness to produce to such court books, plans, papers, documents, articles, goods and things likely to be material evidence on the hearing of any charge, information, or complaint....'
13. Section 29 of the Justices of the Peace Jurisdiction Act, First Schedule Form 15 is the information, and Form 16 is the warrant for the apprehension of a defendant.
14. Per section 29 of the Justices of the Peace Jurisdiction Act, First Schedule Form 17 is the form called summons to a person charged with an indictable offense. Form 18 is the form called warrant where the summons is disobeyed.
15. See the Recognizance and Surety Act, s. 4.
16. See Bail Act, s. 17.

The Clerk is however charged to sign warrants for the commitment of convicted persons to prison,[17] of arrest and for searches.

### Lay Magistrate Court Duties

Under the section, one duty of the Clerk is to attend the Lay Magistrate Court. This Court was previously called the Courts of Petty Session. By virtue of the Renaming of the Courts of Petty Sessions Miscellaneous Amendments 2018, the name of the court was changed to the current nomenclature. The Clerks assist the sitting Justices of the Peace with matters of law. In furtherance of these duties, the Clerk is also empowered to issue summonses, warrants, or subpoenas for compelling the appearance of defendants or witnesses at court sessions. Usually, either a deputy Clerk or an assistant Clerk is assigned to this court.

### Indictment Form

The Clerk signs the indictment form for indictable trials in the requisite place.[18] This is done where a defendant has pleaded guilty and is to be sentenced or if he has pleaded not guilty and the indictable trial has started and he has been pleaded to the count(s).

## Cases that are Being Appealed to the Court of Appeal

Where a case is being appealed by the now convict, the requisite documents must be sent to the Court of Appeal within 14 days. The Clerk of the Courts signs the certificate stating that the documents are certified as true copies of the original. The documents are noted under section 299 of the JPCA which also stipulates that the record of the case together with the certified notes of evidence as well as any material admitted into evidence should be transmitted.[19] The notes of evidence consists of the evidence taken by the Judge of the Parish Court along with any documents so admitted as exhibits in the case. All of these are sent to the Court of Appeal.[20]

## Other Issues

Under the JPCA, the Clerk of the Courts 'has no authority to take the preliminary examination, or depositions on informations for indictable offences under the Justices of the Peace Jurisdiction Act or to commit for trial under that Act.'[21] Indeed, the Act further states that the Clerk 'shall not be competent to act as a Justice either alone or with any other Justice, in anything which is to be done at the Lay Magistrate Court or Special Petty Session.'[22] The Clerk of the Courts is also prohibited under section 25 of the JPCA from engaging in

---

17. Per section 16 of the Judicature (Parish Courts) Act.
18. Per section 289 and 290 of the Judicature (Parish Courts) Act, the Clerk of the Courts prosecutes indictable and summary cases before the court. Please also examine section 27 of the Judicature (Parish Courts) Act that deals with notes of evidence.
19. Per section 27 of the Judicature (Parish Court) Act, the Clerk of the Courts, or in his absence the Assistant Clerk, or such Clerk as may be directed by the Judge of the Parish Court, shall take notes of evidence in every case heard summarily before either the Court or the Lay Magistrates' Court; and the Judge of the Parish Court shall take notes of the evidence in the trial of all indictments and in all civil suits, and such notes, heretofore taken, or hereafter to be taken, by the Judge of the Parish Court, or a copy thereof, purporting to bear the seal of the Court, and to be signed and certified as a true copy by the Clerk of the Courts, shall at all times be admitted in all Courts and places whatsoever, in the trial or hearing of all civil proceedings suits and matters, for the purpose of impeaching the credit or contradicting the evidence of any person in accordance with the provisions of sections 15 and 17 of the Evidence Act, as prima facie evidence that the statements therein appearing to have been made by such person were so made.
20. Per section 299 of the Judicature (Parish Courts) Act.
21. Per section 16 of the Judicature (Parish Courts) Act.
22. Ibid.

'mercantile pursuits' or practising at the private bar.[23] Instructively, the Judge of the Parish Court is also so prohibited from such pursuits.

## Immunities of the Clerk of the Courts

One crucial feature of section 16 of the JPCA is that a Clerk of the Courts while executing his office is 'entitled to all the immunities, privileges and protection, conferred on Justices.' The Clerk of the Courts, thus, should fearlessly and fairly exercise his or her duties under the protection of the law. With the repeal of section 25 of the JPCA, there is no longer a requirement that the Clerk of the Courts reside within such parish as the Governor-General may from time to time approve. This is a clear and practical recognition of the fact that often times Clerks of the Courts reside outside of the parish where they perform their duties.

## Broad Administrative Duties

The statutory duties of the Clerk of the Courts will dictate all of the administrative duties that are performed and as such the descriptors following below are really for ease of reference.

There is a wide gamut of administrative functions that are related to the duties of the Clerk. These include:

### Writing Correspondence to the Director of Public Prosecution (DPP)

The Clerk of the Courts may have to write the DPP for advice on matters, to request *nolle prosequis*,[24] and the like. The DPP's office may also have to be updated about matters in the Parish Court that it may have made a ruling on.

Under section 290 of the JPCA, the Clerk of the Courts may be required to take instructions from the DPP or the Minister in the prosecution of certain matters.[25]

### Rulings on Files

The Clerk of the Courts may occasionally be requested to provide opinion rulings on files from the Jamaica Constabulary Force (JCF). Complete rulings are provided on files presented formally to the Clerk of the Courts.

### Duties under the Drug Court (Treatment of Offenders) Act

The Clerk of the Courts undertakes the related duties arising under the Drug Court (Treatment of Offenders) Act. The Drug Court assists drug-addicted persons who are willing to undertake a programme of detoxification.

### Writing Correspondence to Other Agencies

There are many other government and non-governmental organizations that the Clerk of the Courts might find it necessary to correspond with regarding case files. These include the Police Commissioner's Office, police stations, Immigration and Passport Services, Companies Office, Registrar's General Department, and correctional facilities. Formal correspondence to these agencies is important, especially if there are original or certified copies of documents being requested. If documentation is requested as part of case preparation, it is also crucial to make formal requests to such agencies and bodies.

---

23. Per section 25 of the Judicature (Parish Courts) Act. Clearly there could easily be conflicts of interest if the Clerk of the Courts were to engage in practice at the private Bar. The evil is cured by the strict prohibition of such practice. The Canons of Ethics also speak to general conflicts of interest and how they should be addressed by all Attorneys.
24. Section 4 of the Criminal Justice (Administration) Act.
25. Section 290 of the Judicature (Parish Courts) Act indicates that the Clerk of the Courts may be required to take instructions from the DPP or the Minister in the prosecution of certain matters. These matters can be those with grave national security implications, regarding matters such as extradition and the like.

### Verbal Communication

Verbal communication with various agencies about matters before the court is also a part of the duties of the Clerk of the Courts. In this way, case files can be updated to provide information with which to advise the Court on the next court date.

### Documentation Regarding Case Outcome

Dependent on the outcome of a matter before the court, the Clerk of the Courts may be required to oversee the preparation of 'results letters'. These are letters that detail the outcome of matters before the particular Parish Court (whether of recent disposal or of matters long completed). The results letters include certificates of acquittal, certificate of convictions and status letters among others. It is the duty of the Clerk of the Courts to sign and seal these documents.

### Service of Documents from a Case File on Defence Attorneys

These, ideally, must be served (or collected by the attorney) on defense counsel or his designate before the date set for the matter to be dealt with. Therefore, the Clerk of the Courts should give instructions for the documents to be photocopied or otherwise prepared, to be made ready for collection, and to be acknowledged appropriately for the service effected.

### Verification of Documentation Content

There are a myriad of documents that the Clerk of the Courts will be required to peruse and sign in executing his or her administrative duties. It is incumbent upon the Clerk of the Courts to verify adequately the content of all relevant court sheets, case files, etc.

### Medicals

Per section 31CA of the Evidence Act, notwithstanding the provisions of other law, in a criminal proceeding, the court may, with the written or oral agreement of each party, admit into evidence any document that is an expert report. The expert need not be called to give evidence (s. 31CB).

If however, a party intends to put such a report into evidence, that party shall, no later than 30 days before the start of the trial, serve written notice of such intention. A copy of the expert report is also to be served.

The Court may require on its own motion, or on an application by either party, that the expert who signed the report attend and give evidence.

So while section 50 of the Evidence Act is repealed, there still appears to be a requirement for the signing by the medical practitioner in the presence of a Justice of the Peace or the Clerk of the Courts.

As a cautionary note, the Clerk of the Courts must ensure that the medical or other expert report is admissible whether or not it is intended to utilize the procedure in section 31CA.

## Historical Matters for the Clerk of the Courts

The Clerk of the Courts must address any matter that arises which predates his or her appointment. As such, Clerks need access to all relevant documentation and to peruse properly all documents before signing or making a decision on a matter. If the Clerk of the Courts is unsure how to proceed, advice should be sought.

## Effecting the Orders of the Judge of the Parish Court

As the Judge of the Parish Court disposes of matters on any particular day, s/he may make court orders to assist in the timely completion of the case file. It is the primary responsibility of the Clerk of the Courts to ensure that these instructions are carried out either personally or by the relevant administrative or police officer. A few examples of what a Judge may order on any given court date include: interviewing the defendant for legal aid or ensuring that documents, such as post mortems or forensic certificates, are received on the case file.

## The Future of the Clerk of the Courts

There is currently a proposal to change the name of the 'Clerk of the Courts' to Parish Court Prosecutor.[26] The Parish Court Prosecutor would report to the Director of Public Prosecutions.[27] The prosecutorial duties would remain the same, with a significant reduction in the current administrative tasks of the position. The title 'Clerk of the Courts' would become, in effect, the current deputy Clerk of the Courts.[28] The administrative duties of the Parish Court Prosecutor would be assumed by the Clerk of the Courts.[29]

---

26. Proposed Bill – An Act to Further Amend the Judicature (Parish Courts) Act in Order to Provide for the Appointment of Parish Court Prosecutors and for Connected Matters.
27. Ibid.
28. Ibid.
29. Ibid.

# Chapter 3

# The Judge of the Parish Court

## Summary

The Judge of the Parish Court is the lifeblood of the Parish Court system, which accounts for a substantial percentage of the cases, particularly the criminal cases across the island. Prior to 2016, the Parish Court Judge was formerly known as the Resident Magistrate under the then Judicature (Resident Magistrates) Act. In 2016, per the Judicature (Resident Magistrates) (Amendment and Change of Name) Act, the relevant Act became the Judicature (Parish Courts) Act (JPCA) to reflect the name change.

It, therefore, changed the name of the court from the Resident Magistrate's Court to the Parish Court and the Resident Magistrate to the Judge of the Parish Court. Section 3 of the JPCA now reads to reflect this change. The Resident Magistrate is titled 'Judge of the Parish Court', and all cognate expressions referring to Resident Magistrates or the Resident Magistrates' Court, all rules, and other enactments made are also amended.

Thus, for clarity, the term Magistrate as appearing in any and all statutes is now 'Judge of the Parish Court'. The Magistrate is now the 'Judge of the Parish Court'; the Resident Magistrate's Court is now the Parish Court; and the Resident Magistrate is now the 'Parish Court Judge'. The terms Parish Court Judge, Judge of the Parish Court and Judge will be used interchangeably throughout this book.

Finally, any reference to the Resident Magistrates is to be replaced with the word 'Judges'. The amendments to the Act also make a number of other substantial changes throughout the Parish Courts concerning Judges.

## Terms

Qualifications and Jurisdiction

Immunity of the Judges of the Parish Court

Judge of the Parish Court – Roles and Functions

Specific Role of the Chief Judge of the Parish Court

### Qualifications and Jurisdiction

To become eligible for the position of Judge of the Parish Court, per section 12(1)(b) of the JPCA, Judges must now be qualified for no less than seven years as an attorney-at-law. However, Judges who were admitted before this amendment, by a qualification period of five years or more, are not invalidated by this new change according to section 12(1)(3) of the JPCA.

Every Judge of the Parish Court is assigned to a specific jurisdiction. Under the JPCA, the jurisdiction of the Parish Court Judge is usually a single parish.

In some jurisdictions, the Judge of the Parish Court may sit at different venues on certain days. Therefore, in the parish of Clarendon, for example, the Judge of the Parish Court can sit at the courthouse located in May Pen, Frankfield, and Lionel Town all in a single week.[1] Importantly, the parishes outside of the Corporate Area usually see the Parish Court dealing with a wide range of matters across the criminal and civil law.

### The Corporate Area Court

Notably however, the parishes of Kingston and St Andrew comprise the Corporate Area per section 3A of the JPCA. As such, the court's jurisdiction is for the two parishes (for criminal matters, which is the subject of this book, as well as for all civil, traffic, and family matters). In the Corporate Area, the Parish Court is divided into the following physical courts: Criminal, Civil, Revenue, Traffic, as well as Children and Family.

### Powers of the Judge of the Parish Court

Per section 65 of the JPCA:

> ...the judge of the Parish Court shall preside in the Parish Court of the parish, and shall there, to the amounts, and to the extent, and in the manner hereinafter provided, have and exercise the civil and criminal jurisdiction hereinafter assigned to the said Court, and shall, also have and exercise a jurisdiction in all cases in bankruptcy under the provisions of the Bankruptcy Act and in the recovery of all penalties or forfeitures to the Crown, and of fines in the nature of penalties, under all Statutes now or hereafter to be in force relating to the public revenue, and in cases under the Maintenance Act, and in all such causes, enquiries, and matters civil or criminal in which by any law any special jurisdiction, duty or power is given to or imposed on any Judge of a District Court, the judge of the Parish Court shall, within his parish, have, exercise and perform such jurisdiction, duty, or power....

The Judge of the Parish Court has the general jurisdiction to sentence convicted defendants to a maximum of three years imprisonment and or a fine. There is specific legislation which indicates that there is the power to increase this custodial sentence to five years under specific legislation.

### Types of Matters Heard in the Criminal Jurisdiction

The criminal court jurisdiction of the Parish Court includes the taking of evidence in both summary and indictable matters, having a hearing in certain stipulated matters, as well as conducting committal proceedings. The full extent of the powers and duties of the Judge of the Parish Court is outlined in the JPCA.

## Immunity and Constitutionality of the Judges of the Parish Court

The JPCA now stipulates that all Judges of the Parish Courts are immune from liability as are the Judges of the Supreme Court. Section 7A is inserted into the Act to ensure that Judges of the Parish Court can carry out their duties without the added burden of fear of liability.

Under section 112 of the Constitution and in tandem with the relevant legislation, the Governor-General (acting on the advice of the Judicial Services Commission) has the power to make appointments, and to remove and to exercise disciplinary control over persons holding the post of Judges of the Parish Court.

---

1.  See earlier discussion in the chapter on jurisdiction. The Judicature (Parish Courts) Act delineates the constitution and jurisdiction of the Court at section 3; the appointment of judges of the Parish Court at section 4; the assignment of more than one Parish Court Judge per section 5; and the assignment of more than one parish to a Parish Court Judge per section 6.

## Judge of the Parish Court – Roles, Powers, and Functions

### General Court Sitting

The Judge of the Parish Court is responsible for and sits either in a specialized court or in a court that covers the gamut of areas under the auspices of the JPCA and other relevant pieces of legislation. In parishes where there are several Parish Court Judges, each may be assigned to a particular court. They sit in these courts on a daily basis unless they are requested to work in another part of the jurisdiction or in another jurisdiction.

The Judge of the Parish Court is responsible for a wide variety of matters as per the JPCA, which outlines their duties.[2] Thus, within the Lay Magistrates' Court jurisdiction, the Judge of the Parish Court has the power and authority of two or more Justices of the Peace.[3]

### Enquiry Power of Judges of the Parish Court regarding Detainees

Under the Jamaica Constabulary Force Act, the police may detain persons pending an identification parade. The Judge of the Parish Court is to enquire about the status of these detainees at least once a week.[4] After this enquiry, the Judge of the Parish Court can then remand detainees for a further period. However, if it appears that an identification parade will not be held, the detainee should be brought before a court within 24 hours. When a detainee is brought before a Judge of the Parish Court, the Judge can make the appropriate order after reviewing all circumstances of the case.

### Applications/Considerations Regarding Bail in Court

Where an application for bail has been refused by a Justice of the Peace or police officer, the Judge of the Parish Court should review the refusal when the defendant first appears in court. A Judge of the Parish Court shall carry out, at least once per week, a review of cases involving defendants who were granted bail but were unable to take up such bail.[5] This review of custody cases is conducted at the various remand centres. The Judge of the Parish Court may enquire of the remandees, as to such reasons for their continued detention or status or any areas deemed necessary. They can also make orders for remandees to be taken for specific medical attention. The Judge of the Parish Court then signs the requisite entries regarding each remandee at the lockups.

### Committal Proceedings in Brief

The Committal Proceedings Act amends portions of section 64 of the JPCA. Section 64 of the JPCA, which deals with committal proceedings (previously known as preliminary enquiries), indicates that the Judge of the Parish Court shall conduct all committal proceedings regarding charges or information for indictable offences triable in the Circuit Court of the parish. Sections 29–46 of the Justices of the Peace Jurisdiction Act, as amended by the Committal Proceedings Act, illustrate how a committal proceeding is to take place.

The Judge of the Parish Court must bear in mind that every accused, committed to stand and take his trial before the Circuit Court at the end of the committal proceedings, shall be brought before such Circuit Court no later than the second circuit. This is a standard practice unless the Court or a Judge orders otherwise.[6]

---

2.  Sections 63–70 of the Judicature (Parish Courts) Act examine several areas that form part of the Parish Court Judge's general duties.
3.  Section 63 of the Judicature (Parish Courts) Act.
4.  Section 63A of the Judicature (Parish Courts) Act.
5.  Section 12 of the Bail Act; Section 286 of the Judicature (Parish Courts) Act.
6.  Section 5 of the Criminal Justice (Administration) Act. The section also indicates that regard is to be had to sections 3 and 4 of the Act.

However, following this practice depends whether the Director of Public Prosecutions (DPP) has directed that an accused, who has been committed for trial in the Circuit Court, should be tried before a Parish Court or Justices in the jurisdiction where the offence occurred.[7] Of course, the DPP has to notify both the witnesses and the accused of this change of venue. If no notice is given, the accused takes his trial in the Circuit Court.

The DPP may also enter a *nolle prosequi* in a matter before any Justice or court. As such, if the Crown intends to discontinue the proceedings, then the proceedings are over. If there are other criminal matters pending for the accused, which are not mentioned by the *nolle prosequi*, those matters will proceed.[8]

Crucially, the Committal Proceedings Act provides that, where a person is committed for trial, s/he may be indicted not only for the offence for which s/he was committed for trial, but also for any offence which, in the opinion of the DPP, is disclosed by the evidence before the Judge of the Parish Court at the committal proceedings.[9]

### Court Days

Regarding the days and dates of the sitting of the Parish Court, these are to be fixed by the Parish Court Judge, with the *proviso* that the Chief Justice can change them.[10] The Judge of the Parish Court can also sit at any place within the parish or parishes within his remit – that is outside of the Parish Court building itself – if deemed necessary to administer justice as the particular case demands.[11] As such, the court will be wherever it is so convened for the purpose. Visits to *locus in quo* are obviously included here.

The *Gazette* publishes the dates and times of the sittings of the Parish Court and is placed in an obvious and conspicuous place in the precincts of the courthouse as well as in the Clerk of the Courts' office. Such prime placement is deemed to be adequate notice, but the proceedings taken by the Court would still be valid without any public notice.[12]

### Sitting in Chambers

Sitting in Chambers, and thus constituting the Court, is also permissible by the Judge of the Parish Court. While in chambers, the Parish Court Judge can make orders concerning the mode of trial for the accused charged with an indictable offence. The Court can also hear and determine any application for a change of venue from one locale/outstation to another within the parish or parishes under the jurisdiction of the Judge of the Parish Court.[13] The change of venue application can be oral and or in writing.

### The Court Sheet

There is one section that is reserved for the Parish Court Judge to write on the court sheet. It is not to be written in by anyone else without more (such as if there is a natural disaster and the Judge of the Parish Court is absent). In it, the Judge of the Parish Court writes the salient points about the matters before the court on each and every occasion. Therefore, the court sheet is to be carefully secured as it forms part of the records regarding matters before the court.

---

7. Section 3 of the Criminal Justice (Administration) Act illustrates the power of the Director of Public Prosecutions regarding matters committed to the Circuit Court.
8. Section 4 of the Criminal Justice (Administration) Act.
9. Section 10(4) of the Committal Proceedings Act.
10. Section 66 of the Judicature (Parish Courts) Act.
11. Ibid.
12. Ibid.
13. Section 67 of the Judicature (Parish Courts) Act: change of venue applications.

## Hearing of *Habeas Corpus*

Writs of *habeas corpus* can also be heard in chambers.[14] However, in most instances, they are heard in open court. The provision empowers the Judge of the Parish Court to make enquiries into the circumstances and reasons for the person's detention.[15] The officer in charge of the facility or another relevant officer can be ordered to attend court to satisfactorily explain the reason for the person's detention.

The Judge of the Parish Court may also hear applications for stays of execution in chambers.

Figure 3.1    Sample *Habeas Corpus* Application

---

**NOTICE OF APPLICATION UNDER SECTION
286 OF THE JUDICATURE
(PARISH COURT) ACT**

IN THE RESIDENT MAGISTRATE'S COURT
FOR THE PARISH OF SAINT ANN
HOLDEN AT SAINT ANN'S BAY

IN THE MATTER OF  JOHN BROWN

AND

IN THE MATTER OF AN APPLICATION
UNDER SECTION 286 OF THE (JUDICATURE
PARISH COURT) ACT.

**TAKE NOTICE** that on 27TH day of February, 20-- at 10:00 o' clock in the forenoon the Parish Court for the parish of Saint Mary will be moved to issue an Order for the upbringing of  JOHN BROWN  before the Court for the purposes of making enquiries into the circumstances and reasons for his detention at the Saint Ann's Bay Hospital in custody of the Port Maria Police and subsequent detention at the Annotto Bay Police Station Lock-ups and for such Orders as the Court thinks fit.

Dated the 27th day of February, 20--

PER  *Les Craw and Co.*

**ATTORNEYS-AT-LAW**

TO:        The Clerk-of-the-Courts
           Parish Court
           Saint Ann's Bay
           Saint Ann

AND:       The Officer in Charge
           Port Maria Police Station Lock-ups
           Port Maria Police Station
           Saint Mary

**FILED by Les Craw and Co of 3 Port Maria Street, Port Maria, St. Mary, Attorney-at-Law for and behalf of the Applicant herein.**

---

14. Ibid.
15. Section 286 of the Judicature (Parish Courts) Act.

## AFFIDAVIT IN SUPPORT OF NOTICE OF APPLICATION
## UNDER SECTION 296 OF THE JUDICATURE
## (PARISH COURT) ACT

IN THE PARISH COURT
FOR THE PARISH OF SAINT ANN
HOLDEN AT SAINT ANN'S BAY

> IN THE MATTER OF   JOHN BROWN
> AND
> IN THE MATTER OF AN APPLICATION
> UNDER SECTION 286 OF THE (JUDICATURE
> PARISH COURT) ACT.

I, Les Craw, being duly sworn make oath and say as follows:-

1.      That my address for this purpose is 3 Port Maria Street, Port Maria, St. Mary.

2.      That I am an Attorney-at-Law and represent   JOHN BROWN   and authorized to depone this Affidavit.

3.      That I am informed and do verily believe that on or about the 20TH day of February, 20--, JOHN BROWN   was detained by Officers from the Port Maria Police Station and subsequently taken by them to the Saint Ann's Bay Hospital. Upon discharge from the Saint Ann's Bay Hospital on the 23RD February, 20--, he was taken to the Annotto Bay Police Station Lock-ups by Officers from Port Maria where he has been detained.

4.      That to date he has not been released neither has he been charged nor has any satisfactory reason been given for his continued detention.

5.      That no information has gone before the Court by any of the Officers of the Port Maria Police Station and as a result   JOHN BROWN   still remains in custody at the Port Maria Police Station Lock-ups.

6.      I pray that the Court issues an Order for the upbringing of the said   JOHN BROWN   for the said purposes of making enquiries into the circumstances and reasons for his detention and for the purposes of making such Orders as the Court thinks fit.

SWORN to by Les Craw

At

*Les Craw*
.........................
Les Craw

In the parish of

This   day of February 20--  Before me :-

------------------------------------------
 **JUSTICE OF THE PEACE /**
**CLERK OF-THE -COURT**

**FILED by Les Craw and Co of 3 Port Maria Street, Port Maria, St. Mary, Attorney-at-Law for and behalf of the Applicant herein.**

### Visiting Judge of the Parish Court

The visiting Judge of the Parish Court could be a Parish Court Judge who has been transferred to another jurisdiction but returns to his former jurisdiction to hear incomplete matters. Alternatively, the visiting Parish Court Judge could be assisting in the jurisdiction for a specific reason, such as the assigned Judge of the Parish Court being ill. When a visiting Parish Court Judge sits, the matters are listed in a visiting court sheet. Arrangements must be made for a Clerk of the Courts or deputy Clerk of the Courts to be before the visiting Judge of the Parish Court. The court police officers must also be alerted so that they can perform their duties accordingly. A courtroom should then be prepared for the matter to be heard, and the appropriate chambers for the Judge of the Parish Court to use should also be prepared.

### Absence of a Parish Court Judge

When there is only one Judge of the Parish Court for all matters in the jurisdiction, and s/he is absent, another Parish Court Judge should be requested (often through the Chief Justice's chambers) to assist with the particular court lists. Section 7 of the JPCA advises on the procedure to be followed. When a Judge of the Parish Court is absent from the usual court in which s/he sits, another Judge hears the matters in his or her specific courtroom, or in the courtroom of the absent Judge. This is so when there are multiple courts in one building and several judges.

The Clerk of the Courts must make the physical arrangements to have the matters heard before another Judge of the Parish Court. These arrangements include asking another Judge of the Parish Court to hear the matters and significantly, ensuring that the name of that Judge of the Parish Court is recorded on the appropriate section in the court sheet. It is also the duty of the Clerk of the Courts to give appropriate instructions to the police personnel, clerical, and administrative staff so that they can assist with apprising persons with interest in various matters where these will be heard.

When a Judge of the Parish Court hears matters that are not in his usual court assignments, there are three possible actions to be taken. Firstly, that Judge can have the matters fully distilled before him or her on that day.

Secondly, the Judge can adjourn the matters, meaning that they will be set down for dates when the assigned Judge will be sitting, using as a further guide, for example, the next court dates that have been agreed between the prosecution and defence. The Judge then makes the relevant notations in the court sheet about the matter.

Thirdly, the Parish Court Judge can order the transfer a matter to his or her court on a subsequent date. This is usual if there are with multiple courts on a court building. In this latter event, the relevant notation is also made in the court sheet by the Judge of the Parish Court.

### Court Orders

Judges of the Parish Court make a variety of court orders regarding the matters before them. Whenever an order is made in a matter, the Judge of the Parish Court signs it after the Clerk of the Courts endorses the order on the number one or on the indictment. The Judge of the Parish Court also notes the content of the order in the court sheet.

### Trials in the Parish Court vs Committal Proceedings in the Parish Court

When a Judge of the Parish Court begins a committal proceeding, s/he writes the deposition of all the witnesses on deposition paper.[16] A deposition paper forms part of the information that is sent to the Supreme

---

16. Sections 29–46 of the Justices of the Peace Jurisdiction Act discuss Committal Proceedings (as amended by the Committal Proceedings Act).

Court if there is a prima facie case for the defendant to answer at the next circuit. Under the Committal Proceedings Act, there may be no actual depositions taken, but the legislation does provide for it. Since the Judge of the Parish Court oversees the committal proceedings, s/he actually sees, reads, and considers the various documents on the Crown's case, for example, statements, forensic statements, and others.

This is unlike a trial or a hearing matter where the Judge of the Parish Court cannot see these documents unless and until they are put into evidence by either the prosecution or the defence.

When a Judge of the Parish Court begins a trial or a hearing, s/he writes all the notes of evidence in a notebook.[17] It is now permissible for electronic notes to be taken in the Parish Court. These notes in whatever form are the official record of the matter. If there is an appeal in the matter of any aspect of the verdict – or any preliminary point – these notes are provided to the Supreme Court or Court of Appeal, depending on where jurisdiction lies, by the Parish Court's administrative arm.

### The Taking of Notes of Evidence by the Parish Court Judge

The pages in the notebook are called folio, and the Judge of the Parish Court usually indicates to the Clerk of the Courts the folios for particular matters so that these can be noted appropriately on the indictment form or the number one information. Writing down the various pages from the Judge's notebook where the evidence of a particular matter is taken is very useful. The Judge can easily refer to the previous evidence taken, especially for matters that take a long time. When there is need to check the actual notes or to produce an electronic version, as for an appeal, the pages can easily be found. The notes are then electronically produced and forwarded along with whatever other documents were tendered into evidence.

When a Judge begins a trial, a hearing, or committal proceeding, it is this said Judge who must finish that matter. No other Judge of the Parish Court has the power to so do unless the matter is ordered to begin *de novo*. As such, where there are part-heard matters, the Clerk of the Courts must ensure that it is not incorrectly listed before a Judge of the Parish Court who did not begin the matter.

A particular process has to be followed when appealing a matter that the Judge of the Parish Court has decided. The handwritten notes of the Judge of the Parish Court are electronically produced and certified as a true copy and sent to the Court of Appeal as part of the official record of the case. Any statements, exhibits, and other relevant documentation are also submitted.[18]

### Contempt of Court in the Parish Court

There has been significant revision to the power of a Judge of the Parish Court regarding contempt in court. Section 194 of the Judicature (Resident Magistrates) Act has been repealed and replaced by section 194 of the JPCA. It states that any person before the Court who use indecent, violent, or threatening language; displays gestures or conduct of an indecent, violent, or threatening nature; or commits assault or battery on a Judge, any other officer of the court, or any other person in Court has committed a contempt of court.[19] The section makes it clear, however, that this is not an exhaustive list.

---

17. Section 291 of the Judicature (Parish Courts) Act stipulates how records in criminal cases are to be made up and kept. It states that all the information or indictment with the record thereon and any notes affixed shall constitute the record of the case. Such record is to be carefully preserved. Section 27(2), (3), (4), and (5) also indicate the manner in which notes may be taken electronically.
18. Section 292 of the Judicature (Parish Courts) Act says that entries made under section 291 or any signed and certified copy (by the Clerk of the Courts) of these entries that bear the Court's seal can be admitted as prima facie evidence. See too section 27 of the Judicature (Parish Courts) Act.
19. Section 194(1) of the Judicature (Parish Court) Act speaks to some types of behaviour that are considered contempt of court.

Such contempt of court empowers the Judge of the Parish Court to order that a bailiff or an officer of the Court detain the offender until the rising of the Court.[20] The Judge of the Parish Court may impose a fine upon such an offender. For language that is indecent, violent, or threatening the fine shall not exceed $100. For gestures or conduct of an indecent, violent, or threatening nature, the fine is a maximum of $1,000. However, where the offence is an assault upon a Judge, any officer of the Court, or any other person in the court, the penalty shall not exceed $500,000.[21]

Notably, there is no custodial sentence for such an offence. The fines now enumerated replace the paltry sum of $20 that had been the penalty for many years. Indeed, the new section gives much clarity to the issue of contempt of court in the Parish Court. It offers guidance on the manner in which the Judge of the Parish Court should assess acts to determine whether or not there has been a contempt of court.

## Specific Role of the Chief Judge of the Parish Court

The JPCA provides for a Chief Judge of the Parish Courts.[22] This is a wholly new position in the court system and serves to augment the vital functions of the island's Judges of the Parish Courts. The Chief Judge of the Parish Court can also be called 'Judge' as can any other Judge of the Parish Courts.[23] Throughout this work, any reference to the 'Chief Judge of the Parish Courts' shall be styled as the 'Chief Judge of the Parish Courts' or the 'Chief Judge' interchangeably.

## Functions of the Chief Judge of the Parish Court

The Chief Judge of the Parish Court has all the functions of a Judge of a Parish Court and is, in fact, appointed from among the persons qualified to be appointed as a Judge of the Parish Court.[24] In addition, the Chief Judge of the Parish Courts is responsible for the general administrative supervision of the work assigned to Parish Courts and any other functions delegated by the Chief Justice of Jamaica to whom the Chief Judge of the Parish Courts reports directly.[25]

For clarity, every Judge of a Parish Court is responsible and subject to the direction of the Chief Judge of the Parish Courts concerning the administrative duties to be performed.[26]

---

20. Section 194(2)(a) and (b), Ibid.
21. Section 194(3), Ibid.
22. Section 2 of the Judicature (Parish Courts) Act.
23. Ibid.
24. Section 4A(1) of the Judicature (Parish Courts) Act. Section 4A(2) of the Judicature (Parish Courts) Act speaks to the pool of persons from whom a Chief Judge of the Parish Courts can be appointed.
25. Section 4A(5)(a) and (b) of the Judicature (Parish Courts) Act. Section 4A(4) deals with the reporting structure regarding the Chief Judge of the Parish Courts.
26. Section 4A(6) of the Judicature Parish Courts Act.

Chapter 4

# Other Court Staff

## Summary

While the Parish Court Judge and the Clerk of the Courts are the most visible legal staff in the Parish Courts, there are many other positions, both legal and administrative, that are crucial to the effective administration of justice.

## Terms _____

Deputy Clerk of the Courts

Executive Legal Officer

Court Administrator

Assistant Clerk of the Courts

Administrative Staff

The Future of Other Court Staff

_____

## Deputy Clerk of the Courts[1]

It is usual practice for the deputy Clerk of the Courts to be referred to as the 'deputy Clerk'. That practice will be followed here. The deputy Clerk of Courts is not an attorney-at-law but does have legal training under the Judicature (Parish Courts) Act (JPCA)[2] and is appointed for each parish. They also marshal evidence on behalf of the Crown and attend to many administrative matters in the courts.[3] In the courtroom when a deputy Clerk of the Courts is appearing for the Crown, s/he is nevertheless styled as 'Clerk'. The JPCA places some strictures on the powers of the deputy Clerk.[4]

## Executive Legal Officer[5]

This is a new position in the court structure, and the appointed officer must be an attorney-at-law. This officer's main duties include providing legal research and other support services for the Chief Judge of the Parish Courts to whom s/he reports.

_____

1. Section 21 Judicature (Parish Courts) Act speaks to the appointment of deputy Clerks of the Courts.
2. See section 22 Judicature (Parish Courts) Act regarding the qualification of deputy Clerks of the Courts.
3. Section 23 Judicature (Parish Courts) Act details the powers of the deputy Clerk.
4. Section 24 Judicature (Parish Courts) Act illustrates the limits of the deputy Clerk's powers.
5. The executive legal officer, per section 15A of the Judicature (Parish Courts) Act has a wide mandate to provide legal support for the chief of the parish courts. One important function, per s. 15A(3)(b) is that this officer liaises with the director of court administration at the Supreme Court on behalf of the Chief Judge of the Parish Courts.

## Court Administrator[6]

Each court has a court administrator who is appointed by the Governor-General. The court administrator is responsible for the administrative staff of the court's office as well as general administrative matters. The court administrator may be assigned duties in relation to more than one parish and the scope of the duties of the court administrator is governed by the JPCA.

## Assistant Clerk of the Courts[7]

Assistant Cerks usually have some paralegal training. Their duties are extensive and range from writing up court sheets, filing away case files, doing preliminary preparatory work for matters, and making checks regarding the status of files. The JPCA also provides that it is 'lawful for the Assistant Clerk to perform any duties belonging to the office of the Clerk of the Courts, including the conduct of the prosecution in criminal cases,'[8] and as assistant Clerks gain more experience, they do prosecute matters usually beginning in the Lay Magistrates' Court.

The Act, however, makes it abundantly clear that the assistant Clerk *shall not* (emphasis added) perform those duties of the Clerk of the Courts that are the Clerk's by virtue of the fact that s/he is a justice (ex officio).[9]

### Administrative and Ancillary Staff

Like any other organisation, the Parish Court employs administrative staff - secretaries who electronically produce appeals and documents for matters committed to the Circuit Court as well as accountants, receptionists, and telephone operators. Groundskeepers and attendants make up the ancillary staff and are responsible for the general maintenance and upkeep of the court and surroundings.

## The Future of Other Court Staff in the Judicial System

There is currently, a proposal to amend the Judicature (Parish Courts) Act that would effect, at the very least, name changes for the post of the deputy Clerk of the Courts. The draft bill, 'An Act to Further Amend the Judicature (Parish Courts) Act in Order to Provide for the Appointment of Parish Court Prosecutors and for Connected Matters', would amend some of the duties assigned to the deputy Clerk and rename the post 'Clerk of the Courts'. Section 16 of the Judicature (Parish Courts) Act would be amended to read that the Clerk of Courts (that is the phrase in the draft bill) may not perform any function of a Parish Court Prosecutor (presently the Clerk of the Courts) except under the direction of the Parish Court Prosecutor.

So at least theoretically, the Clerk of the Courts might stand in the shoes of the Parish Court Prosecutor and thereby prosecute a case. Section 13 of the Judicature (Parish Courts) Act when and, if amended, would delete the reference to 'deputy Clerk of the Court'. Notably, section 18 of the Judicature (Parish Courts) Act when and if amended, would delete reference to the deputy Clerk of the Court as well as to repeal the proviso that now states that: "Provided that in the case of a Deputy Clerk such powers shall be exercised subject to the direction of the Judge of the Parish Court for the parish, or for the portion of the parish, in which such powers are to be exercised."

---

6. By virtue of sections 41A and 41B of the Judicature (Parish Courts) Act, the court administrator shall, subject to the directions of the particular Judge of the Parish Court, be responsible for the administrative affairs of the court.
7. Section 20 of the Judicature (Parish Courts) Act.
8. Ibid.
9. Ibid.

Sections 21, 22, 23, and 24 which also speak directly to the appointment, qualifications, powers, protection, and immunities and limitations of the powers of the deputy Clerk of Court would also be repealed under the draft bill. Seemingly, as the post would no longer be a prosecutorial one, there would be no further need for these safeguards.

Furthermore, sections 46, 58, and 143, when and if amended, would delete all references to the 'deputy Clerk of the Court'.

Regarding the current position of assistant Clerk of the Courts,[10] these duties remain unchanged in the draft bill. However, it appears that where the term 'Clerk of the Courts' appears, it will be amended to be 'Parish Court Prosecutor' as the current Judicature (Parish Courts) Act now reads:

> Provided that an Assistant Clerk shall not perform such of the duties of the Clerk of the Courts as belong to that officer by virtue of his being a Justice.
>
> And such Assistant Clerk, while acting under any such order, shall have the like powers and privileges and be subject to the like provisions, duties and penalties for misbehaviour, as if he were the Clerk of the Courts for the time being.

---

10. Ibid.

# Chapter 5

# Court Types in the Parish Court System

## Summary

The Parish Court system, while appearing a monolith, is actually a conglomeration of multiple courts. The courts in this conglomeration vary according to issues ranging from the mundane such as the physical structure of the courthouse, which may house only one courtroom, to the legislative provisions in each court.

Regardless of the court type, the overarching practice is essentially the same for certain preliminaries in the daily structure of the court.

## Terms_____

How Case Files Enter the System

Daily Process Book

General Court Proceedings

Types of Courts:
> Return Day Court
>
> Summary Court
>
> Committal Proceedings Court
>
> The Gun Court
>
> Night Court
>
> Drug Court
>
> Lay Magistrates
>
> Traffic Court

_____

## How Case Files Enter the Court System

Case files begin their life in the court system in one of two ways. They can be brought by police officers who have either arrested or served summons on an accused person to attend court; or, a case file may begin when members of the public bring private prosecutions against other private citizens.

Most new case files come to the court via police officers. The officer tells the accused the date on which s/he is to come to court or will be brought to court if in custody, for the first mention of the matter. The accused might have been offered station bail before the first court date and so would be bailed to attend court on the date indicated by the investigating officer.

In the case of private prosecutions, individuals institute the proceedings by bringing criminal charges against others. The basic documents needed to start a private prosecution are the Statement of the Complainant and the number one information(s). The complainant's statement should be recorded by an authorized court administrative officer such as an assistant Clerk. The assistant Clerk or other authorized officer takes the complainant's statements and the statements of any witnesses who may have attended the court office with the complainant. When all the information is gathered, the court officer should write up the number one information and the Clerk of the Courts is to ensure that the offences are made out correctly.

The complainant should be given the requisite summons to serve on the accused, indicating when s/he is to come to court for the first mention of the matter. Examples of types of private prosecution include threats, common assaults, and breaches of the Rent Restriction Act.

## Daily Process Book

All new case files are received by the court office's front desk, entered into the daily process book, and given the next consecutive number. As such, the daily process book is crucial to the effective administration of the court system as it details the intake of new cases. Each new case is assigned an information number. This number consists of the order and the year in which the case enters the court system. The order number is written first, followed by a slash and the year the matter was opened. An example of an information number would be 1121/2019, which means that this case is number 1,121 for the year 2019, in a particular location.

The New Case Numbering Protocol for Jamaican Courts which was outlined in early 2019 details the manner in which new case files going forward would be numbered upon receipt into the court system: parish code, then the year, followed by the case type code and the actual number which can be up to five numerals long and in sequence. Therefore, for example, a criminal case in the Westmoreland Parish Court would be WL2020CR00001. WL represents the parish code for the Westmoreland Parish Court; 2020 represents the year when the matter was first brought before the court; CR indicates this is a criminal matter, and 00001 represents that this is the first case of this type for 2020. If there are multiple informations laid charging more than one offence then the number(s) would be written WL2020CR00001 - 1, WL2020CR00001 - 2, WL2020CR00001 - 3.

## General Proceedings in Court

### The Court Takes the Bench

As the Parish Court Judge approaches the bench at or about 10 a.m.,[1] everyone is required to rise when instructed by the court officer. The Judge bows in greeting and all attorneys present should reciprocate. As the Judge takes the bench, the court is opened by the court police officer who is in charge of the courtroom.

### Opening of the Parish Court

The assigned court police officer then opens the court as follows on a Monday morning:

> Oyez, oyez, all manner of persons having anything to do or say here in her Majesty's Parish Court and Lay Magistrates' Court before Her Honour Justicia Justice, Judge of the Parish Court for the Corporate Area/ Parish of — draw near and give their attendance and they shall be heard. God Save the Queen. You may be seated.

On subsequent days in the week, the opening is as follows:

> *'This Court now resumes its sitting, God save the Queen.'*

---

1. The sitting of court is set out in the Jamaica Gazette. The usual hours are from 10 a.m. to 1 p.m., with the luncheon adjournment lasting until 2 p.m. The rest of the day is from 2 p.m. to 4 p.m. Notably, in the Circuit Courts, the period of days that the Court sits is also gazetted.

The daily opening and closing of the court is important, and the court police officer is expected to know the correct oath for each occasion.

### Adjourning the Court Day

When the matters have all been dealt with, so indicate to the Judge in words such as '*May it please you, Your Honour, that is Your Honour's list for the day.*'

Unless the Judge of the Parish Court has something to say to the Clerk or another personnel in the court, s/he will say: '*Very well, please adjourn the Court.*'

The Court is adjourned by the court officer until the following day in the following terms:

> '*This Court is adjourned until 10 a.m. tomorrow morning, God save the Queen.*'

At the end of the week, the adjournment takes the following form:

> '*This Court now stands adjourned until 10 a.m. Monday morning.*'

If a visiting Judge presides in the Parish Court, the Court is adjourned until the next date that s/he is set to return to hear matters.

### Greeting the Court

The Court is greeted every day the Court sits and almost every time the Court is addressed. Here, the term the 'Court' refers to the person of the Judge of the Parish Court sitting as such. The Clerk of the Courts rises and begins with the court list for the day, having greeted the Parish Court Judge as follows: '*May it so please the Court, Your Honour, on the (new, CP [Committal Proceedings], Summary Trial, etc.) list, the Queen against John Binnz.*' A similar such traditional and formal style is perfectly acceptable.

It is unseemly and far too familiar to address the Court by saying '*Good morning, your Honour.*' The proper protocol is the traditional style. If the Judge greets counsel and everyone else in the courtroom informally, the lay persons may respond. However, an attorney should not reciprocate, knowing the preferred style to address the Court.

It is also inappropriate for any attorney to address the Court from outside of counsel's bench. If it appears that that might happen, the attorney should immediately return to counsel's bench and another attorney should immediately yield his seat so that the courtesies can be observed.

### The Office of the Director of Public Prosecutions (DPP) and Senior Counsel

Sometimes an officer from the DPP or a senior attorney such as a Queen's Counsel is present in court. When this happens, it is the practice to extend the courtesy of allowing that attorney to address the Court first. That attorney will usually indicate to the Court that s/he does so with the permission of the learned Clerk of the Courts.

The Clerk of the Courts should call the matters on the copy of the court sheet. Traditionally, the defence counsel calls up their matters first, followed by the prosecution. The matters on the Clerk's copy can be called according to the convenient order in which the files are arranged. Guiding examples include:

- the state of readiness;
- the age of the matters;
- the matters with multiple accused or witnesses;
- if persons are in custody and not yet before the Court.

Another method is to simply go chronologically.

### Accused in the Dock

Matters are not to be called if the accused is not present in the dock or discussed if the accused is not in the courtroom. When the accused takes the dock, s/he should be asked whether they have a legal representative if this is unknown. The Clerk, at this time, can call for the investigating officer, complainants, and any other witnesses or parties necessary.

### Interposing Matters

Where the Clerk of the Courts is in the middle of dealing with one matter and it becomes necessary for another to be dealt with (i.e., 'interposed'), the Clerk must seek the leave of the Court by asking *'if this would be a convenient time to "interpose" with the matter of ....'*

Leave may or may not be granted, and the Clerk of the Courts must be prepared to proceed accordingly.

### How to Make Enquiries about the Status of the Case File in Court

Ideally, these should be done prior to the court date. However, exigencies may arise and when they do, the Court is be respected. The Clerk of the Courts, therefore, must get the necessary information from investigators, witnesses, attorneys, or other persons without appearing to disrespect the Court.

To do this, the Clerk should seek the leave of the Court. A simple: *'If the Court is so minded, might I have a minute to confer with the —?'* is sufficient.

Only when that leave has been granted should the Clerk speak with the relevant party. Only sparing enquiries should be made at this time regarding outstanding statements, further investigations, and the like. If necessary, advise the particular witness that s/he is being requested to stay behind to confer with the Clerk or the police officer, or make some other arrangements to get the necessary information.

### Requests from Defence Attorneys to Peruse Files in Court

If the defence attorney wishes to peruse the case file before the Clerk has copied the documents in it, the Clerk of the Courts can respectfully decline this request and instead make immediate arrangements to have the documents copied. The Clerk of the Courts is the custodian of the records in the Parish Court and should not readily hand over files to anyone or leave their files unattended. They must safeguard the integrity of all documents at all times.

### Adjournments of a Case

If a matter is not fully distilled in the Court by a particular day (e.g., trial), then another date, agreed upon by the defence attorney, police, and civilian witnesses, should be chosen. The date set should be subject to the pre-existing fixtures in the court's diary as well as convenient for all parties involved. Choosing a date to everyone's liking is determined by:

- the Judge's agreement;
- the number of cases previously set for the proposed date;
- whether the case has been listed as having a particular date as a 'final date' or 'priority';
- whether the proposed date is convenient to all concerned.

### Endorsements on the Case File

As the matters are disposed of, the necessary endorsements are to be written on the number one information. The endorsements include any court orders or offers of bail variations. Orders of the Court are written on the number one information and signed by the Judge of the Parish Court.

Where there are multiple accused, the endorsements should reflect the status of each accused on every occasion the matter is heard, and if the Court makes an order regarding a particular accused, it should be endorsed on the number one after on which s/he is charged.

## Sentencing Cases

Matters set for verdict or sentencing can be left until late in the list or even at the end/foot of the list.

## Cases Ready for Trial/Hearing

Quickly conclude matters on the court sheet not ready for trial or a hearing. Only focus on matters that are to be distilled on the day.

## Absence of the Assigned Sitting Judge of the Parish Court

If a particular Judge of the Parish Court is not sitting on a given day, the matters must still be dealt with by a court.[2] The court system cannot fall apart with the absence of any one Judge. Matters should be taken before another Judge on the building and dealt with in that courtroom.[3] Sometimes another Judge from a neighbouring parish will be dispatched to sit.[4]

The Clerk of the Courts takes the court sheet before the new Judge, and his or her name should be written in the place reserved for the Court. Before all of this, the Clerk should have notified all defendants and relevant parties of the Court's new location for the day (as necessary).

If the sitting Judge is absent and there is no other Judge able to deal with the matters, such as in a rural outstation, the Clerk of the Courts can adjourn the matters and give the attorneys, defendants, witnesses and others with business before the court new dates.

## Types of Courts

- Return Day Court
- Summary Court
- Committal Proceedings Court
- The Gun Court
- Traffic Court
- Night Court
- Drug Court
- Lay Magistrate Court

In some parts of the island, one courtroom may serve various functions in the court system and many matters may be heard within them. For example, in some parishes, one courtroom may serve as the Return Day Court, the Trial Court, or the Committal Proceedings Court. In other parishes, there are multiple courtrooms on a court building, each serving as a specific type of court.

---

2. Section 4 of the Judicature (Parish Courts) Act deals with the appointment of the judges of the Parish Court by the Governor-General. In section 5 of the Judicature (Parish Courts) Act, it states that it is lawful 'for the Governor-General from time to time to assign any court to more than one Judge of the Parish Court.'
3. The Judge of the Parish Court of a particular parish may be assigned to more than parish under section 6 of the Judicature (Parish Courts) Act.
4. The Judge of the Parish Court for one parish may lawfully act for the Judge of the Parish Court for another parish under section 7 of the Judicature (Parish Courts) Act.

**Return Day Court**

This court hears 'new' matters and 'mention' matters. A matter is 'new' when it first goes before the Court and so falls under the jurisdiction of the Court. Matters that are not yet ready for trial are also heard in the

Return Day Court, for 'mention'. Where matters are mentioned, the case file is often incomplete. When no formal Return Day Court exists, there may be specified days for such matters to be heard.

**Summary Courts**

The Summary Court is a trial court in the main. Matters ready for trial are sent to this court. The court therefore tries mainly summary matters including those under the Dangerous Drugs Act and Offensive Weapons (Prohibitions) Act.

However, a number of indictable matters, hearings, and committal proceedings may also be placed occasionally in this court. This may be as a result of another courtroom having many matters on their list.

**Committal Proceedings[5]**

Committal proceedings were previously known as preliminary enquiries, but the Committal Proceedings Act repealed and amended the specific provisions of the Justice of the Peace Jurisdiction Act related to this. However, there may still be a few summary, indictable matters as well as hearings before this court.

The limit of the Judge of the Parish Court's custodial sentencing power is three years except where so particularized[6] – such as for forgery offences. Committal proceedings are therefore conducted in the Parish Courts for certain offences where the possible custodial sentence falls outside the jurisdictional maximum custodial sentencing power of the Judge of the Parish Court.

For example, under the Offences against the Person Act, offences such as murder, wounding with intent, and causing grievous bodily harm require committal proceedings in the Parish Court. Under the Sexual Offences Act, there are several offences such as having sexual intercourse with a minor that stipulates the necessity for a committal proceeding.

**The Gun Court**

The Gun Court Act gives the Judge of the Parish Court particular powers related to firearm offences. In the Gun Court Act, as it relates to the Parish Court Division of the (Gun) Court, the jurisdiction is as set out below:[7]

a. to conduct any committal proceeding relating to a firearm offence which is murder or treason, whether committed in Kingston or St Andrew or any other parish, *other than* (emphasis added ) the parishes referred to in section 8(a)(3) or a parish designated under section 8d, and to commit the accused to a Circuit Court Division of the Court;

b. to hear and determine any offence under subsection (3) of section 13;

c. determine all matters appearing to be ancillary to trial in any division of the Court

---

5. The Committal Proceedings Act at section 3(2) indicates that committal proceedings may be conducted wholly on the basis of written statements submitted to the Judge of the Parish Court. After examining all statements, the Judge of the Parish Court may commit the accused to stand trial or discharge him or her.

6. The Forgery Act speaks to five years imprisonment at hard labour. The offences triable in the Parish Court are described under section 268 of the Judicature (Parish Courts) Act.

7. The Gun Court Act, section 5.

Murders that were committed with firearms also come within the purview of the Parish Court's (Gun Court) Division under committal proceedings. *All other firearm* (emphasis added) related matters are heard in the High Court Division of the Court for the particular parish.[8]

At section 4 of the Gun Court Act, it states that there are three divisions, namely:

1. a Parish Court division;

2. a Supreme Court judge sitting without a jury – the High Court Division of the Gun Court; and

3. a Supreme Court judge exercising the jurisdiction of a Circuit Court – the Circuit Court Division.

The Parish Court has further powers under the Gun Court Act. In the parishes of Kingston, St Andrew, or St Catherine, the Judge of the Parish Court shall forthwith transfer any case involving 'a firearm offence'. Such a case is to be sent for trial in the Gun Court.[9]

In such a situation, the Judge of the Parish Court is to endorse the number one information (the record) stating: 'Let this matter be transferred to the High Court Division of the Gun Court where jurisdiction lies.'

The Judge of the Parish Court's jurisdiction in other parishes is also set out for firearm offences under section 6(2) of the Gun Court Act. The other parishes as well those specifically noted under section 8(a)(3) are also required to treat firearm offences in a particular manner.[10] Where the offence before the court is not murder or treason, the Judge of the Parish Court may ask the Clerk of the Courts to ascertain whether the Court has jurisdiction to hear the matter at all.

The Clerk of the Courts, therefore, must know the nuances of the Gun Court Act and the jurisdiction of the Judge of the Parish Court. If the procedure to be taken is unclear, the Clerk must do the necessary research to assist the Judge of the Parish Court to make a proper decision.

Having so made enquiries, the Judge of the Parish Court can exercise any of the powers so vested under the section. The Judge of the Parish Court can direct that the defendant be tried in the Parish Court, not hold a committal proceeding, and forthwith make an order that the defendant be committed to stand and take his trial in a High Court Division or direct that the case be transferred for trial to the Gun Court.

The Western Regional Gun Court is established in Montego Bay and its geographical jurisdiction extends throughout St James, Hanover, Trelawny, and Westmoreland. As such, all other firearm offences except for murder and treason are heard in this court by a single Judge of the Supreme Court. The Parish Court Division of the Regional Gun Court (Western) has the jurisdiction to conduct committal proceedings into gun murders or treason in the parishes of St James, Hanover, Trelawny, and Westmoreland. This Parish Court exercises all of the powers as noted above.

The proceedings of the Gun Court are in camera and, as such, the Judge of the Parish Court's has jurisdiction to try persons who contravene the Gun Court Act regarding publicizing in camera sessions. Notably, the Judge of the Parish Court in the Gun Court has the power to try persons who publish information about such Gun Court proceedings.[11]

---

8.  Ibid., section 5(2).
9.  Section 6(1) Gun Court Act.
10. Ibid., section 6(2).
11. Section 8A of the Gun Court Act deals with the establishment of the Western Regional Gun Court. Section 8B deals with the sittings of the Gun Court. Section 13(3) sets out the power of the Parish Court Judge to try persons who publish information relating to the particulars of witnesses or the intimate details of the proceedings of a trial in the Gun Court.

## Night Court of the Parish Court[12]

The Night Court is presided over by a Judge of the Parish Court. The Clerk of the Courts usually marshals the cases, but sometimes the deputy Clerk or an assistant Clerk marshals the cases. The formalities are the same as for court held in the daytime. Matters are 'transferred' or 'sent to' the Night Court after they have first come before the Return Day Court.

The Judge of the Parish Court has discretionary power to deem a case fit to be tried in the Night Court. Generally, clear-cut cases involving an unrepresented defendant are transferred to the Night Court.

The Night Court also presides over matters involving certain types of private prosecutions, domestic disputes, assaults, and the like. Essentially, the court deals with matters that appear capable of fast disposition.

## Drug Court[13]

The Drug Court is a sitting of the Parish Court. It is declared to be a drug court as stipulated by the Drug (Treatment and Rehabilitation of Offenders) Act, often referred to as the Drug Court Act. The Court may sit separately and may be opened to hear matters and then closed at the end of the list when another court is opened. This often happens when there are a limited number of courtrooms or available Parish Court Judges.

Persons who appear before the Drug Court are those arrested for the possession of not more than one ounce of prepared opium, between two and eight ounces of ganja, and one-tenth of an ounce of cocaine, heroin, or morphine, according to section 7(3) of the Dangerous Drugs Act. Persons in possession of pipes or other paraphernalia used to smoking ganja or opium also fall within the Drug Court's jurisdiction.

Anyone smoking or so otherwise using ganja or prepared opium or frequenting places where opium is smoked, also fall within the Parish Court's jurisdiction.[14] Such accused persons must appear to have a persistent drug habit with which the Drug Court's prescribed rehabilitation programme can assist.[15]

The objects of the Drug Court, at section 3, are crucial to ensuring that the Drug Court is not abused. One significant aim is to reduce the incidence of drug use amongst those whose criminal activities are found to be clearly linked to their dependence on such drugs. As such, persons who are generally found with drugs or drug utensils are outside the contemplation of the Act.

The consent form is used for any person recommended for the drug court and shows the perceived role the Court plays in reducing the person's dependency on the illicit substance.

See Figure 5.1 for an example of the consent form in the Drug Court.

The Clerk of the Courts, the arresting officer, or the investigating officer usually indicates to the Court that the accused has a drug habit and recommends Drug Court. The defendant is then referred to the Drug Court by the Judge of the Parish Court.

The prosecution of offences is put on hold while a person is before the Drug Court. At the end of a successful rehabilitation programme, the accused is brought back to the Parish Court where the Clerk of the Courts advises the Judge whether the Crown intends to prosecute the offence. If the programme was not successfully completed, the Judge of the Parish Court is empowered to hear the matter, order another programme of

---

12. The Night Court sits as a part of the Parish Court, on designated days often between 5 p.m. and 9 p.m. Several parishes convene a night court.
13. The Drug Court (Treatment and Rehabilitation of Offenders) Act at section 2 defines the scope of the court. At section 4, the jurisdiction of the Drug Court is delineated.
14. Section 7(3) of the Drug Court (Treatment and Rehabilitation of Offenders) Act outlines of the classes of offences that fall within the purview of the Act.
15. Section 3 of the Drug Court (Treatment and Rehabilitation of Offenders) Act sets out the objects of the Drug Court Act and are critical to ensuring that the legislation is not abused.

Figure 5.1     Sample Consent Form in the Drug Court

---

**THE DRUG COURT ACT, 1999**

**Consent of Person Arrested and Charged with a Relevant Offence to be**

**Transferred to the Drug Court**

**(Under Regulation 4 (2) (c))**

I, _____John Doe_____

of _____1 Main Street_____

having been arrested and charged with the office of _____smoking marijuana_____

_____being the relevant offence,

do hereby signify my consent to be referred to the Drug Court to be dealt with in accordance

with Section 8 of the Drug Court Act, 1999.

*John Doe*                                                          September 13, 20–
.............................                                    .............................
Signature of person arrested and                                         Date
charged with relevant offence

*Lila Clarke*                                                       September 13, 20–
.............................                                    .............................
Signature of Clerk of the Courts                                         Date

Declared before me this  13th  day of      September 21,      20–

Signed:        *Joe Brown*
              .............................
              Parish Court Judge, Justice of the Peace
              Clerk of the Courts, Registrar *(delete as necessary)*

---

treatment, sentence the accused evidenced on the particular offence (after as guilty plea or a guilty verdict), or refer the matter back to the regular court sitting.[16] Under section 14 of the Act, the Clerk of the Courts shall keep a register with the prescribed particulars of persons who are before the Drug Court.

## Lay Magistrate's Court

The Lay Magistrate's Court was formerly known as the Petty Session Court or the Court of Petty Sessions. It was renamed in 2018 by the passage of the Renaming of the Courts of Petty Sessions (Miscellaneous Amendments) Act. Justices of the Peace preside in this court as is prescribed by the Justices of the Peace Jurisdiction Act.[17] Sometimes the Judge of the Parish Court has a Lay Magistrate's Court matter on his or her list and, in such a situation, is actually sitting in the Court in a Lay Magistrate capacity. The Clerk of the Courts marshals the evidence before this court. Notably, a Judge of the Parish Court has the power of two Justices.

## Traffic Court

The Road Traffic Act[18] governs a myriad of traffic offences within the jurisdiction of the Parish Court. While the Corporate Area has a specialized traffic court, all other parishes may have special days dedicated to deal exclusively with traffic cases.

Section 109 of the Road Traffic Act provides that unless expressly stated, all offences or contraventions of the act shall be tried summarily. The section further states that to determine jurisdiction, the offence or contravention shall be deemed to have been committed either at the actual place or in the parish in which the offender resides.[19]

The Corporate Area has a specialized Traffic Court that hears only traffic maters occurring in that jurisdiction.

---

16. Section 7 of the Drug Court (Treatment and Rehabilitation of Offenders) Act examines the persons who may be brought directly before the Drug Court. Section 8 discusses the assessment procedure for offenders. Section 9 indicates that the Drug Court has very wide powers once an offender accepts the conditions imposed for his participation in any prescribed treatment programme. Under section 10, the Drug Court programme can be terminated. Section 13 illustrates the fact that the act allows the Judge of the Parish Court very wide powers to assist in the rehabilitation of such offenders.
17. The Justices of the Peace Jurisdiction Act sets out the offences under the jurisdiction of the Lay Magistrate's Court.
18. The Road Traffic Act deals with the regulation of motor vehicles at sections 9–11; the licensing and regulation of motor vehicles at sections 12–15; the matter of driving connected offences at sections 26–38; the duty to stop in the case of an accident at section 39; lights, reflectors, horns, and noise at sections 40–43; seatbelts and protective helmets at 43A–48; the weighing of vehicles at 49–50B; driving rules at 51–58; the points system at 59A–59C; the regulation of Public Passenger Vehicles at 60–68; conductors licence at 69–70; provisions as to licences at 71–77; the regulation of commercial motor cars at 78–89; roads and vehicles generally at sections 92–105; the special powers of enforcement and administration regarding the traffic ticketing system at section 116 and section 120, and the proof in summary proceedings of the identity of the driver of a motor vehicle. The amendments to the Road Traffic Act were passed in the Upper and Lower Houses of Parliament. However, as of this writing, there was no Gazetting.
19. Section 109 of the Road Traffic Act stipulates that: 'Every offence under, and every contravention of, this Act shall, except where otherwise expressly provided be tried summarily and the offence or contravention shall be deemed to have been committed either at the place at which the same was actually committed or in the parish in which the offender resides.'

# Chapter 6

# Return Court

## Summary

This chapter describes the way in which the Return Court is conducted and builds on the chapter discussing the types of courts in the system.

## Terms

- Types of Matters in Return Court
- File Status
- Accused in Custody
- Outlining the Case File to the Court
- Representation
- Bail and Other Issues in the Case
- Pleading the Accused
- Guilty Plea
- Not Guilty Plea
- Mixed Plea
- Mention Matters
- Applications
- Return Day Ends

### Types of Matters on the Return Court List

Case files start in the Return Court. The type of matter will determine where they are later sent. Case files, therefore, come to the trial courts from the Return Court.

Current case files are kept in date order in the 'dip', which is really a storage area such as a filing cabinet for each court. This means that all the cases for a particular day are kept together. They are also written in the court diary in order of the date upon which they are scheduled to be heard in the court. Therefore, it is possible to know ahead of time what matters are slated to be heard on any particular day.

The matters that are heard in Return Day Court vary. They include new matters, and for every day that there is a return day, there will be new matters on the list. There are also mention matters, applications to re-list, *habeas corpus*, and re-issued summons among others. The Return Court may be a dedicated court or only a dedicated day. The latter is often the case in parishes where there are fewer resources, both human and physical.

Matters remain in the Return Court until they are at a stage where they can be sent for trial, for hearing in one of the trial courts, or for committal proceedings. The Return Day Court, therefore, acts as a gatekeeper. Its aim is to ensure efficiencies by only sending cases to trial that are ready.

## File Status

The Clerk of the Courts would have previously conducted file preparation to determine various aspects of the case files. How the accused has been brought before the court is important to determine how both the prosecution and defence proceed. The accused first comes before the Court in one of several ways:

- On Bail: - having been granted station bail. The person who is on bail should be either inside the court or outside waiting to be called.
- By summons: - for private trial matters, summons, or re-issued summons. The person who was summoned should be either inside the court or outside waiting to hear her name.
- In custody: - this person would be held at a police station or correctional facility. In this case, the accused should have been already brought by the police to the court building and kept in the holding area until the matter has been called up.

## Accused in Custody

The Clerk of the Courts must make enquiries of the court police officers if the custody accused are in the holding area. This helps to control the list, so matters will not be called when the accused are absent from the courtroom. A good rule of thumb for the Clerk of the Courts is to call such matters later in the list. Alternatively, the court police officers may indicate to the Clerk of the Courts that the accused persons in custody have been brought up from the police lock ups and processed in the holding area. In that event, the accused are basically waiting to be escorted into court. Sometimes the defence attorney indicates that the client is in custody and has been brought. In such a scenario, this case can be called up earlier than where the accused person has not been brought from whatever facility where s/he is being held.

## Outlining the Case File to the Court

The Clerk of the Courts must indicate to the Court the details of the charges, presence or absence of the police liaison officer, the investigating officer, and any witnesses. If the accused has legal representation and it has been indicated, the Clerk of the Courts also advises the Parish Court Judge. It is useful to assist the Court by asking the accused if s/he is represented if there is no indication. The status of the accused is crucial, and so it should always be indicated to the Parish Court Judge. The accused may be on bail, on bail in this instant matter but in custody in others, in custody, or has a bail offer. All of this should be relayed to the Judge.

The Judge writes all of the information that is conveyed on the court sheet and as such, accuracy from the Clerk of the Courts is absolutely important.

## Representation

If there is an attorney representing the accused and s/he is present, the attorney will rise and address the Court on the matter. Issues such as bail (see chapter on bail), applications (see chapter on applications), and the like can be canvassed at this time. Where there are persons in custody there may be no representation when the matter comes first before the court. Time can be given by the Parish Court Judge to an accused to settle his representation with a private attorney, or an order might be made for the accused to be interviewed for a legal aid assignment of an attorney under the Legal Aid Act. However, it is not unusual in the Parish Courts for an accused to be remain unrepresented throughout the life of his/her matter.

## Bail and Other Issues in the Case

When the Clerk of the Courts has no opposition to bail after the requisite due diligence and based on the allegations, it should be so indicated to the Court. Where a person with interest in the matter is present in the court (such as someone whose vehicle was used in an offence), it is the duty of the Clerk of the Courts to so indicate. Such a person may wish to get their property back and an appropriate bond can be ordered by the Judge of the Parish Court.

If an accused is offered bail by the Court, the conditions are to be written on the number one information by the Clerk of the Courts and sent up to the Judge for signing. The Judge also writes the various conditions in the court sheet.

## Pleading the Accused (Arraignment)

When the accused enters the dock, the Clerk of the Courts should plead him by reading directly from the number one information detailing the offences (s) as follows:

> Mr John Brown, you are charged that on the first day of January 2008, at the Norman Manley International Airport, in the Corporate Area, you did have ganja in your possession contrary to section 7C of the DDA. How do you plead sir, guilty or not guilty?

It may be the case that the accused does not understand the specific language used in the offence. It is proper to use ordinary words that closely follow the actual wording to explain the allegations. So, for example the above, the Clerk could properly state 'the police say that you had ten pounds of ganja in your suitcase at the airport, guilty or not guilty?'

The accused should be pleaded on *all* of the offences that are on the number one information. If the plea is not guilty, the accused is, therefore, joining issue with the Crown's case. It is the taking of the plea that determines what procedure is followed thereafter.

## Guilty Plea

If the accused pleads guilty, sentencing can be immediate or postponed. Where sentencing is to be at a later date, it is to be before the same Judge of the Parish Court.[1] If the matter is as such that the sentence can be given immediately, the Judge will hand down the sentence. The cases of *R v Pearlina Wright* and *Gaynair Hanson v R* as well as the Criminal Justice Administration Act are very useful in this regard.[2]

The Clerk of the Courts writes the sentence of the court on the number one information on the case file. Immediately after, the file is handed to the court police officer who will, in turn, give it to the Judge of the Parish Court for signing. The Parish Court Judge will also write the sentence in the court sheet. The Clerk of

---

1. The Judge of the Parish Court who takes a guilty plea is the Judge who is to sentence the accused.
2. *R v Pearlina Wright* (1998) 25 JLR 221; *Gaynair Hanson v R* [2014] JMCA Crim 1. The Criminal Justice (Administration) Act at section 42D deals with reducing sentences after a guilty plea to an offence.

the Courts then ensures that the file is returned and placed in the batch of files that have already been dealt with on the list, to avoid confusion.

> ...cases where a guilty plea is entered by an accused, the learned [Parish Court] Judge must note clearly what has transpired before the court. Any statement made by the Clerk of the Court or other prosecuting officer should be noted, and any statement made by the accused or by his counsel should also be noted as forming part of the record of the trial, otherwise, it will be impossible for the Court of Appeal to know what in fact did transpire in the court below.[3]

## Not Guilty Plea

Where the accused pleads not guilty, there are several options available to the Clerk of the Courts.

- Set another date by agreeing a date with the defence attorney who is present. If the accused is unrepresented, set a date that is convenient to the court's diary. In any event, the main issues to bear in mind include if the accused is in custody, witness availability, and the state of the court's diary. Once the case has been heard, it is automatically removed from the new list. It should go on the mention list in the Return Court if it is not a ready file.

- If the file is ready for trial, the Clerk must set a date for trial in one of the trial courts. It is a good idea to canvass with those courts the state of their diaries so that the matters are not set for dates that are in reality inconvenient to them. The Parish Court Judge will make the notation in the court sheet that the file is 'transferred for trial to court # —.' This notation is also endorsed on the file.

## Mixed Plea

- When this occurs, the Clerk must make accurate and appropriate notations on the file as to the guilty plea and then transfer the other matters to another court if that is appropriate at the time. Appropriateness is determined by the readiness of the file. Thus, the file could remain in the Return Court for some time even where an accused has pleaded guilty to one or more of the offences, which have been disposed of by the Parish Court Judge.

## Mention Matters

All dates subsequent to the first date that a matter is dealt with, i.e., 'mentioned', in the court are called mention dates. As matters come up again for mention in Return Day Court, their state of readiness must be checked. The procedure is basically the same as for new matter cases.

## Applications

A wide range of applications, such as to relist, *habeas corpus*,[4] re-issued summons, private prosecutions, and others come before the Parish Court Judge in the Return Court. The manner in which these are dealt is dictated by what documentation is before the Court. As an example, applications for *habeas corpus* can be made orally and or in writing.

---

3. See *Canterbury v Joseph* (Police Constable) (1963) 6 WIR, *R v Cecil Green* (1965) 9 JLR 254 and *Michael Francis v R* [2021] JMCA Crim 5.
4. Section 286 of the Judicature (Parish Courts) Act indicates that when an application for *habeas corpus* is made for anyone detained, the Judge of the Parish Court can make enquiries into the circumstances and reasons for the detention.

## After Return Court Day Ends

At the end of the return day, the case files must all be accounted for by the Clerk of the Courts. Notably, files that are fully disposed of in Return Day Court are to be sent to the back desk after the outcome has been noted on the number one information. The outcomes are noted in the appropriate court record books (see the chapter on court record books).

**Figure 6.1    Return Day Court Sheet**

Holden at Corporate Area Parish Court this ___2nd___ day of ___January___ 20--,
before ___Her Honour Miss Stephle Jones,___ Parish Court Judge

### Mention Cases

| Number of Information * | Prosecutor * | Defendant | Offence * | Fine ** Costs |
|---|---|---|---|---|
| 9135/20– 9139/20– | Regina    v | Strokes, Tom | Unlawful Poss. of Prop | John Johnson Rep. Not Guilty Plea. IO to complete file by NCD. <br><br> IOBO <br><br> Bail offer -$50k, 1/2 S |
| 9100/20- | Regina   v | Brenn, Hick | Murder | Paul Smith Rep. <br><br> No Post Mortem Report <br><br> RIC |

### Re-Issued Summons

| | | | | |
|---|---|---|---|---|
| 2001/07 | Regina v | Hopnes, Havia | Larceny/ Servant | No returns for Summons |
| | Regina v | Hopnes, Havia | Uttering F/ Docs | No return for Summons |

### Application to Re-List

| | | | | |
|---|---|---|---|---|
| 3000/90 | Regina v | Jones, Tom | Mal. Inj. to Prop. | Case dismissed |
| | | | | |

### *Habeas Corpus*

| | | | | |
|---|---|---|---|---|
| | Re: | Doe, Jane | | Charge or release by 4pm today |
| | | Bills, Tomas | | Charge or release by 4pm today |
| | | | | |

### New Cases

| | | | | |
|---|---|---|---|---|
| CA20– CR00001 | Regina v | Harris, Robin | Possession of Ganja | Not guilty plea. <br><br> Bail – $150,000 w. <br><br> 1/2 surety. <br><br> Transferred to Court 5 <br><br> NCD 10.2.20-- |

\* These are written in the court sheet beforehand by the assistant clerk.
\*\* The Parish Court Judge writes in this section, recording the salient points regarding the matter.

Where the sentence is or includes a fine, it must be paid immediately, unless the accused was granted additional time to pay it. In the alternative, the accused must serve the custodial sentence. Fines are paid in to the accountant's office[5] and a receipt is issued to the payee. The accountant writes the sum of the fine that was paid, the requisite receipt number related to that payment and the date when it was paid in the return day court sheet beside the name of the accused. If there are custodial sentences, the committal forms are completed, and the sentence information is written in the commitment book.[6]

## Status of the Accused at End of Return Day

For custodial sentences, the accused is returned to the holding area and is then transferred to the facility where the custodial sentence will be served. The committal forms accompany the accused. Where an accused has been fined, when the fine(s) has been paid, the accused is released provided s/he has no other matter for which s/he is in custody. If the prosecution offers no evidence against him or her, the accused is discharged and the case dismissed and can request a certificate of acquittal from the Court.[7]

Figure 6.2    Case File in Return Day Court with Endorsement about Bail and Showing a Transfer to a Trial

To be Holden at St. Catherine Parish Court

On 12.1.20--

Brown, Dudd }Williams

for  Assault     Joeh

Sgt. #1000

On 12.1.20--

Bail conditions

Bail in the sum of $30,000

With one surety.

*(Judge's signature here)*

Parish Court Judge

Transferred to Court # 3

NCD 21.1.20--

Statements to be copied for Attorney

---

5.  Section 41C of the Judicature (Parish Courts) Act.
6.  Section 288 of the Judicature (Parish Courts) Act states that where an accused is committed to prison, the requisite form of commitment is to be used.
7.  Section 280(3) of the Judicature (Parish Courts) Act speaks of the certificate of acquittal and the certificate of conviction for the accused once a matter ends.

The case files are usually folded with the number one informations on the outside, and so these examples are for illustration purposes only, showing the relevant part of the number one information. The Clerk endorses all information on the file and the Parish Court Judge signs in the requisite section.

**Figure 6.3    Case File in Return Day Court with Guilty Plea on a Summary Trial Matter and Showing Payment of Fine**

On 2. 1. 20–


Before Her Hon

Liana Crassly

St. Elizabeth Parish Court


Arraigned: 2.1.20--

Plea:

Tried:                    } Guilty

Verdict

Sentence:


$24,000 fine

*(Judge's signature here)*

St. Elizabeth Parish Court Judge

Fine PAID ON 2.1.20—

Receipt # 123

Accountant: Tom Strokes

# Chapter 7

# Committal Proceedings[1]

## Summary

Committal proceedings are held to determine whether sufficient evidence exists in a criminal case to bring the matter to trial. They may take place in a dedicated courtroom or within a larger court list, depending on the court's resources. Committal proceedings were previously called preliminary enquiries, and the Judge of the Parish Court was responsible for marshalling the evidence in the matter, even though, in reality, the Clerk of the Courts took on this responsibility. Prosecution witnesses were also deposed in preliminary enquiries.

However, significant changes have been made in the way matters are examined in the committal proceedings phase. The Judge of the Parish Court now examines only the document case file (with exceptions being allowed for by the Committal Proceedings Act) and determines thereon, whether or not a prima facie case has been established against the accused. If a prima facie case is established after reading the case file, the matter should be committed to the Circuit Court for trial in the upcoming term.

Since the Committal Proceedings Act allows for either a paper decision (a decision by the Judge after reading the case file) or an actual proceeding, it is prudent that Clerks understand how to marshal evidence in a committal proceedings should the Judge embark on a full proceeding.

In this chapter, all references are to the Committal Proceedings Act (CPA) unless otherwise stated.

## Terms

Initial Enquiries by the Judge of the Parish Court

The Court Sitting for Committal Proceedings

Committal Proceedings for Indictable Offcences

### Initial Enquiries by the Judge of the Parish Court

The Judge of the Parish Court has the power to make an enquiry to ascertain if the offence charged is within the Court's jurisdiction and if the accused could be adequately punished upon a trial if found guilty. The Judge can, therefore, make orders which are to be duly endorsed on the number one information and signed by him or her. The orders can be one of two: that the accused should be tried; or that committal proceedings should be held with a view to a committal in the Circuit Court if a prima facie case is made out against the accused.[2]

---

1. The Committal Proceedings Act and attendant Committal Proceedings Rules repealed and replaced the preliminary enquiry under the Justices of the Peace Jurisdiction Act.
2. Section 272 of the Judicature (Parish Courts) Act gives the Judge of the Parish Court the power to make an enquiry as it seems necessary to ascertain jurisdiction of the indictable offences thereon in the information. If the offence is within the Judge's

## The Court Sitting for Committal Proceedings

The Judge of the Parish Court sits as an examining justice in the Lay Magistrate's Court when committal proceedings are being heard (CPA section 2). Any room or building where the Judge of the Parish Court conducts committal proceedings should be deemed an open court (CPA section 14(1)) subject to two situations.

Firstly, the Judge of the Parish Court may consider if it is necessary or expedient, in the interest of justice, to exclude from the proceedings, persons other than the relevant parties and their attorneys at law (CPA section 14(2)).

Secondly, dependent on specific provisions in other Acts, the categories of persons who may be present during committal proceedings are in any event restricted (CPA section 14(5)).

## Committal Proceedings for Indictable Offcences

Under the Justices of the Peace Jurisdiction Act at section 29, as amended by the CPA, any person who has committed or who is suspected to have committed any treason, felony, or indictable misdemeanour or other indictable offence, should be brought to answer that charge. An indictable offence is an offence that is triable in the Criminal Division of the Supreme Court (CPA section 2(3)).

Warrants should be issued for such persons charged, or summons as the case requires, compelling their attendance upon the court, under section 32 of the Justices of the Peace Jurisdiction Act.

### Committal for Trial on Written Statements

Under the Committal Proceedings Act, the Judge of the Parish Court can order that committal proceedings be held. Section 3(2) of the CPA provides that the proceedings may be conducted wholly, on the basis of written statements submitted to the Court in the case file.

For a committal, the Judge of the Parish Court must be satisfied that all the evidence tendered, in respect of the offence(s) from either the prosecution or the defence, consists of written statements, with or without exhibits *and* that those statements are compliant (CPA section 3(2)(b)). Upon examination of all the evidence, the Judge of the Parish Court may commit the accused to stand trial or discharge him or her (CPA section 3(2)(b)).

### When are Written Statements Compliant?

Section 6(1) of the CPA indicates that a written statement should be admissible as evidence in the *same manner as oral evidence by that person* (emphasis added).

- **Recording the Statement**

    For a written statement to be admissible, it should be recorded by a member of the Jamaica Constabulary Force, who is called the recorder, and done in the presence of a Justice of the Peace (to reduce bias and protect the integrity of the record). If no Justice of the Peace is present, the statement may be recorded in the presence of a senior member of the Jamaica Constabulary Force, not below the rank of Sergeant.

    The statement is to be read over to the maker or communicated to him or her in any other effective manner required, for example, through sign language for persons with a disability (CPA section 6(2)(a)).

---

jurisdiction, the trial can proceed. If the Judge has no jurisdiction, then a committal proceeding should be held in accordance with the Committal Proceedings Act with a view to committal to the Circuit Court.

- **Signing the Statement**

  The statement is to be signed by the maker and the recorder – in each other's presence – and in the presence of the Justice of the Peace or the senior member of the Jamaica Constabulary Force (CPA section 6(2)(b)).

- **The Declaration in the Statement**

  The statement must contain a declaration by the maker, stating that all of its content is true to the best of his or her knowledge and belief, that the maker is at least 14 years old and knows that s/he may be prosecuted if s/he wilfully gave false statements or said anything s/he believed to be false (CPA section 6(2)(c)).

- **Age of the Maker**

  The statement should state whether the maker is over 18 years old and if under age 18, then the particular age should be stated (CPA section 6(3)(a)).

  If the maker is under 14 however, then the Judge of the Parish Court has to refer to the provisions of the Child Care and Protection Act which stipulates that the Judge must receive evidence from an independent assessor to determine whether the child understands the nature of an oath and the duty of truth telling. This evidence is collected either by oral examination of the assessor or via the assessor's written statement submitted to the court (CPA sections 6(3)(c) and 6(3)(b) (ii) and (iii)).

  Section 6(4) of the CPA also indicates the persons a Judge of the Parish Court may consider as being qualified to assess a child.

- **Safeguards where the Maker is Unable to Read**

  The Act provides that where a maker cannot read, the statement is to be read to the maker or otherwise effectively communicated to him or her. This is to be done before s/he signs the statement or makes their mark. The accompanying declaration is to state that the maker made his or her mark. See section 6(3)(d) for additional details.

- **Safeguards where the Maker is Incapable of Signing or Making a Mark**

  Where such a situation exists, the statement is to be read to or otherwise effectively communicated to such a maker so that s/he can affirm or negate the content of the statement. The *recorder* (emphasis added) must provide a declaration that said statement had been made with the maker's affirmation and there should be a clear indication of the nature of the affirmation. See section 6(3)(e) of the CPA.

- **Where Statements Refer to Other Documents as Exhibits**

  Statements that refer to other documents as exhibits should be served on the other parties to the proceedings. In the alternative, the information required to allow the other party to inspect such documents and to get copies must be furnished (CPA section 6(3)(f)(i) and (ii)). If a statement refers to an exhibit that cannot be conveniently copied, such a statement must include information as to where the exhibit is available for inspection (CPA section 6(3)(g)).

- **Treatment of Documents or Objects Referred to as Exhibits in Written Statements Admitted into Evidence**

  Any such document or object is inadmissible as evidence in the committal proceedings *unless* (emphasis added) it has been produced in court as an exhibit and marked as having been produced. The accused person (and/or an attorney) must also have had the opportunity to inspect the exhibit per section 6(5)(a) of the Act. Furthermore, if an exhibit cannot be conveniently produced in court, the parties must have been served with notice of the location of the particular exhibit (CPA section 6(5)(b)).

### Treatment of Written Statements

Where a written statement has been admitted in evidence in a committal proceeding, such statement should be treated as a witness who has given evidence in said proceedings (CPA section 6(6)).

Any maker of age 14 and above, whose written statement has been tendered in evidence has wilfully made a statement material to the proceedings, and who knows that the statement given is false or does not believe the statement made to be true, is guilty of an offence.

Upon summary conviction before a Parish Court, such a maker is liable for a fine not exceeding $3 million or to imprisonment not exceeding three years or to *both* (emphasis added) such fine and imprisonment.

Under sections 6(11)(a) and (b), if the conviction is in the Circuit Court on indictment, then the penalty is a fine or imprisonment or *both* (emphasis added) fine and imprisonment for a term not exceeding seven years.

- **Signing of Statements and Documents Tendered**

  Every written statement tendered and every document tendered as an exhibit should be signed by the Judge of the Parish Court when s/he is sure they comply with section 6 (CPA section 9).

- **Witness Orders**

  The Judge of the Parish Court conducting committal proceedings may make witness orders regarding all the witnesses who gave evidence in the proceedings. These witness orders essentially require the witness to attend in person and give their evidence before the Circuit Court where the accused will be tried (CPA section 12(1)).

  Every witness order is to be served by a constable or other authorized person upon the witness. The witness order is to be delivered to the witness personally, or if s/he cannot be found, by leaving it with some person at the usual or last place of abode. The constable or other authorized person is to attend on the court, if necessary, to prove the witness order was served (CPA section 12(2)). The authorized person is appointed by the Judge of the Parish Court (CPA section 12(4)).

  According to section 12(1), no witness order is made for accused persons.

- **Disobedience of a Witness Order**

  Unless a person has just cause to disobey a witness order, s/he is guilty of contempt of court (CPA section 12(3)). The offence is a summary one and is punishable by the court that the person should have attended. Notably, there is no definition in the Act of what should constitute just cause in contempt of court; it is left to the discretion of the sitting Court. The witness is liable to face a maximum of three months' imprisonment for disobeying a witness order. This is, therefore, a powerful tool that the Court has to ensure that witnesses attend court, give evidence after a matter has been committed, and assist in the disposal of cases within a reasonable period of time.

  The Court also has another option that can be prayed in aid where a witness fails to comply with a witness order. The Court can order that a notice be served on the witness demanding his attendance on a particular day (CPA section 13(1)(a)). If the Court is satisfied that there are reasonable grounds to believe that the failure to attend is without just cause or if the witness fails to attend per any notice served, then a warrant can be issued for his or her arrest to bring the witness before the court (CPA section 13(1)(b)).

Any witness brought into court upon a warrant may be remanded into custody or admitted to bail (with or without sureties, at the discretion of the Court). The remand or bail should secure the witness's presence on the requisite date that the matter will be heard (CPA section 13(2)).

- **When Witness Attends Court per a Notice**

   The witness who attends court, having been served a notice, may be bound over by the Court to attend on a later date to give evidence or for the Court to deal with the witness as necessary. Therefore, it should be as if the initial notice itself required the witness to attend on the later date (CPA section 13(3)).

## Production of Statements to Parties

Section 6(2)(d) requires that all statements be served on the parties to the proceedings, according to the terms of section 8.

Interestingly, under section 8(1) of the CPA, steps shall be taken by the prosecution and *each accused person* (emphasis added) to make available to the other and to any other accused person in the proceedings, copies of such statements or other documents that they intend to rely on at the committal proceedings in relation to the offence(s) charged.

So the Act places some burden on an accused person to ensure that s/he serves, and is served statements and documentary evidence. This is especially so in multiple accused matters. The parties must serve on every other party not less than seven days before the committal proceedings or on any specified date of adjournment of such proceedings (CPA section 8(2)).

Notably, the Judge of the Parish Court may vary the seven-day period if s/he is not satisfied that a particular party has had adequate time to consider any statement or document (CPA section 8(3)). The affected party usually applies to the Judge to vary this time period, but the Judge may vary the seven-day period without any such application by a party.

## The Committal Proceedings in Practice

There is no plea taken from the accused in committal proceedings. Instead, the Parish Court Judge asks the Clerk of the Courts to find out whether the offence charged is within the Court's jurisdiction and can be adequately punished under the Court's powers per section 272 of the Judicature (Parish Courts) Act. If it is permissible to try the offence, the proceedings follow that format. Where there is no jurisdiction, the Judge should sign the order for the committal proceedings to be committed to the Circuit Court. This order should have been previously endorsed on the number one information as a matter of proper preparation by the Clerk of the Courts.[3]

- **Where Only Written Statements and Documentary Exhibits are Considered**

   The Judge of the Parish Court (having previously perused all pertinent statements and documentary exhibits) generally asks the defence attorney if s/he agrees that the statements and any documentary exhibits are compliant. If there is agreement, the Judge should rule whether the accused is to be committed to stand trial or be discharged. If there is no representation, the Judge must doubly ensure that all of the strictures of section 6 are met before any decision regarding committal is made.

---

3. Ibid.

- **Submissions by Attorney/Accused**

  Section 3(3) of the CPA provides that the accused or the attorney may make a submission to the Judge that the evidence is not sufficient to commit the accused to the Circuit Court for trial for an indictable offence.

  If there is no attorney on record for the accused, the Judge should inform the accused that s/he has the right *to himself or herself* (emphasis added) make a submission about the insufficiency of any evidence (CPA section 3(4)).

  The Judge should take such submissions into consideration when determining whether to commit the accused for trial. In essence, the Judge must establish on the statements and documents tendered if there is a *prima facie* case for the accused to answer.

- **Oral Evidence from Persons Other Than Accused**

  The Judge of the Parish Court may hear a submission from either an attorney or an accused (CPA section 4(4) and 4(5)) and may also allow that oral evidence be taken at the committal proceedings from any person other than the accused (CPA section 4(1)).

  The basis of the decision to allow this type of oral evidence is that it may help the Judge decide whether the accused is to be committed to stand trial.

  If the Judge of the Parish Court determines that oral evidence is required, s/he may issue a summons or warrant (CPA section 4(6)).

  The oral evidence must be under oath and must be subject to cross-examination (CPA section 4(2)). An unsworn statement may be allowed where legislation permits.

  Where such evidence is taken, it is to be recorded, either in writing or electronically, in the form of a deposition and read over to the witness at the end of the deposition. After that, it should be signed by both the witness and the Parish Court Judge (CPA section 4(3)). Any changes made by the witness are to be endorsed accordingly. Traditionally, each witness signs and dates the bottom of each page of the deposition and initials any changes (errors, additions, corrections, deletions).

  Since a committal proceeding is not a trial, the deposition of a witness is recorded by the Parish Court Judge on what is called the 'committal proceedings papers.' Such blank papers with the requisite heading should be placed on the file and be easily available so that the Judge may have them if and when a deposition commences.[4]

  Where an oral statement is to be recorded, in the form of a deposition, from any witness other than the accused, the committal proceedings papers are completed as follows: 'In the Parish Court for the Circuit Court Committal Proceedings held at the Corporate Area Parish Court (Criminal Division) before Her Honour Miss Justicia Justice, Judge of the Parish Court on the 2nd day of September 20–.'

- **Option of an Accused**

Section 5(1)(a)-(d) of the CPA indicates that an accused may exercise one of four options at the committal proceedings.

Option 1 - Tender his own written statement into evidence.

---

4. Section 4(1) of the Committal Proceedings Act deals with the oral evidence of someone other than the accused.

This is a new addition to the committal proceedings. Previously, an accused was unable to tender such a statement. Where a statement is tendered by an accused, it must presumably conform to the strictures of section 6.

Option 2 - Make an unsworn statement.

If an accused elects to make an unsworn statement, s/he does it from the dock, but without the assistance of an attorney. There is no cross-examination by the prosecution and the Judge is prohibited from asking the accused any questions, except to ask that s/he repeats whatever the Court did not hear. This unsworn statement should be written down by the Parish Court Judge, after giving the accused the requisite warning (see below regarding oral evidence).

Option 3 - Give oral evidence.

Any accused who chooses to give oral evidence does so on the same footing as every other witness who gives oral evidence. Therefore, the accused must swear or affirm before giving evidence. Notably, if the accused elects to make an oral statement, the Judge of the Parish Court has a duty to caution the accused *before* s/he exercises this option as any statement made at this point may be used against the accused at trial.

The caution that the Judge should give per section 5(2) and the First Schedule is as follows:

**"You are not obliged to say anything in answer to the charge unless you desire to do so, but whatever you say will be taken down in writing and may be given in evidence upon your trial."**

The oral statement must be recorded (in writing or by electronic means); it must be read over to the accused; and it must be signed by the accused and the Judge of the Parish Court.

If the matter is committed and the accused is to be tried in the Circuit Court, that oral statement and any other statements and any witness depositions and other documentary evidence should be transferred to the Director of Public Prosecutions (CPA section 5(3)(a) to (e)).

Option 4 - Remain silent.

The Parish Court Judge, in such a scenario, should note that there was no statement from the accused. Traditionally, the accused said 'I reserve my defence' and nothing more is noted by the Judge of the Parish Court; this is still the adopted procedure.

- **Dismissal/Discharge**

At the end of the committal proceedings, regardless of the procedure adopted, the Judge of the Parish Court must decide if there is a prima facie case to commit the accused (CPA section 7). The Parish Court Judge must examine all of the evidence before the Court and if satisfied that the evidence against the accused is insufficient to establish prima facie proof of the charge, dismiss the case.

If the Court is, however, satisfied that the evidence against the accused is sufficient to establish *prima facie* proof of the charge for the particular indictable offense, the Judge may remand the accused in custody or admit the accused to bail for the offence charged or for any other indictable offence disclosed by the evidence, according to section 7(b). Any bail offered is pursuant to the Bail Act and sections 41 and 43 of the Justices of the Peace Jurisdiction Act. The Judge may extend the accused's bail at this time or remand him in custody. As such, a fresh bail application would need to be made. If the accused is offered bail, s/he must be bailed again according to the terms and conditions ordered by the Parish Court Judge. The Court may be requested to accept the same surety as before, but the Parish Court Judge will have to decide whether to accede to the request.

**Figure 7.1    Warning to Accused**

---

**14**

**Statement of Accused**

**JAMAICA SS.**

John Brown ......................................................................................... stands charged

before the ....... Hon Jon Tomms ....... one of her Majesty's Justices of the Peace in and for the Parish undersigned and aforesaid

This .................... day of .................... in the year of our Lord Two Thousand and .................... and the said charge being read to the said John Brown and the witnesses for the prosecution and being severally examined in his presence, the said John Brown is now addressed by ....... His Hon Jon Tomms ....... as follows:

"Having heard the evidence do you wish to say anything in answer to the charge? You are not obliged to say anything unless you desire to do so, but whatever you say will be taken down in writing and may be given in evidence against you upon your trial," and you are clearly to understand that you have nothing to hope from any promise of favour and nothing to fear from any threat which may have been holden out to you to induce you to make any admission or confession of your guilt, but that whatever you shall say may be given in evidence against you upon your trial notwithstanding such promise of threat.  Do you desire to call any witnesses? If you do, it must be done after you have made your own statement.

WHEREUPON the said John Brown

saith as follows:

I acted in self-defence. He had the machete and I got it from him and chop him.

Taken before me, Hon Jon Tomms at St James Parish Court on the day and year above mentioned.

The accused calls the following witnesses: - Tom Strokes

---

- **Multiple Accused at a Committal Proceedings**

  If there are multiple accused, the order of committal is read out to each accused. In essence, the accused is told that s/he will be committed to stand and take trial at the next circuit commencing on a particular day.

- **Use of Accused Oral Evidence, Statements, Depositions, and Exhibits at Trial**

  Section 5(3) indicates that all of these documents are to be transmitted to the Director of Public Prosecutions upon the committal of the matter. The information or complaint, the written statements, any depositions, all documentary exhibits, the warrant of commitment for trial, and any recognizance entered into are also to be transmitted as stated in section 10(1) of the Act.

  All of these can be admitted into evidence without further proof thereof at the trial of the accused (CPA section 5(3)). Therefore, it is no longer necessary that the particular Clerk of the Courts has to give evidence in the Circuit Court regarding any of these documents before they can be put into evidence at the trial.

  The assigned investigating officer is the designated officer to take charge of all other exhibits and is to produce them at the trial (CPA section 10(2)). Unless the Judge of the Parish Court directs otherwise, the investigating officer is the designated officer. However, under the same section, the Commissioner of Police may also designate another member of the Jamaica Constabulary Force to be the investigating officer.

- **Keeper of the Committal Proceedings Records and Powers**

  The DPP retains the committal proceedings case file (consisting of the written statements, depositions, and other documents) sent from the Parish Court. The indictment is drafted and thereafter the case file is transmitted to the proper officer of the court in which the accused is to be tried (CPA section 10(3)). It is also usual for the documents related to any bail, subpoenas, to be transmitted in the committal proceedings case file.

  Upon perusal of the evidence from the committal proceedings, the DPP may decide to indict for any other offence that is disclosed on the face of the proceedings (CPA section 10(3)). The offences can be tried jointly with any offence for which the accused was committed or the offences can be tried independently as allowed by relevant statute or precedent.

- **The Forms Used in Committal Proceedings**

  Section 15 of the Committal Proceedings Act provides all the forms utilized under the previous dispensation, under the Justices of the Peace Jurisdiction Act, are still applicable with the relevant changes as noted in the Second Schedule for particular forms. For the most part, the changes are minor, but it is still prudent to ensure that all forms conform to the specific changes before using them.

# Chapter 8
# File Preparation

## Summary

This chapter examines the way in which a case file from the court's office should be prepared upon receipt by the Clerk of the Courts. It outlines the basic documents that should be on a case file and how they are to be examined. Information on how to disclose information to the defence as well as how to treat witnesses in the matter is provided. The manner in which an offence is to be proven is also examined in this chapter.

## Terms _____

Daily Court Preparation by the Clerk of the Courts

Statutes

Case Law

Case File

Basic Documents on a Case File

_____

## Daily Court Preparation by the Clerk of the Courts

Final preparations for court each morning should include ensuring:

- That the court sheet is listed correctly to reflect all the matters to be heard on that day.

- That the court sheet has been copied and given to the police officers assigned to the court. This list helps police officers to write up their own court books and for them to call the names of accused persons.

- That a list of witnesses is also provided to the officers to call those names. However, the names of persons in witness protection or for in camera cases should not be provided. Instead, arrangements should be made by the Clerk to have these persons stay in a private office in the court building until they are needed.

- That the court police officers are alerted about persons in custody so that they can check to see if they have been brought. The accused status can be written on the police officers' copy of the court sheet.

- That the court diary is ready to be taken into court.

- That the day's case files are all in the possession of the Clerk and match the listing in the court sheet.

The Clerk of the Courts should have these items daily:

- the court sheet

- copies of the court sheet to be distributed

- the court diary
- the case files for the day
- any statutory or other authorities that are needed.

The court sheet should be placed on the Parish Court Judge's bench before s/he arrives in court; the Judge should not have to request the court sheet while court is in session. This is a major oversight, and it shows a lack of due preparation by the Clerk of the Courts.

## Statutes

The Clerk of the Courts must keep abreast of the latest legislation. If any Act was amended, the Clerk is expected to have a copy of it. Therefore, Clerks should check the Jamaica *Gazette* regularly for any new amendment, acts, or regulation. Websites such as www.moj.gov.jm and www.japarliament.gov.jm usually have the statutes in force as well as Bills. Jamaica Printing Services (1992) Limited, colloquially known as the Government Printing Office, is the official printer of all Acts in force.

## Case Law

There are certain key cases for some matters that the Clerk should have to hand (See chapter 9 on Case Law).

## Case File

The case file on an accused 'travels' with him throughout the life of the case. As such, great care must be taken to ensure that the documents are kept properly and that all relevant notations are made on the file. The court sheet does not move about in the same way that the file does and so it is the file that will be used to capture all that occurs in the case. Therefore, it is vital that this file is accurate.[1] The case file is retained in the court's filing room at the back desk when the case is finally disposed of in the courts.

When the Clerk of the Courts first receives a file – whether as the return day Clerk of the Courts or as the clerk in one of the trial courts – it must be carefully read. For best practice, an allegation page should be produced briefly outlining the allegations, the accused status, the role of each accused in multiple accused cases, the availability of the various witnesses, any documentation on file, and any that are outstanding. The allegation sheet assists the Clerk of the Courts to answer questions of law and/or fact from the Judge of the Parish Court. It also helps Clerks to respond to any issues that may arise from any defence counsel's submissions to the Court when the matter is called up.

## Basic Documents

The basic documents on any case file are a variation of some or all of the following which will be examined in turn:

- The Number One Information(s) (this is usually called the 'Number One').
- The Indictment (if it is applicable).
- The Criminal Record Form (formerly the Criminal Investigation Bureau [CIB 4] Form is now the Jamaica Constabulary Force Profile Form, commonly called the CR-12.

---

1. See section 291 of the Judicature (Parish Courts) Act which indicates among other information that 'in all proceedings...there shall be recorded on or in the fold of the indictment or information...the plea...the sentence...the presiding Parish Court Judge shall sign his name once at the end of the record...each record shall be carefully preserved in the office of the Clerk of the Courts, and an alphabetical index shall be kept of such records.'

Figure 8.1    File Summary/Crown's Allegation Page

| File Summary/Crown's Allegation Page | |
|---|---|
| **R v Jon Doe** <br> **for Breaches of the Corruption Prevention Act contrary to s. 14 (1) Corruption Prevention Act** | |
| Status of Acc: | Bail/Custody |
| Status of File | Ready |
| Investigating Officer | Det. Sgt. Tom Strokes Constant Spring PS. Cell no. 300-0000 |
| Virtual Complainant | Robert Outrage <br> Cell no. |
| Witnesses | Robert Outrage will say . . . <br><br> Inspector Sting Operation will say... <br><br> Det. Sgt Tom Strokes will say... <br><br> Supt. Standard Bran will say... |
| Allegations | On Jan. 3, 20– A. approached Mr Outrage and demanded $5,000 in return for him not to write Mr Outrage a traffic ticket on HWT Road. Outrage reported it to Internal Affairs. Sting operation carried out on the same day. A. seen taking the marked money from Outrage. Approached by the officers. Arrested. |
| Issues/Law | - Corruption Prevention Act <br> Credibility |
| To Proceed | - File complete |
| Documents on File | 1 Number One Information, CIB 4, IO Statement, Statements from the three witnesses, copy of the money handed over by Outrage to Accused, Summary of allegations |
| Exhibits | Money collected - original bills in sealed and labelled envelope |
| Put Exhibit in Thru | Outrage and Det. Sgt Tom Strokes |
| Order of Witnesses | 1.  Robert Outrage <br> 2.  Supt. Standard Bran <br> 3.  Inspector Sting Operation <br> 4.  Det. Sgt Tom Strokes |

- Police (Investigator's) Statement
- Statements
- Other Documents to Ground the Offence
- Police Summary of Allegations

### The Number One Information[2]

The following details should be outlined in the Number One Information:

- the name of the officer (usually the investigating officer);
- the date the number one information was taken out;
- the date of the offence or a particular period during which the offences allegedly occurred;
- the place of the offence;[3]
- the name of the alleged offender(s);
- the particulars of the offence(s);[4]
- the section of the relevant statute.

The Clerk of the Courts must ensure that the information has been laid properly and that the appropriate legislation or common law offence is being used. It is crucial to ensure that the statute is still in force.[5] If this is not done, the result could be that the accused is not properly before the Court.

After reading the statements and documentation on the case file, the Clerk is at liberty to advise the police officers that there are other offences being shown on the face of the allegations and to instruct that the other charges be included or that the offence charged be changed. It is always best to discuss with the investigating officer if there are statements and/or documents outstanding.

The Clerk of the Courts can make and initial simple amendments to the Number One Information. Common amendments include the spelling of a name or amending the section and subsection of the Act. More substantial amendments may require the leave of the Judge and sometimes submissions by the Clerk and the Defence Attorney. This leave is discretionary under section 278 of the Judicature (Parish Courts) Act.[6]

An amendment or alteration can be granted at any stage for an indictable offence *before sentencing*. In fact, if it appears necessary from the evidence being adduced or otherwise, the Parish Court Judge can direct that the trial be adjourned for a future date, if in the interest of justice it appears that that is necessary (for either the prosecution or the defence to make submissions about said amendment being

---

2. The number one information is found in Part 2 Form 15 of the schedule to the Justices of the Peace Jurisdiction Act.
3. This is important to ensure that the particular Parish Court has jurisdiction to hear the matter.
4. The Clerk of the Courts can research the applicable statute(s) to ensure the wording is correct or look to the ingredients of the offence if it a common law offence. It is also very useful to peruse recognized authorities such as an Archbold Criminal Pleading, Evidence and Practice (usually called simply Archbold).
5. As legislation is repealed or amended it is critical that the clerk is abreast of these changes. Acts such as the Vagrancy Act and the Juvenile Act have been repealed. Amendments have been made to acts such as the Evidence Act, Indictment Act, and the Judicature (Parish Courts) Act.
6. Under section 278 of the Judicature (Parish Courts) Act, the Judge of the Parish Court may grant any application for an amendment. This is a discretion that the Judge of the Parish Court has and s/he may choose to not exercise this discretion if the arguments in favour are not cogent. As such, it is important that the Clerk of the Courts has prepared the matter well so that only minor amendments are needed. The accused will also have to be re-pleaded after the amendment has been granted, to answer the charges in the new terms.

sought). Therefore, if the proposed amendment does not fall within the strictures of the section, the Judge of the Parish Court is at liberty to refuse the application.

**Figure 8.2    Sample Number One Information**

**1**

**INFORMATION**

PAGE 2

Parish of ......... Kingston

The Information and Complaint of ...... Cons. Tom Adams #112

of the parish of ........... Kingston                                made and taken upon oath

before the undersigned, this ...... 21st ...... day of ...... May ........... in the year of our Lord

two ...... thousand ...... and --                                         who saith that

on

the ............. 21st ............ day of ............. May ........... in the year

aforesaid, one ............. John Brown ...........                of the said parish

of                                          with force                          at

Duke Street ...........................                in the parish aforesaid, and within

the

jurisdiction of this Court unlawfully did threaten this Complainant, in the words following, to wit: -

Assaulted Mary Clarke

and that from the above and other threats used by the said ...... John Brown ......

                                                                 towards this Complainant he is

afraid that the said ...... John Brown ......

will do him some bodily harm or injury and therefore prays that the said ...... John Brown ......

may be required to find sufficient sureties to keep the Peace towards this Complainant. And this Complainant further said that he doth not make this Complainant against nor requires sureties from the said ...... John Brown ......

from any malice or ill-will, but merely for the preservation of his person from injury against the form of the Statute in such case made and provided, and against the Peace of our Sovereign Lady the Queen, her Crown and Dignity, and thereupon the said Complainant prays that the said

John Brown ........................... may be summoned to answer unto the said Complainant, according to Law.

Taken and sworn to before me at the Corporate Area Parish Court (Criminal Divisions)

In the parish of ........... Kingston ........... this ...... 21st ...... day of

May ...........    two thousand and --

*Carl Dewaar*
...........................
*Clerk of the Courts*

**Figure 8.3    Endorsement on the back of the Number One Information**

| PAGE 1 | |
|---|---|
| In the parish of   Kingston | In the parish of   Kingston |
| REGINA        }<br>     vs       } Information of<br>John Brown    } | REGINA              }<br>     vs              } Information of<br>Cons Tom Adams #112} |
| | For        Assault<br>Tried on    July 22, 20– |
| | Before      Her Hon Lucy Gale |
| | Plea       Guilty |
| | Verdict     Guilty |
| | Sentence    $10,000 or 30 days<br>           imprisonment |
| | *Here fill in place at which Court was held |

In *R v Hazel Grant* and another,[7] the Court of Appeal held that the Resident Magistrate as the he then was, was duty bound to amend if the strictures of the section were met.

The number one information is needed to plead the accused for all summary offences and so the details must be accurate.

The signature of the Justice of the Peace before whom the information was sworn should be affixed and the seal affixed. The number one information can also be sworn before the Clerk of the Courts and sealed accordingly with the court seal.

**The Criminal Record Form (formerly the CIB 4, now the CR 12)**

This is an administrative document utilized by the police to gather information about the accused. It is useful to the Clerk if s/he did not get an opportunity to peruse the file beforehand. However, it does not to replace the due diligence the Clerk is expected to exhibit when preparing court files.

The Form outlines:

- the name of the accused;
- the date of birth of the accused;
- address of the accused;
- information on the offence.

The form includes a detailed description of the defendant to include such features such as tattoos.

---

7. *R v Hazel Grant and anor RMCA 68/89* and delivered March 19, 1990.

Figure 8.4    Sample Form CR 12

---

**Jamaica Constabulary Force    Profile Form (CR -12)    (Please Attach Photo)**

Date _____

☐ **Wanted**  ☐ **Suspect**  ☐ **Person Charged**  ☐ **Convicted**  (Tick appropriate box and complete relevant sections below)

| Offence(s) | Crime Ref. No. | CRO No. |
|---|---|---|
| When and where offence was committed | Dairy No. | |
| Investigative Officer | Contact Nos. | Station |

**Particulars of Present Conviction** *(THIS SECTION IS TO BE COMPLETED IF ACCUSED IS CONVICTED)*

Offences_____    Court _____    Date _____

Sentence _____

**Previous conviction, give date if CRO Number is not known** _____

Surname: _____    First name(s): _____    Middle name: _____

Aliases: _____    Maiden name: _____    Corrected name: _____

Occupation: _____    Permanent Address: _____

Tel. Nos. (H) _____ Cell _____ Business(s) _____ E-mail: _____

Business Address: _____

Gender: ☐ M   ☐ F   Nationality: _____    Resident Status: ☐ Tourist ☐ Foreign National/Work permit

☐ Foreign Student  ☐ Other: _____    Repeat offender: ☐ Yes ☐ No    D.O.B_____ Age: _____

Place of Birth _____    Hobbies: _____

Deportee: ☐ Yes   ☐ No    If "yes", state country deported from and date _____

Mother's Name: Surname: _____ First(s): _____ Middle:_____ Maiden: _____

Address _____ Tel No. _____ Place of Birth _____

Father's Name: Surname: _____ First(s): _____ Middle:_____

Address _____ Tel No. _____ Place of Birth _____

**Description of Person**

Height: _____    **Build:** ☐ Light   ☐ Medium   ☐ Other, state _____

Weight: _____    ☐ Heavy   ☐ Obese   ☐ Muscular   ☐ Round Shoulder

| | |
|---|---|
| Complexion:  ☐ Dark ☐ Medium ☐ Other _____<br>☐ Light ☐ Black | Eye Colour:  ☐ Black ☐ Brown ☐ Green<br>☐ Grey ☐ Other |
| Handed:  ☐ Left ☐ Right  ☐ Both ☐ Unknown | Teeth:  ☐ Normal ☐ Crooked ☐ Broken<br>☐ Missing ☐ Other |
| Voice:  ☐ High Pitched  ☐ Other Impediment<br>☐ Low Pitched  ☐ Stammer | |

| | |
|---|---|
| **Scars:** ☐ Face _____ (Describe)<br>☐ Torso _____<br>☐ Arms _____<br>☐ Other _____ | **Tattoos:** ☐ Face _____<br>☐ Torso _____<br>☐ Arms _____<br>Other Marks: _____ |

| | |
|---|---|
| **Ethnic Group:** ☐ Oriental ☐ Indian ☐ Caucasian<br>☐ Negroid ☐ Other _____ | **Chin:** ☐ Dimpled ☐ Cleft or Doubled ☐ Pointed ☐ Round<br>☐ Protrudes ☐ Recedes ☐ Square ☐ Other_____ |

| **Hair Style:** | ☐ Bald/Shave | ☐ Natural | ☐ Curly/Wavy |
| | ☐ Dreadlocks | ☐ Straight | ☐ Dyed |

**Hair Length:** ☐ Short   ☐ Medium   ☐ Long

**Hair:** ☐ Black  ☐ Brown  ☐ Blond  ☐ Other _____
**Colour:** ☐ Beard (shape & colour)

**Hair on Face:** ☐ Moustache (*size, shape and colour*)

_____

☐ Dark Chin   ☐ Sideburn

**Weapon Used:**                **Description**
☐ Handgun     _____
☐ Rifle          _____
☐ Shotgun     _____
☐ Long Knife
☐ Short Knife        ☐ Hands/Feet/Bodily Force

**Conveyance:**          **Description**
                              (See Supplementary Form)
☐ Car           _____
☐ Bicycle      _____
☐ Foot          _____
☐ Bus
☐ Other, state   _____

**Head:** ☐ Large  ☐ Narrow  ☐ Small  ☐ Square
**Nose:** ☐ Large  ☐ Small  ☐ Long  ☐ Short
          ☐ Bulbous  ☐ Broad Base  ☐ Wide  ☐ Narrow
          ☐ Other _____

**Eyebrows:** ☐ Thick  ☐ Thin  ☐ Bushy  ☐ Plucked
                  ☐ Penciled  ☐ Arched  ☐ Meet in Centre
                  ☐ Sparce  ☐ Other _____

**Face:** ☐ Round  ☐ Oval  ☐ Wrinkled  ☐ High Cheek Bone
          ☐ _____

**Forehead:** ☐ High  ☐ Low  ☐ Narrow  ☐ Broad
                  ☐ Wrinkled  ☐ Bulging  ☐ Receding

**Burglary Implements:**  ☐ Pry Tool  ☐ Hack Saw  ☐ Sledge Hammer  ☐ Duplicate Key  ☐ Other _____

**Unusual Deformities – peculiarities of gait etc., speech or figure, known habits or weaknesses**

_____
_____
_____

**Full Details of Methods Used in Committing Offences**

_____
_____
_____

**Names and Addresses of relatives, giving relationship**

_____
_____

**Mode of Travelling**

**Names and Addresses of persons who stood surety for accused when bailed**

_____
_____
_____

**Usual Associates**

_____

**Communities and Places Frequent by Suspect**

_____
_____
_____

**Specimen of Handwriting:** 1. _____ 2. _____ 3. _____

☐ Authority to declare a person wanted (Minimum of DDI) Signature _____

### Police Investigator's Statement

Police Statements should outline:

- the date of the alleged offence;
- allegations against the accused;
- the name(s) of virtual complainants, if any;
- the surrounding circumstances of the offence;
- the date of the arrest of the accused;
- the certificate of truth; and
- the signature of the Investigating Officer, date, and regulation number.

All other police officers' statements should reflect their roles in the matter, and should bear their certificate of truth, signature, regulation number, and date that the statement was written.

### Civilian Statements

These should outline:

- the name and other personal details of the witness;
- the relevant dates of the incident;
- what the witness did, saw, said, and any other information that is relevant to the date of the alleged offence(s);
- the certificate of truth; and
- the signature of the witness and the date.

### Other Documents to Ground the Offence(s)

These are all the supporting documents that assist in proving the offence(s). For ease of reference, the information here is subdivided and speaks to the areas of witnesses, certificates, potential exhibits, and other important aspects. Examples of supporting documents and statements include forged cheques, receipts, forensic certificates, and medical certificates for persons.

### Police Summary of Allegations

This gives a brief outline of the offences and the involvement of the accused. It is often produced by the investigating officer in the case.

### Types of Offences

The offence (s) outlined in the file can be for one, some, or even all of the following types of offences:

| | | |
|---|---|---|
| Summary Trial | - | S |
| Indictable Trial | - | I |
| Committal Proceedings | - | CP |
| Hearing | - | H[8] |

---

8.  Note that extradition matters are termed hearings. The various categories of offences are not joined together for the purpose of trial or hearing. As such, if an accused has multiple types of matters, the Clerk of the Courts elects which proceed on the particular day. After the matter has been disposed of, the other matters are transferred to other courts (where possible). This

It is always good practice to make a notation on the outermost number one information of how many and what types of offences are on the file. This is crucial when deciding which offence to proceed with first as dissimilar types of offences cannot be grouped together and would create a misjoinder.

Also, write on the related number one information the relevant order to be signed by the Parish Court Judge when the matter begins in court. Bear in mind that there are separate orders for indictable trials, hearings, and committal proceedings.

However, there is no order for the start of summary matters, but the summary trial information is made on the file regarding the date that the matter starts and how the accused pleaded.

Notably, no orders are made in the matter at the start of an extradition hearing.

### Endorsements/Notations

Endorsements on the case file are critical to guide all subsequent Clerks handling the matter. The case file travels with the defendant until a matter is disposed of, even as court sheets finish and close, and new ones are opened. Therefore, the Clerk of the Courts must ensure that accurate and complete notations are taken each time the matter goes before the Court.

Basic endorsements can be placed on the file jacket. However, orders of the Court that are to be signed by the Judge are best written on the number one informations. If necessary, place a new 'backing', which is simply another number one information, on a case file when there is no space left to write on the old ones. Remember to place the basic details on it – the information number, name of defendant(s), and police officer/complainant.

The following notations/endorsements are useful for every occasion the matter goes to court:[9]

- the Parish Court Judge;
- the investigating officer;
- the attorney(s);
- the next court date (NCD);
- the complainant;
- the witnesses; and
- any comments.

The Clerk should note carefully which attorney is on record for multiple accused cases.

The following indicates the witnesses who may be called first in particular matters:

| *Examples* | *First Witness* |
| --- | --- |
| Simple Larceny | - virtual complainant |
| Receiving Stolen Property | - investigating officer |
| Assault | - virtual complainant |

---

transfer reduces the possibility of bias on the part of the Judge of the Parish Court, wherein an accused is tried before the same Judge of the Parish Court for multiple matters.

9.   These are just suggestions as to how to keep a careful track of the files' life on each occasion the accused is before the court. The style shown is attractive as it can give a quick overview of the progress or lack thereof of the file.

| Murder | - identification of the body witness.[10] |
| Committal Proceedings | - eyewitness |
| Dangerous Drugs | - the person who found the drugs. Where it is a complex case the necessary foundation must be laid. |

**Figure 8.5    Notations/Endorsements for Each Occasion a Matter is Called up, on a Case File**

| | |
|---|---|
| Parish Judge: | Her Hon Mrs. Justicia James, Ct. 5 |
| IO: | D/Sgt. Tom Strokes BO/IOBO |
| ATTNY: | Mr Minis Justice pres |
| W'SS: | Supt. Standard Bran BO Inspector Sting Operations BO |
| (T) NCD: | February 2, 20– |
| COMMENT: | Defence adjmnt. |
| | Matter is priority on TNCD |

**Next Court Date (NCD)**

The notation on the NCD should reflect whether a matter is for 'mention' (M), 'trial' (T), 'hearing' (H), or committal proceedings (CP). This notation helps the assistant Clerk to write up the court sheet for the new date and also assists the Clerk of the Courts with custody of the matter to know the status of the file.

A mention 'M' date means that something is still outstanding or something is to be done. The file is, therefore, incomplete or not ready for trial, a hearing, or committal proceedings. When this happens, write what is to be done for the next occasion.

The trial 'T' date means that the file is ready as all documents are on file, the defence has been or will soon be served, and a firm trial date is being set. To determine whether a file is ready, look at the type of offence that is alleged and the proof available to ground the offence.

The same is true if a hearing or committal proceeding is set, unless one of the many vagaries that beset the court happens and a matter cannot start on an appointed date.

**Comment**

This section is for general information about the matter. For example, it is useful to write whether the Crown or defence is seeking an adjournment, if the matter could not be reached due to some other particular circumstance, or if documents are to be copied for defence counsel in the matter.

---

10. The person who identifies the deceased is often called the "ID body witness," i.e. the witness who has actually identified the deceased body at the funeral home/the scene and who comes to court to give that evidence.

**Attorney**

It is always useful to note which attorney appears for an accused. Representation can change and, in some cases, the accused may need the assistance of the Court with the assignment of a defence attorney under the Legal Aid Act.

**Perusal of Statements on File**

Statements on the case file should be read with a view to:

- establishing the nexus between the accused and the offence;
- ensuring that the offence is made out;
- ensuring that any perceived gaps in the case are closed (for example by instructing the investigating officer to get a further statement from someone or by researching other areas of law);

**Figure 8.6**     Notice of Intention to put into Evidence a Statement under section 31 of the Evidence Act

---

### NOTICE OF INTENTION TO TENDER INTO EVIDENCE
### STATEMENT OF JOHN BROWN
### UNDER SECTION 31 (A/B/C/D/E) OF THE EVIDENCE ACT

IN THE PARISH COURT

FOR THE PARISH OF
CLARENDON
HOLDEN AT
MAY PEN

| REGINA | )( | FOR |
|---|---|---|
| VERSUS | )( | ROBBERY |
| TOM STROKES | )( | |
| | )( | |

**TAKE NOTICE** that at the trial of the above-mentioned accused to be holden at the Clarendon Parish Court at May Pen, on the ___19th___ day of ___May___ 20—

It is intended to tender into evidence the statement of ___John Brown___ a copy whereof is attached.

*Pitney Bowe*

CLERK OF THE COURTS
FOR THE PARISH OF
CLARENDON

---

- ensuring that the witnesses who gave the statements are available to give evidence;

- determining if a paper trial (per section 31D of the Evidence Act) is being contemplated as certain preliminary steps are critical to this type of trial; and

- ensuring that that all corrections are initialed, that the statements are signed and dated at the foot of each page and that there are no empty spaces, and that they contain the certificate of truth.

## Statements of Particular Types of Witnesses

Arresting and/or investigating officers should write these basic details in their statements:

- the circumstances that led to the accused being charged relative to that officer's knowledge;

- the dates of incident, arrest and charging of accused and other dates as appropriate;

- the names of virtual complainants, if any;

- the specific actions of the officer related to his role in the matter;

- the grounding of the offences under the relevant Acts (if necessary in this statement);

- the informing of the accused of the allegations;

- the cautioning of the accused;

- any words said by the accused;

- the arrest of the accused;

- the transportation of the accused and any relevant potential exhibits together;

- the proper labelling and sealing of possible exhibits (if necessary or possible in accused presence) where necessary and or possible;

- the handing over of accused to custody officer;

- the signature of the officer and date that the statement is written; and

- the certificate of truth of the officer.

## Virtual Complainants

Virtual complainants are varied but the Clerk of the Courts should ensure key elements are included when a case is placed before the court:

- For property, such as motor cars, try to establish that there was no permission to do anything with the property.

- For sexual matters, it is necessary to negative consent where the complainant is an adult.

- The age of minors should be recorded.

- For matters where identification might be important, ensure that the necessary *Turnbull* directions are noted.

- The acts of any and all accused persons must be noted.

- The date of the offence must be shown or an approximate time period.

- The signature of the witness and date that the statement is written must be noted.

- The certificate of truth of the virtual complainant should be present.

- The certificate of the police officer who recorded the witnesses' statement(s).

**Other Witnesses**

- Other witnesses should identify, if necessary, accused persons.
- They should establish support for the offence.
- They should establish how they came to be requested to do certain things as regards the matter.
- The signature of the witness and date that the statement is written is needed.
- The certificate of truth of the witness should be provided.
- The certificate of the police officer writing down the witness's statement is also necessary.

**Expert Witnesses**

The credentials of expert witnesses should be established to prove that they are experts in the area and so can give the evidence. The proper foundation when laid means that the expert's testimony can be received as such and relied on by the Judge of the Parish Court.

Section 31CB of the Evidence Act provides that:

(1) any report signed by an expert shall, in any criminal proceedings, be admitted as evidence of the matter stated therein, without the expert being called upon to attend and give evidence on oath.

(2) where, in any criminal proceedings, a party intends to put into evidence a report as provided in subsection (1), that party shall, no later than 30 days before the commencement of the trial, serve upon the other party (or in the case of an accused, his attorney-at-law) written notice of such intention, together with a copy of the report, and the other party may, not later than five days before the commencement of the trial...require the attendance of the expert...

(3) The Court may...on its own motion require the expert...to attend and give evidence...in the interest of justice.

Figure 8.7    Witness List

| Order of Witness | Name of Witness | What Witness Will Say | Potential Exhibit to Put in Through Witness | Comment |
|---|---|---|---|---|
|  |  |  |  |  |
|  |  |  |  |  |

**Statements Made by the Accused**

While the Jamaican Constitution guarantees the right to silence, sometimes an accused decides to proffer an explanation in a committal proceeding or before the case even comes to the court. The Judges' Rules indicate that the accused should be advised that any such statements will be taken down in writing and may be used against him or her in any trial. Where an accused, having been so advised, still wishes to proceed, then the statement is to be reduced to writing. In the committal proceedings, this is called the statement of the accused. See chapter 7 on committal proceedings.

The most usual forms of statements by an accused before the matter is heard in a courtroom are caution statements and question and answers.

For a caution statement, a question and answer session or any words said on being cautioned by the police officer the words of the caution that are generally used by the officer are based on the Judges' Rules. *Judges' Rules* [1964] 1 All ER 237.

## Figure 8.8    Question and Answer of Suspect

Name Of Interviewee: Micky Jones.          D.O.B.: 02/10/20--; Age: ---

Place Of Interview:    Metcalfe Street Juvenile Detention Centre

Date: 20/08/20--; Time Commenced 1:15 P.M.; Time Completed:  2:15 P.M.
Persons Present:  Julz Mckay (Mother), Elbow Brown (Lawyer), Cons. Lew, Del Thoms, C.D.A., Cons. Mich Daye, W./Det./Cpl. Micha Duggy #12345

Caution: you are not obliged to say anything unless you wish to do so but anything you may say will be taken down in writing and given in evidence.

Q1.      What is your full name?

A.       Micky Jones

Q2.      Are you called by any other name?

A.       On the advice of my attorney I have nothing to say

Q3.      What is your mother's name?

A.       On the advice of my attorney I have nothing to say

Q4.      What is your address?

A.       9 Clance Road, Kingston 22

Q5.      Who do you live with?

A.       On the advice of my attorney I have nothing to say

Q6.      Was Mr Omi Lands, who is now deceased your cousin?

A.       On the advice of my attorney I have nothing to say

Q7.      How long have you known that Mr Omi Lands was your cousin?

A.       On the advice of my attorney I have nothing to say

Q8.      Did you stab your cousin Mr. Omi Lands during a dispute on Monday 11.07.20-- About 10 a.m.?

A.       On the advice of my attorney I have nothing to say

Q9.      Where did you get the knife that you used to stab Mr. Omi Lands?

A.       Same answer

Q10.     Was Mr Omi Lands carrying a weapon?

A.       Same answer

Q11.     Who were there with you when you stabbed Mr Omi Lands?

A.       Same answer

Q12.     What did Omi do to you before you stabbed him?

A.       Same answer

Q13.     Was Omi ever abusive to you?

A.       Same answer

Q14.     Who took you to the Admiral Town Police Station on the night of 11/7/20--?

A.       Same answer

Q15.     Are you comfortable with this interview?

A.       Yes

| S/ | SUSPECT | MICKY JONES |
|----|---------|-------------|
| S/ | WITNESS (MOTHER) | JULZ MCKAY |
| S/ | WITNESS | CONS. LEW |
| S/ | WITNESS | W/DET/CPL MICHA DOTTY #12345 |

THE FOREGOING QUESTIONS AND ANSWERS NUMBERING 1–15 WERE READ OVER

TO ME BY MY ATTORNEY, ELBOW BROWN. THE QUESTIONS WERE ASKED BY CONS. D. LEW AND THE ANSWERS GIVEN BY ME ON THE ADVICE OF MY ATTORNEY. I WAS TOLD THAT I CAN ADD, ALTER, CORRECT OR DELETE ANY PART OF THE ANSWER GIVEN. THE ANSWERS ARE TRUE. I GAVE THEM OF MY OWN FREE WILL.

| S/ | SUSPECT | MICKY JONES |
|----|---------|-------------|
| S/ | WITNESS (MOTHER) | JULZ MCKAY |
| S/ | WITNESS | CONS. D. LEW |
| S/ | WITNESS | W/DET/CPL. MICHA DOTTY #12345 |

THE FOREGOING QUESTION AND ANSWERS NUMBERING 1–15 WERE RECORDED

BY ME. THE QUESTIONS WERE ASKED BY ME, DET CPL. DUGGY, AND THE ANSWER GIVEN BY THE SUSPECT IN THE PRESENCE OF HIS ATTORNEY-AT-LAW MR ELBOW BROWN. HE WAS TOLD BY ME, DET CPL. DUGGY THAT HE COULD ADD, ALTER OR CORRECT ANY OF THE ANSWERS GIVEN. NO PROMISE, OFFER OR THREAT WAS MADE TO THE SUSPECT DURING THE INTERVIEW. THE ANSWERS WERE GIVEN BY THE SUSPECT OF HIS FREE OWN FREE WILL. PRESENT WERE ATTORNEY, ELBOW BROWN, CONS. LEW, DEL THOMS, C.D.A., CONS. MICH DAYE, W./DET./ CPL. DUGGY

S/      DET CPL DOTTY #12345          -          22.07.20--

## Further Statements

Further statements become necessary when a statement reveals some lacuna, the offence is not properly made out on the information given, and when there are ambiguities or omissions in the earlier statement. In these cases, a clear notation is to be made on the heading of the subsequent statement to read that John Doe 'further states'.

**Figure 8.9    Further Statement from Investigator**

| | | |
|---|---|---|
| Name | : | Lucien Panes |
| Occupation | : | Inspector of Police |
| Address | : | 00 Ocean Boulevard, Kingston Mall |
| Telephone | : | 920-0000 |

Further States:

On Monday the 1st day of December 20-- I obtained a ruling from the Director of Public Prosecutions indicating that Constable John Honey is to be charged for the offence of Breach of the Corruption Prevention Act.

Based on the ruling I prepared warrants on information and on Tuesday the 2nd day of December 20-- I executed same on Constable John Honey by arresting and charging him for the above mentioned offence. When cautioned, he replied "I'm innocent".

He was later handed over to the Sub-Officer in charge of Duhaney Park Police Lock-ups and scheduled to attend the St. Catherine Parish Court, at Spanish Town on Friday the 5th day of December 20--.

s/      Inspector Lucien Panes -           03-12-20--

This statement consisting of half a page signed by me is true and correct to the best of my knowledge and belief and I make it knowing that if it is tendered in evidence I shall be liable to prosecution if I have willfully stated in it anything I know to be false or do not believe to be true.

s/      Inspector Lucien Panes -           03-12-20--

## Potential Exhibits

- Potential exhibits come in various forms and so their availability and whereabouts must be ascertained beforehand by the Clerk.

- For paper exhibits, the originals should be on the file. If they are not, find out if they are with the investigating officer or with another person. Ensure that they can be brought to court when required. It is only when proper a foundation is laid that copies of paper documents may be admitted in trial matters before the Court.

- Exhibits such as drugs, marked dollar bills, and ammunition are usually kept in secure storage by the police until required at court. The store keeper is the custodian of these items and is usually a senior police officer.

- Potential exhibits should be duly sealed and labelled in the presence of the accused wherever practicable. The Clerk should see this in the related statements. If it was not done, the Clerk must request a further statement as to what happened so as to ensure that the chain of custody does not become an issue at trial.

- If there is any defacement or destruction of packaging or labelling subsequent to the initial sealing and labelling, evidence must be led about this to preserve the chain of custody of the potential exhibit.[11] The chain of custody of the potential exhibit must be clearly established.

- The type of item will, of course, dictate the way in the evidence regarding the chain is led.

- Drugs, ammunition, and offensive weapons are usually small enough for both such sealing and labelling on the same package.

- For potential exhibits such as recovered stolen vehicles, these can be in storage at a police station or released on bond[12] and, as such, brought to court when required. Where an exhibit is released on a bond, the appropriate notation must be on the file to alert the Clerk of the Courts with conduct of the trial list.

- For exhibits that are voluminous or cumbersome, the Crown may make an application to the Court,[13] at the relevant time, to visit the location where the exhibits are being kept. Such exhibits include containers of drugs or vehicles.

- Potential exhibits are to be brought to court (as best as possible) and so the Court is not obligated to grant this application without a proper foundation and basis for the application.

- The investigating officer must be alerted in good time to make the requisite arrangements for the potential exhibit to be viewed at the site or be brought to court.

A specific procedure is observed when the Court visits a site to view (potential exhibits, locus, etc.). First the Court must be adjourned. Next, the Court is re-opened at the site by the court police who must also attend with the Court. All other protocols must be observed as when the Court is in session at the courthouse.

## Certificates

The certificates that are necessary in a trial matter will vary depending on the nature of the case before the court.

---

11. Chain of custody is crucial in criminal cases. The case of *Clyde Grazette v R* [2009] CCJ 2 (AJ) and *Chris Brooks v R* [2012] JMCA 5 are instructive on this area.
12. See applications for court orders.
13. Ibid.

A prescribed form is used for medical certificates in proceedings before the Parish Court, per section 31CB of the Evidence Act. When a medical certificate or report has been duly signed and sworn to, it should be admitted into evidence without the need to call the medical practitioner who signed it.[14]

Where the Crown intends to rely on a medical certificate, the accused must be served a written notice along with a copy of the certificate or report at least 30 days before the commencement of the proceedings.

If the defendant objects to such a certificate being admitted, then s/he may require that the medical practitioner give evidence.

The effect of section 31CB of the Evidence Act is that in criminal proceedings before any Judge of the Parish Court, where a medical certificate is accompanied by a sworn statement by the medical practitioner who signed it, the certificate becomes admissible in evidence; it is irrelevant whether the prosecution or the defence tenders the certificate.[15]

The island chemist certificates are crucial to ensuring that matters are ready in the court.[16] Island chemist means any government chemist, government pathologist, or analyst appointed under any relevant legislation. The island chemist is an expert, and his or her evidence is regarded and accepted by the Court as such.

Island chemist certificates or forensic certificates are issued when items have been examined and the results reduced to writing. The certificate of the island chemist, once signed, becomes prima facie evidence and the Clerk of the Courts must lead evidence that there was no injury to the any seals or other fastenings on the item when it was delivered to the island chemist.[17]

There are many types of certificates that are island chemist certificates and they all come under the nomenclature of 'forensic certificates'. The defendant has a right to require that the particular island chemist attend and give evidence about the content of a certificate.[18]

Certificates may also be necessary for cases involving drugs, gunshot residue, vehicles, alcohol, and petroleum. Other such certificates include:

- ballistic certificate (for firearms and ammunition);
- handwriting certificates (for testing of handwriting samples);
- post-mortem reports (on deceased persons); and
- reports (accident reconstruction, fire).

---

14. The now repealed section 50 of the Evidence Act illustrated that medical certificates and reports are admissible in court without the maker attending court if the necessary conditions are met. Section 31CB of the Evidence Act (as delineated above) has replaced this section. The tenor is basically the same with the main change being that such reports *are now admissible without more being necessary* (emphasis added).
15. See *R v Ezra Hall* (1980) 17 JLR 146; also instructive is *Sheldon Heaven v Regina* [2010] JMCA Crim 33 where the medical certificate was not sworn to by the doctor and wrongfully admitted into evidence. In Heaven, the Court of Appeal, at paragraph 50, stated that: 'There is a principle to be extracted from the circumstances of this case. It is that Clerks of Courts, Resident Magistrates (as they then were) and indeed, defence counsel, must be alert to ensure that medical certificates and the like are in compliance with the provisions of section 50, before they are tendered and admitted into evidence.' See too *Regina v Nickoy Grant* [2013] JMCA Crim 30 regarding the nondisclosure of the medical certificate.
16. Evidence Act, section 52.
17. Section 54 of the Evidence Act.
18. Ibid.

**Figure 8.10    Example of a Certificate from a Motor Vehicle Certifying Officer**

---

### Statement of Certifying Officer

I, Jack Toms, states: I am a Certifying Officer of Motor Vehicles, and I am employed by the Island Traffic Authority, Ministry of Transport and Works, and stationed at Swell Hope, in the parish of St James.

My address for the purposes of this report is Ministry of Transport and Works, Swell Hope, in the parish of St James.

At the request of the Dunns Road Police Station, St James, on March 1, 20–,

I carried out examinations at the said station on the below mentioned vehicles.

1.    A 2006 Toyota Hiace, registered 0000 EW,

2.    A 2004 Nissan Sunny, registered 0000 AB

Upon examination I found and recorded the following defects:

Vehicle 1: Front windshield broken.  Vehicle 2: Front bumper broken

*Jack Toms*
Signature

---

**Figure 8.11  Example of a Fire Report**

# FIRE REPORT

ST THOMAS (SUB)               FIRE STATION

DATE: TUESDAY, MAY 1, 20--

---

TYPE OF PREMISES     OCCUPIED DWELLING HOUSE, No. 4 RAND ROAD KINGSTON 10

TIME OF CALL        1:10 PM       HOW CALLED    TEL. No. 926-0000

TIME OF LEAVING     1:21 PM TIME OF ARRIVAL  1:26 PM TIME OF RETURN  3:00 PM

OWNER             JACK SMITH:  4 RAND ROAD

OCCUPIERS         JACK SMITH

                       JUNE SMITH

DISTANCE           FIVE (05) KILLOMETERS

NO. OF MEN PRESENT   SUPT JOE YOUNG AND A CREW OF FIFTEEN (15) FIREFIGHTERS

APPLIANCES PRESENT  No 5-96 & 5-92 FIRE UNITS, NO.8-4 WATER TANKER & NO.3-11

                       AUXILARY CAR

HOW EXTINGUISHED   TWO (02) MEDIUM JETS

HOSE IN USE         FOUR HUNDRED (400) FEET

ESTIMATED LOSS      APPROXIMATELY NINE HUNDRED THOUSAND DOLLARS ($900,000.00)

ESTIMATED VALUE

OF PROPERTY AT RISK APPROXIMATELY  FOUR MILLION DOLLARS ($4,000,000.00)

                       BUILDINGS _____

                       INSURANCE OFFICE _____

                       CONTENT $_____

INSURANCE          NONE

CAUSE OF FIRE      "UNKNOWN"

GENERAL REMARKS

    1.    On Tuesday, May 1, 20--, this call of Dwelling House on fire at No. 4 Rand Road, Kingston 10 was received at Half Way Tree Sub-Station at 1:20 p.m. through telephone number 926-0000. Response was made at 1:21 pm in the No.0-96 fire unit with a crew of six (6) firefighters, under the command of District Officer Burry Bossini.

    2.    On arrival at the given location, the brigade observed a four (4) bedroom house constructed of concrete, brick cement and the roof of lumber and zinc fully engulfed in flames. Two (02) medium jets were quickly brought into operation to contain and extinguish the fire whilst Divisional Headquarters, High Park was contacted and informed of the situation and additional units were requested.

KSA/100

## UNOCCUPIED DWELLING HOUSE, No. 4 RAND ROAD, KINGSTON 10

3.  Shortly after District Officer Herb Brown and men and also Contracted Driver Gower Haze and men arrived in No.0-92 fire unit and No.. 8-4 Water Tanker from Trench Town and York Park Fire Station respectively. Immediately the operation was transferred to the No. 0-92 fire unit with water being supplied from the No.- 8-4 Water Tanker as the No.-0 5-96 unit's tank was exhausted and left to replenish its tank.

4.  The same operation continued using two (2) medium jets from the No.05-92 fire unit until the fire was brought under control. Sometime during the operation Firefighter Gibbs Brown received injuries to his head and other parts of his body from a collapsed wall. The Police who were on the scene, assisted in transporting Firefighter Gibbs Brown to the Kingston Public Hospital.

5.  Sometime later Superintendent Joe Young and Firefighter Cessie Coe arrived in the No. 0-11 Auxiliary car from High Park. Superintendent Joe Young was then briefed of the situation by District Officer Herb Brown. Superintendent Joe Young being satisfied and seeing that the operation was under control and cooling down operation commenced, left in the No. 0-11 Auxiliary car along with Firefighter Gibbs Brown to the Kingston Public Hospital.

6.  Cooling down operation continued, using one medium jet from the No.0-92 fire unit. At this point the No. 5-96 had returned to the scene and the operation was then transferred to the No. 5-96 fire unit. District Officer Burry Bossini then instructed the Nos. 8-4 and 5-92 fire units to return to their respective stations.

7.  Investigating the cause of the fire, the Brigade was unable to get any information because the dwelling house was abandoned. However, speaking to Sergeant M. Mango from the Short Way Tree Police Station, the Brigade learnt that there was a feud going on in the area and the occupants had moved out, the Brigade also tried to speak to persons who were milling around but no one was willing to talk. With the Brigade's own investigation and information obtained from the Police there was not enough evidence or possible clues to determine the cause neither could the origin be found. Hence, the cause is listed as "UNKNOWN".

8.  Damage done as a result of the fire was estimated at approximately Nine Hundred Thousand Dollars ($900,000.00), whilst the estimated value of property at risk was Four Million Dollars ($4,000,000.00).

9. Seeing that all was correct the Brigade concluded its operation and returned to station.

Sign: _Burry Bossini_

District Officer

**Figure 8.12   Example of a Post Mortem Report**

# POST MORTEM EXAMINATION REPORT

I hereby report that on the _____5th_____ day of _____April, 20–_____

I viewed and examined the body of a _____PETE WASHAABLE_____ at the _____ALLPERSONS_____ UNIVERSITY HOSPITAL OF THE WEST INDIES (AUHWI) in the Parish of ST. ELIZABETH and have noted the following particulars after careful enquiry and examination.

## PARTICULARS OF ENQUIRY

a. When, where and by whom body was discovered?

The patient was pronounced dead at 1:30pm on the March 21, 20– on Ward 0, of the Allpersons University Hospital of the West Indies (AUHWI) by Dr Cossnip.

b. The position of the body when discovered and its surroundings.

The body was in the supine position on a bed on the same ward.

c. If the body had been moved thereof and by whom caused.

The body was transported from the ward to the morgue and from the ward to the post-mortem room for examination.

This was done by porters employed to the hospital.

d. The name, address, calling, sex, age and colour of the deceased.

WASHAABLE, Pete

Palm River

May Pen

May Pen P.O. Clarendon

Sex:  Male, Age: 70 years

(Retired Postmaster)

e. The name, calling and address of the person identifying the body.

Merl Washaable

Palm River

May Pen

May Pen P.O.

Clarendon

(Wife of the deceased) (Retired)

* All statemenrts made in this Report should be to the personal knowledge of the Operator

## PARTICULARS OF EXAMINATION

a. The time and place of the Examination and the number hours after death.

The post-mortem examination is being conducted at 8:00am on April 5, 20– in the post-mortem room of the Pathology Department, AUHWI.

b. The result of the examination of the position of the clothing or coverings, and of the external appearance of the body with special reference to any marks or signs of violence or injury

The body is that of an unclad black man with 93% partial thickness burns to most of his body including face, chest, abdomen, back, upper and lower limbs and groin.

The particulars that I have been able to ascertain by enquiry and external examination of the body being insufficient to enable me to determine for legal purposes the cause of death, I have made such dissections as were necessary and have observed and noted the following appearance –

1. The head, brain, spinal cord, organs of special sense &c.

The brain is swollen with blood noted in the skull cavity, most likely associated with head trauma.

2. The thorax and contents.

Both lungs are swollen and fluid filled and associated with fluid in both lung cavities. The heart is overweight and exhibit features of hypertension.

3. The abdomen and contents.

The abdominal contents are autolysed, but unremarkable except for enlarged prostate gland, mild infection of the urinary bladder secondary to catheter placement and mild congestion and inflammation of the stomach.

4. The extremities

Please refer to "b".

Having reason to believe that death may have been caused or accelerated by poison, I have placed the following substances in separate                    which I have carefully

Stopped and secured and handed to

For transmission to the Government Analyst at

 a.
 b.
 c.
 d.
 e.

Information obtained respecting the history and symptoms before death.

The patient sustained trauma to the head and flame burns after having been allegedly attacked on March 20, 20– He was brought to the Accident and Emergency department of the AUHWI on the following day, diagnosed with partial burns, 90% with inhalational lung injury and had tracheostomy tube placed on the same day. He died six hours later.

---

### SUMMARY OF OPINION AS TO CAUSE OF DEATH

From the abovementioned information and appearances I am of opinion that:-

Death is due to the inhalation injury secondary to the extensive flame burns and blood in the intracranial cavity secondary to the head trauma.

(Signed) *Dr. C. Cossnip*
..............................

Resident
Department of Pathology

PLACE

Allpersons University Hospital of the West Indies
St Elizabeth

---

## Fitness to Plead Certificates

Fitness to plead certificates are needed where the accused is said to be or appears to be of unsound mind. The Judge of the Parish Court can order a psychiatric evaluation to determine if the accused is capable of giving instructions to counsel and understanding the nature of a plea.

## Disclosure to Defence Counsel

It is the duty of the Clerk of the Courts, as the representative of the Crown, to ensure that the accused's attorney has all documents on file that are relevant to the case. An unrepresented accused is also fuly entitled to know the case against him so that he can prepare to meet the allegations. The accused should be provided with copies of everything the Crown intends to rely on in the case. *R v Linton Berry and Sangster/ Dixon v R PC #8/2002* address disclosure of material in the prosecution's possession.[19] If it is not feasible to copy these at once, copy them as they come to hand. It is quite useful to write out the list of documents that are being served on counsel or the defendant.

Defence counsel (or the accused himself) should be asked to acknowledge, sign, and date the receipt of all documents served. This acknowledgement of service should be kept on the file. The Clerk of the Courts should ensure disclosure documents are copied and served before the matter goes to court. Of course, disclosure of documents does not extend to the research the Clerk of the Courts does in preparation for a trial or to the Crown's theory of the case.

## Witnesses

Generally, witnesses should attend court on each court date that they are bound over to do so, and the investigating officer should be in touch with witnesses to ensure they attend court when required.

Realistically, however, it is not possible to have all witnesses in all trial matters on each day. As such, the Clerk of the Courts should also keep in touch with the witnesses and inform them about the dates to attend court.

---

19. *R v Linton Berry and Sangster/Dixon v R* PC #8/2002.

The Clerk of the Courts can also request subpoenas from the Judge of the Parish Court to serve on witnesses where necessary.

All witnesses should be on standby, ready to give their evidence, on the day they were subpoened or advised, even when it appears they will not be able to testify. The Clerk of the Courts must ask beforehand if the witnesses will swear or affirm and indicate to them that if they affirm they will have to explain their reasons to the Judge of the Parish Court.[20]

When the matter begins it might become clear that an additional witness/material is needed to further underpin the Crown's case. In such a situation, the Clerk of the Courts, at the appropriate time, should alert the Court and seek a brief adjournment – a day or two – to obtain the necessary witness or material. The adjournment is at the Judge's discretion.

### Subpoena *Duces Tecum*

Where it appears that a particular potential exhibit is in the possession of someone or an entity, the Clerk of the Courts, can apply to the court for a subpoena *duces tecum* for that potential exhibit to be brought to the court. The Judge of the Parish Court, on his own motion, can also order a subpoena *duces tecum*.

**Figure 8.13    Sample Subpoena *Duces Tecum***

---

**SUBPOENA DUCES TECUM**

IN THE PARISH COURT
FOR THE PARISH OF  ST. ANN   HOLDEN AT   ST. ANN'S BAY

REGINA VS TOM STROKES

FOR   FRAUD

QUEEN ELIZABETH II, By the Grace of God, of Jamaica and of her Other Realms and Territories, Queen, Head of the Commonwealth.

TO:   JOHN BROWN, THE PEOPLES BANK

GREETINGS

**WE COMMAND** you and every of you to be and take your proper person at the Parish Court, for the parish of  ST ANN  holden at ST. ANN'S BAY on the 25th day of   SEPTEMBER Two Thousand and --- at  the hour of 10:00 o'clock in the forenoon of the said day and do from day to day until the above case is being tried to give evidence on behalf of the Crown/Defence  and also to bring with you and produce,  at the time and place aforesaid:-

BANKING RECORDS OF TOM STROKES 20– to  20–

Witness the 20th day of  SEPTEMBER, Two Thousand and----
in the parish of St Ann holden at St Ann's Bay

*Emma Spitts*
Clerk of the Courts

---

20. *R v Hines* [1977] AC 195.

## Case Roadmap

It is useful to establish the way in which the evidence will be marshalled when the matter begins.

The usual procedure is to let the case unfold in a logical manner that ties the allegations and the accused together on the Crown's case. If there is a virtual complainant, s/he is usually the first witness. However, the surrounding circumstances of the allegations may dictate what is followed. Notably, since the Parish Court Judge is a trained legal mind, sitting alone, there is no need for a specific witness order.

**Table 8.1  Elements to be Proved by the Prosecution**

| Offence | Prove/Note | Potential Exhibit |
|---|---|---|
| Assault<br><br>Contrary to common law | Unlawful touching<br><br>Fear<br><br>Apprehension of injury by complainant | |
| Unlawful Wounding<br><br>Assault Occasioning Bodily Harm (OBH)<br><br>Offences Against the Persons Act | Breaking of skin<br><br>Wound that bled<br><br>Any swelling or bruising<br><br>Negative self-defence by Accused | Medical certificate for complainant<br><br>Weapon or implement if available |
| Dangerous Drugs, e.g., ss. 7 and 8 of the Dangerous Drugs Act | See s. 2 Dangerous Drugs Act for definitions<br><br>For the offence of dealing, per s. 22 (7) (e) of the Dangerous Drugs Act the amount must be eight ounces minimum. The type of packaging might also suggest dealing, such as many sticks or bags.<br><br>Possession – actual or constructive:<br><br>• Prove knowledge – that item is dangerous drugs<br><br>• Exclusive control – take note of the place and or thing where drugs found<br><br>• Prove custody<br><br>• Prove that the item is a dangerous drug (done through tests at the Forensic Laboratory and the Forensic Certificate is prepared) | Actual dangerous drugs<br><br>Chillum pipe<br><br>Forensic certificate |
| Corruption<br><br>s.14 Corruption Prevention Act | Public official offered not to, or declined to do his duty and that he should be paid to do so | The 'gift', e.g., money |

| Offence | Prove/Note | Potential Exhibit |
|---|---|---|
| Unlawful possession of property under s. 5 of the Unlawful Possession of Property Act | Accused is a 'suspicious' person per section 2 of the Act<br><br>Police officer's suspicion aroused | The item |
| Unlawful possession of property under s. 8 of the Unlawful Possession of Property Act | Search warrant's existence | 1. Search Warrant duly executed at the time and place of the search<br>2. The item |
| i. Abstracting Electricity<br>ii. Trespassing on NWC works s. 15 Larceny Act | Accused is the owner and/or occupier of premises.<br><br>JPS/NWC technician should speak to the fact that when he went to the premises he observed a breach | |
| Rent Restriction Act s. 27(1) | Establish the landlord and tenant relationship.<br><br>Establish the act that breaches the quiet enjoyment of the complainant. | Rent receipts<br>Rental agreements |
| Medical Act – s. 3 | That at time of commission of offence, the accused was not a registered member of medical or allied profession | Any prescriptions given to complainant 'patients'<br><br>Results of search from Medical Council or Nurses Association records that accused is not a member |
| Airport Authority Act | The accused was told to leave, not to park, etc. | Gazette that speaks to the offences at airport |
| Simple Larceny s. 5 Larceny Act | Proof that the property is owned by another;<br><br>Proof that the taking was with an intention to permanently deprive the complainant;<br><br>There was no consent given to the accused to take the property | The item, if recovered<br>Proof of ownership of item |
| Receiving Stolen Property s. 41(1) Larceny Act | Accused cannot be guilty of simple larceny and receiving. So decide which is better evidentially to proceed on and withdraw the other as necessary. | The item, if recovered |

| Offence | Prove/Note | Potential Exhibit |
|---|---|---|
| Forgery<br><br>Forgery Act | The accused has in his possession the forged document.<br><br>The accused 'uttered' the forged document | Items such as driver's licences, cheques and other paper documents |
| Fraudulent conversion<br><br>Forgery Act | Accused must have been entrusted with property that he 'converted,' i.e., used for his own purpose | |
| Indecent Assault<br><br>s. 13 Sexual Offences Act | Touching of complainant by accused without permission<br><br>The touching is of a body part that all right minded people would think is indecent. Such as breasts, bottom and sexual organs.<br><br>Age (if a child) | |
| Conspiracy<br><br>Common Law | Prove that two or more persons carried out or planned to carry out an unlawful act or a lawful act in an unlawful manner<br><br>It is the course that is agreed upon that is important (*Mulachy v R* 1866 LR 3 HL 306). | |

Table 8.2     Offences and Basic Documents that Indicate the Crown's Readiness

| Drug Offences | Offences Against the Persons Act | Simple Larceny | Abstracting Electricity/Trespassing on NWC works | Rent Restriction Act | Airport Matters |
|---|---|---|---|---|---|
| Forensic certificate | Medical certificates<br><br>Forensic Certificates (if necessary) | Statement from owner of property | Statement from investigating officer | Complainant's statement | Police Officer's Statement |
| Investigator's Statement | Post Mortem Report (if necessary) | Forensic certificate where necessary | Statement from relevant agency's Technician | Rental receipts | Gazette |
| Other Witnesses' statements | Witness statements – for example, the eyewitnesses ID the body; other witnesses | Investigating statement | | | |
| Documents that relate to the matter, e.g., shipping documents | Complainant's statement | | | | |

# Chapter 9

# Case Law

## Case Law

The cases cited here are not exhaustive on the particular principles being considered. However, they represent areas often considered in the Parish Court and are useful if a quick reference is needed while preparing for a matter. This section indicates the relevant citation and a brief summary of the laws in some instances.

| Type of Offence/ Areas/Act | Authority | Brief Summary of Case Law |
|---|---|---|
| Abuse of Process (delay) | See section 14 of the Charter of Fundamental Rights and Freedoms (Constitutional Amendments), Jamaica Constitution<br><br>*Bell v DPP* [1985] AC 937 Privy Council, Jamaica<br><br>*Prakash Boolell v The State* (Mauritus) PC 39 of 2005<br><br>*Mervin Cameron v The Attorney General* [2018] JMFC Full 1 | Fair trial, within a reasonable time by an independent and impartial court established by law form part of the protection afforded to the individual. The longer the delay...the less likely it is that the accused can still be afforded a fair trial..... |
| Accomplice | *R v Malek and Reyes* (1966) 9 JLR 553 | There is much danger in convicting on the uncorroborated evidence of an accomplice. |
|  | *R v Baskerville* [1916] 2KB 658 | The evidence of one accomplice cannot be corroborated by the evidence of another accomplice. |
|  | Calling a former accomplice for the Crown | Per *Archbold*, 36th ed. at note 1, 297, the practice is to omit such a person from the indictment, take his or her plea of guilty separately, sentence him or her, or enter a *nolle prosequi*. |
| Accused Silence | *R v Laing and Others* RMCA 78/1988<br><br>Delivered November 22, 1988 | Silence after caution cannot be impugned by a tribunal to form the basis of a conviction. |
| Admissibility (of Confessions/Statements) | *R v Seymour Grant* 23 WIR 132 | Admissibility is a question for the judge.<br><br>Voluntariness, as a test of admissibility, is a question for the judge and for the judge alone. |

| Type of Offence/ Areas/Act | Authority | Brief Summary of Case Law |
|---|---|---|
| Admissibility (of Confessions/Statements) | *Ibrahim v R* [1914] AC 599 | The statement must have been shown by the prosecution to have been a voluntary statement in the sense that it was not obtained from the accused either by fear or prejudice or hope of an advantage exercised or held out by a person in authority. |
| Admissibility (of Confessions/Statements) | *Shabadine Peart v R* Privy Council, Jamaica 21 [2006] UKPC 5 | This deals with the admissibility of a statement by a defendant in breach of the Judges' Rules. The overarching criterion of the admissibility of such a statement must be the fairness of the trial. The most important aspect of that would be the principle that a statement made by the accused must be voluntary in order to be admitted. If the statement is not voluntary, it will not be admitted into evidence. |
| | *Barry Wizard v R* (2007) 70 WIR 222 Court of Appeal, Jamaica | The Parish Court Judge, as judge and jury, is obliged to consider the question of voluntariness at the end of the day. This is notwithstanding that the caution statement may have been admitted without objections about its voluntariness. |
| Agent Provacateur | *R v Looseley* [2001] 4 All ER 897 HL | This considers the law of entrapment. |
| | *R v Peter Gordon and Wesley Gordon* (1991) 28 JLR 562 Court of Appeal, Jamaica | An undercover agent is not an accomplice for the purposes of the law. |
| | *R v Sang* 1979] 2 All ER 1222 at 1226, [1980] AC 402 Privy Council, Jamaica | Entrapment is not a known defence in the English law and thus is not in the common law of Jamaica. The court is generally unconcerned with how evidence was obtained. The areas of confession and other admissions are, however, special categories that require particular care. |
| Alibi | *Mills, Mills, Mills and Mills v R* (1995) 46 WIR 240 Privy Council, Jamaica | Where the accused relies on alibi as a defence and makes an unsworn statement from the dock, there is no need for a direction as to the possible impact of the rejection of the alibi. The jury should be told to accord to such statements the appropriate weight they think the alibi deserves. |

| Type of Offence/ Areas/Act | Authority | Brief Summary of Case Law |
|---|---|---|
| Alibi | *R v Balvin Mills* | Where the accused gives evidence and invokes alibi, the jury is to be told that the evidence can convince them of innocence, can convince them of guilt, or raise reasonable doubt. If the jury finds that the accused is lying, that is insufficient to convict. Rather, the Crown's case must be returned to and considered, so that the jury is sure of guilt. |
| | *Oneil Roberts and Christopher Wiltshire v R* SCCA 37-38/2000 November 15, 2001 | The Court need only give an alibi direction where there is evidence that the accused was at some other particular place or area at the material time. |
| Amendment | s. 278 Judicature (Parish Courts) Act | |
| Autrefois Acquit | *DPP v Patrick Nasralla* [1967] 2 AC 238 Privy Council, Jamaica | Proof of a verdict of acquittal (not mere peril of conviction) was essential to found the plea of *autrefois acquit*. |
| | *Dennis Thelwell v DPP* Full Court Division (Constitutional) Miscellaneous 126 of 1997 Heard May 11, 12 and 22, 1998 | There must be some joinder of issue as a condition precedent to the grant of a valid order of dismissal. If the accused was not in peril of being convicted then *autrefois* cannot be obtained. |
| Autrefois Convict | *R v Lloydell Richards* (1987) 24 JLR 142 Privy Council, Jamaica | When an accused pleads guilty (here to manslaughter) and there are no facts in evidence to so support such a plea, the Director of Public Prosecutions may enter a *nolle prosequi* and commence proceedings *de novo*. In such circumstances, the plea of *autrefois* convict is wholly unavailable to the accused. Where there is a guilty plea that is not followed by a sentence, there is no conviction. It is only a 'solemn confession' of the crime and in appropriate cases, with the Court's permission, it can be altered. |
| Bail[1] | | Safety of accused ensured in custody |

1. The Bail Act addresses a number of issues. These include the issue of an entitlement to bail (s. 3), the powers that can grant bail as the case may require (s. 3[1] ), the considerations of the Court (s. 4) and conditions of bail (s. 6), records to be kept regarding decisions on bail (s. 7), reasons for granting or refusing bail (s. 8), issues of absconding bail (s. 14), and procedures related to bail processing (s. 17). See too the Bail Regulations of 2001.

| Type of Offence/ Areas/Act | Authority | Brief Summary of Case Law |
|---|---|---|
| Bail[2, 3] | *Hurnam v The State* PC 53/2004 Delivered December 15, 2005 | Seriousness of offence is not by itself a basis upon which to refuse bail. |
| | *Phillip Stephens v The DPP* HCV 05020/2006 | Principles to be considered |
| | *Huey Gowdie v R* [2012] JMCA Crim 56 | Principles to be considered |
| | *Regina v RM St. James ex parte Michael Troupe and Gladstone Jemmison* 2&4/1992 (February 12,1992) Full Court | Forfeiture of bail recognizance |
| Case and Cross Case | *R v Epsom JJ ex parte Gibbons* [1983] 3 All ER 523 *R v Christopher Thompson* (1990) 27 JLR 50 (CA) | Exists where the defendant and complainant in the two matters are the same and the circumstances are also the same. It indicates that a case and cross case should not be heard together in any circumstance. |
| Caution Statement/ Confession | See Admissibility of Confessions/Statements | |
| | *R v Mushtaq* [2005] UKHL 25 | In the absence of evidence and denials by the police officers that there was actually any evidence of oppression or any other improper means, the fact that the judge did not go further should not affect the fairness of the appellant's trial or the safety of his conviction. |
| Chain of Custody | *Chris Brooks v R* [2012] JMCA Crim 5 | This adopts the position in *Damian Hodge v R* HCRAP 2009/01 Del November 10, 2010 (Court of Appeal of the Virgin Islands) that the purpose of testimony relating to the chain of custody is to prove that evidence which is sought to be tendered has not been altered, compromised, contaminated, substituted, or otherwise tampered with. It ensures the integrity of items from collection to production in court...Proof of continuity is not a legal requirement and gaps in continuity are not fatal...unless they raise a reasonable doubt about the exhibit's integrity. |

2.  Section 15(3) of the Constitution of Jamaica speaks to the right to a trial within a reasonable time.
3.  Bail can be granted by the police per section 23–24 of the Jamaica Constabulary Force Act.

| Type of Offence/ Areas/Act | Authority | Brief Summary of Case Law |
|---|---|---|
| Chain of Custody | *Damian Hodge v R* HCRAP 2009/01 Delivered November 10, 2010 (Court of Appeal of the Virgin Islands) *Regina v Heron Plunkett* [2015] JMCA Crim 32 | The purpose of testimony relating to chain of custody is to prove that evidence which is sought to be tendered has not been altered, compromised, contaminated, substituted, or otherwise tampered with. It ensures the integrity of items from collection to production in court...Proof of continuity is not a legal requirement and gaps in continuity are not fatal...unless they raise a reasonable doubt about the exhibit's integrity. |
| | *Clyde Grazette v R* [2009] CCJ 2 | Where the chain of custody is shown to be problematic, if there is sufficient evidence to persuade a judge who weighs the probability of interference and believes there is no interference, then the evidence is admissible. |
| Character (good) | *Chris Brooks v R* [2012] JMCA Crim 5 | Offers a detailed exposition on the authorities regarding this area. In circumstances where the accused has put his or her good character into evidence, s/he is entitled to a direction as to the relevance of said good character to his credibility and the likelihood of his having committed such an offence. |
| | *Noel Campbell v R* PC 7/2009 Delivered November 3, 2010 [2010] UKPC 26 | The appellant gave sworn evidence. The absence of a good character direction accordingly deprived him of a benefit in precisely the kind of cases where such a direction must be regarded as being of greatest potential significance...the Board does not feel able to treat the absence of a good character direction in this case as irrelevant to the safety of the verdict ... |
| Child of Tender Years Procedure in Court | Child Care and Protection Act Evidence Act regarding statements from children | Establishes definition of child and the treatment of statements from children. "child" is defined as less than fourteen years old (s.31M). The competence of a child to give evidence (s.31N). Determining competence (s.31O). Children may give evidence without an oath being administered (s. 31P). A corroboration warning is no longer necessary (s.31Q). |

| Type of Offence/ Areas/Act | Authority | Brief Summary of Case Law |
|---|---|---|
| Circumstantial Evidence | *Loretta Brissett v R* SCCA 69/2002 Delivered December 20, 2004 | Contains a useful synopsis of cases. Where the prosecution's case is made up of circumstances entirely, before the accused can be found guilty, it must be satisfied that not only were those circumstances consistent with his having committed the act but there must be satisfaction that the facts were inconsistent with any other conclusion other than that the accused is guilty. |
| | *Melody Baugh-Pellinen* [2011] JMCA Crim 26 Delivered July 8, 2011 | Treatment of circumstantial evidence in a no case submission. Cites *Loretta Brisset* |
| Co-accused Statements | *R v Gunwardene* [1951] 2 All ER 290 | Examines the issue of editing the statement of one co-accused against another. |
| Common Design/Joint Enterprise | *R v Sutcliffe and Barrett* SCCA 148&149/1978 (April 10,1981) | Principles |
| | *R v Jackson and others* (2009) 75 WIR 421 | Forseeability |
| | *Powell and English v Regina* [1997] 1 AC 1 | |
| | *Regina v Rahman* [2008] 3 WLR 264 | |
| | *R v Clovis Patterson* SCCA 81/2004 Delivered April 20, 2007 | |
| | *Ruddock v Regina* [2016] UKPC 7 *R v Jogee* [2016] UKSC 8 | *Ruddock* and *Jogee* revisit the principles and held: liability as an accessory required both conduct and mental elements. Here, conduct means that the accessory had assisted or encouraged the commission of the principal offence. The mental element, however, means an intention to assist or encourage the commission of that crime. Foresight alone that the principal might commit the offence charged was not an intent to assist, and it was not the inevitable yardstick of a common purpose. |

| Type of Offence/ Areas/Act | Authority | Brief Summary of Case Law |
|---|---|---|
| Confession | *Ibrahim v Rex* [1914] AC 599 | It has long been established as a positive rule of English criminal law that no statement by an accused is admissible in evidence against him unless it is shown by the prosecution to have been a voluntary statement in the sense that it has not been obtained from him either by fear of prejudice or hope of advantage exercised or held out by a person in authority. |
| Court Functus Officio | *Paynter v Lewis* (1965) 8 WIR 318<br><br>*Cummings (Steve) v The State* (1995) 49 WIR 405<br><br>*Beswick v R* (1987) 36 WIR 318<br><br>*R v Gilbert Henry* [2018] CCJ 21 (AJ) | The court is functus officio after it has made a final order, e.g. upholding a no case submission or a verdict of guilt or acquittal. |
| Corroboration | *Prince Duncan and Herman Ellis v Regina*<br><br>SCCA 147&148/2003 (February 1, 2008)<br><br>*Regina v Rennie Gilbert* (2002) 61 WIR 174 | As regards matters of a sexual nature, the corroboration warning is no longer mandatory. Rather, the court can give the warning in the appropriate circumstances and also determine the strength of any warning to be given. |
| Disclosure | *Linton Berry v R* (1992) 3 All ER 881 | Prosecution has a duty to supply the defendant with relevant statements and other material in the matter before the Court. |
| | *Franklyn and Vincent v R* (1993) 42 WIR 262 | The practice of refusing to provide statements of proposed prosecution witnesses to the defence as a matter of course is inappropriate. |
| | *R v Neville Williams* SCCA 117/01 Delivered March 18, 2005 | Where there are specimens taken in a matter, it is incumbent upon the prosecution in whom knowledge would rest to ensure that the results are ascertained before the trial begins. |
| | *Mark Sangster and Randall Dixon* SCCA 70&81/1998 Delivered October 8, 2003 [2002] UKPC 2 | The prosecution had some evidence (videos) that did not show the appellants were part of the offence. Remitted for reconsideration by Court of Appeal whether a re-trial was in order according to the relevant principles. |

| Type of Offence/ Areas/Act | Authority | Brief Summary of Case Law |
|---|---|---|
| Dying Declaration/Res Gestae | *Mills et al v R* (1995) 3 All ER 865 (1995) 46 WIR 240<br><br>*Regina v Andrews* [1987] AC 281; [1987] 1 All ER 513 | Gives an overview of case law in this area. Where the deceased last words were closely associated with the attack that triggered his statement and that statement was made contemporaneously in a situation where the incident would have dominated his thoughts, the possibility of concoction or distortion could be disregarded. |
| Evidence Act<br>Section 31D<br>(a) Death of Witness | *R v Clarence Peck* SCCA 68/1997 Delivered November 1, 1999 | Examines the principle that the circumstances of the death of a witness whose statement is being sought to put into evidence should not be elicited as it is not relevant to the admissibility of the statement. In fact, such evidence might well be gravely prejudicial to the accused. |
| (b) Mental Incapacity | *R v Setz-Dempsey* (1994) 98 Cr. App 23 | If the witness is unable to recollect events and the medical evidence establishes that the cause was a mental disorder giving rise to anxiety and failure of recall under stress, the test is met. |
| (c) outside Jamaica and not reasonably practicable to secure his attendance | *Henriques and Carr v R* [1990] 39 WIR 253 | On an application to admit the deposition of an absent witness, all factors relevant to its grant/refusal should be examined. Upon admission, the treatment thereof should be to instruct the jury of how to receive it. |
| (d) cannot be found after all reasonable steps have been taken to find him | *R v Michael Barrett* SCCA 76/1997 | The requirement of all reasonable steps being taken to find the maker of a statement is a pre-condition to admission into evidence of such a statement. |
| | *R v Barry Wizard* SCCA 14/2000 Delivered April 6, 2001 | Examines what can be considered as reasonable steps. |
| (e) kept away by threats of bodily harm and no reasonable steps can be taken to protect the person | *Nyron Smith v R* SCCA 241/2001 Delivered April 11, 2003 | That it is not reasonably practical for a witness to go on the witness protection programme (provided for by the Justice Protection Act) and that, as a result, the fears expressed by the witness could not be protected against and so his statement could be put into evidence under the fear prong. |

| Type of Offence/ Areas/Act | Authority | Brief Summary of Case Law |
|---|---|---|
| Exhibits | *Jadusingh and Jadusingh* (1963) 6 WIR 362 | Where an item has been tested but is now no longer available, the forensic certificate that would have been produced can be put into evidence despite that unavailability. |
| Expert Evidence | Evidence Act<br><br>*Myers v R; Cox v R; Brangman v R* [2016] AC 314 | Where the legislation allows, forensic certificates, ballistics certificates and other such certificates are admissible without the maker giving *viva voce* evidence. |
| Fair Trial | Section 20(6) Jamaican Constitution<br><br>*R v Damion Stewart* SCCA 147/07 Delivered March 26, 2010 | An accused is not to be deprived of 'facilities' as contemplated in s. 20 (6)(b) of the Constitution to adequately prepare his defence. |
| Findings of Fact | Section 291 Judicature (Parish Courts) Act | Record in summary form of the findings of facts on which a verdict of guilty is founded. |
| Findings of Fact | *R v Lloyd Chuck* 28 JLR 422 | Addresses the manner in which the Parish Court Judge is to deal with the findings of fact pursuant to s. 291 of the Judicature (Parish Courts) Act. |
| Forfeiture | Section 24 of the Dangerous Drugs Act | |
| | Section 60 of the Betting Gaming and Lotteries Act | |
| Hearsay | *Subramaniam v Public Prosecutor* (1956) 1 WLR 965 | It is not hearsay where the accused seeks to tender evidence showing his own state of mind in circumstances where statements were made to him by others that were relevant to said state of mind. |
| Hostile Witness | Section 15 of the Evidence Act *R v Christopher Parkes* SCCA 32/1990 Delivered August 3, 1991 | Dependent on the circumstances of the evidence led, it is in the discretion of the trial judge regarding leave to cross-examine a witness who has essentially recanted, on the Crown's case. |

| Type of Offence/ Areas/Act | Authority | Brief Summary of Case Law |
|---|---|---|
| Identification<br><br>*Generally* | *R v Turnbull*<br>(1977) QB 224 | Amount of time seen<br><br>Distance<br><br>Visibility<br><br>Obstructions<br><br>Known or seen accused before<br><br>Any particular reason to remember<br><br>Time that observation took<br><br>Error or material discrepancy (from Anthony Heaton-Armstrong, ed., *Analysing Witness Testimony*, 138. |
| *Voice* | *Siccaturie Alcock v R*<br>SCCA 88/1999<br>Delivered April 14, 2000 | Cites with approval *R v Rohan Taylor*, SCCA NOs 50, 51, 52 and 53/1991 and delivered March 1, 1993 which states that in order for the evidence of a witness that he recognized an accused by his voice be accepted as cogent, there must be evidence of the degree of familiarity with the accused, including prior opportunities to hear it. |
| *Video* | *Lynden Levy et al v R*<br>SCCA 152, 155, 156<br>May 16, 2002 | If the accuracy and authenticity of video tape evidence is established, it becomes relevant. |
| *DNA* | *Michael Pringle v R*<br>PC No. 17 0f 2002<br>Delivered January 27, 2003 | Examines the manner in which such evidence is to be received and treated. |
| | *R v Neville Williams*<br>SCCA No 117/2001<br>Delivered March 18, 2005 | In cases where the forensic results are pending, the prosecution has a duty to ensure that they are obtained before a trial commences. |
| *Parade* | *Kevin Tyndale and Brenton Fletcher v R*<br>SCCA No. 15 and 23/2006<br>Delivered October 24, 2008 | Where the defendant disputes knowledge of the witness, there may well be a useful purpose served to hold an identification parade. Where none is held, then the jury is to be warned about the dangers of identification without such a parade. Cites with approval *Pop v R* [2003] UKPC 40. |
| *Recognition* | *Michael Freemantle v R*<br>Privy Council Appeal No. 1 of 1993<br>Delivered June 27, 1994 | If there is cumulative potency in the quality of the visual identification, then that quality may be good enough to eliminate the danger of mistaken identification. |

| Type of Offence/ Areas/Act | Authority | Brief Summary of Case Law |
|---|---|---|
| Joinder of Offences | Section 22 of the Criminal Justice (Administration) Act | Outlines the circumstances wherein matters triable in the Parish Court (whether summary, on indictment, at the Lay Magistrate Court or by virtue of any criminal jurisdiction conferred by statute) can be joined. |
| Jurisdiction of the Parish Court | Section 268 of the Judicature (Parish Courts) Act | |
| Legal Representation and Conduct of Counsel | *Marcus Brown and Valentine Spencer* [2013] JMCA Crim 12 Delivered March 6, 2013

*Christopher Thomas v R* [2011] JMCA Crim 19 Delivered September 30, 2011 | Examines the ways in which both the prosecution and the defence should conduct their cases in trial matters. |
| Locus in Quo | *Warwar v R* (1969) 15 WIR 298 | Regarding applications to visit *a locus*, the object of a view or visit to the *locus in quo* should be to allow the jury to understand the questions being raised, to follow the evidence, and to apply the evidence. Visits to a *locus* is not in substitution for the evidence in court. |
| Lies | *R v Lucas* [1981] 2 All ER 1008 | People sometimes tell lies for reasons other than a belief that they are necessary to conceal guilt. Four conditions were identified which must be satisfied before a defendant's lie could be seen as supporting the prosecution case: (1) The lie must be deliberate; (2) It must relate to a material issue; (3) The motive for the lie must be a realization of guilt and fear of the truth; and (4) The statement must be clearly shown to be a lie by evidence other than that of the accomplice who is to be corroborated, that is to say by admission or evidence from an independent witness. |
| No Case Submission | *R v Galbraith* [1981] 1 WLR 1039 | Examines the issues the tribunal has to consider in deciding if the accused has a case to answer. |

| Type of Offence/ Areas/Act | Authority | Brief Summary of Case Law |
|---|---|---|
| No Order | *Halsbury's Laws of England,* 4th edition, Volume 29:185<br><br>*DPP v Feurtado* [1979] 16 JLR 519<br><br>*R v RM for St Andrew ex parte Ervin Walker* M63/1980 (February 16,1981) Full Court | Examines the effects of a no order in court. |
| Options of the Accused | *DPP v Leary Walker* (1974) 21 WIR 406 | The judge in plain and simple language make it clear...that the accused was not obliged to go into the witness box but that he had a completely free choice to do so or to make an unsworn statement or to say nothing...give the unsworn statement only such weight...think it deserves. |
| Possession Generally | | Knowledge<br>Custody<br>Control |
| | *Bernal and Moore* PC 56/1996 (1997) 51 WIR 241 Privy Council, Jamaica | 'Wilful Blindness'<br>Knowledge |
| | *Monica Williams* (1971) 12 JLR 116 Court of Appeal, Jamaica | 'something more' needed to ground the offence not just mere presence or occupation |
| | *Shawn Phillips* RMCA 6/96 Delivered March 25 and April 15, 1996 | No definition of hashish in Dangerous Drugs Act |
| | *Jadusingh and Jadusingh* (1963) 6 WIR 362 Court of Appeal, Jamaica | Where exhibits were tampered with and cannot be produced at trial but had been previously tested and the forensic certificate indicates that the items were drugs per the act, then the forensic certificate can be tendered and the trial is not vitiated. |

| Type of Offence/ Areas/Act | Authority | Brief Summary of Case Law |
|---|---|---|
| Possession Generally | *Richard Nicholson* (1971) 12 JLR 568 | Where prosecution has adduced evidence in proof of a) fact of possession and b) the thing is ganja, then it may be inferred that the accused knew it was ganja. |
| | | Where a *prima facie* case is made out, the evidential burden shifts to accused to displace the inference of knowledge even though the legal burden remains always on the prosecution. |
| | *Cyrus Livingston* (1952) 6 JLR 95 | To ground a conviction under section 7 of the Dangerous Drugs Act for possession, the accused must have knowledge that s/he has the thing and also know that the thing is ganja. |
| Postponement of Proceedings | Section 280 Judicature (Parish Courts) Act | |
| Previous Statements Inconsistent | Section 16 of the Evidence Act | |
| Reasons for the Findings of Fact of the Judge of the Parish Court | Section 291 of the Judicature (Parish Courts) Act | The Judge of the Parish Court must demonstrate that s/he has considered the various legal principles issues. |
| | | Inscrutable silence is to be decried. |
| | *R v George Cameron* [1985] SCCA 77/88 | |
| | *R v Lloyd Chuck* (1991) 28 JLR 422 | |
| | *R v Vince Stewart* (1990) 27 JLR 19 | |

| Type of Offence/ Areas/Act | Authority | Brief Summary of Case Law |
|---|---|---|
| Self-Defence | *Solomon v* R (1987) 24 JLR 242 (PC) | The test is the reasonableness or unreasonableness of the accused's belief and this is material only to the question of whether the belief was, in fact, held. If the belief was held by the accused, its reasonableness or otherwise is immaterial. Therefore, even if the defendant were labouring under a mistake or misapprehension as to the facts, s/he must be judged according to the mistakes whether or not the mistake was, on an objective view, a reasonable mistake or not. |
| Unlawful Possession of Property | *Whyte* (1974) 12 JLR 659<br><br>*Oscar Robinson* (1971) 12 JLR | Re section 5 of the Unlawful Possession of Property Act<br><br>Re section 8 of the Unlawful Possession of Property Act |
| Voir Dire | *R v Cargill and Roberts* 24 JLR 217 | The trial within a trial is appropriate in cases tried before judges and jury. This is a reminder to Parish Court Judges of this fact.<br><br>See too *Hylton et al.* RMCA 32/05 Delivered February 10, 2006 |
| Witnesses | The Evidence Act deals with absence of witnesses in various situations.<br><br>Section 12 of the Committal Proceedings Act indicates the treatment of witness who had given evidence at such proceedings. The Judge of the Parish Court makes what are called 'witness orders' requiring the witness to attend and give evidence before the court where the accused is to be tried. | |

## Sentencing

Sentencing Guidelines for Use by the Judges of the Supreme Court of Jamaica and the Parish Courts 2017

| See generally<br><br>Consecutive v Concurrent | *Kirk Mitchell v R*<br>[2011] JMCA Crim 1 | Examines the principles that should guide tribunals in determining if sentences should be concurrent or consecutive. |
| --- | --- | --- |
| General Principles of Sentencing | *R v Beckford and Lewis* (1980) 17 JLR 202<br><br>*R v Everald Dunkley* RMCA 55/2001 (July 5, 2002) | The four 'classical principles of sentencing' identified as retribution, deterrence, prevention, and rehabilitation. |
| Factors to Consider | *William Penn v R* HCRAP 2006/001 Delivered September 28, 2009 | This is a judgment of the territory of the Virgin Islands. However, it offers some guidelines as regards sentencing (in this instance regarding domestic burglary). |
| Sentencing of minors | *A v R* [2018] JMCA Crim 26 | Whilst a case dealing with manslaughter, it offers an excellent overview of all the issues that a court should consider regarding the anxious matter of sentencing a minor. |
| | Sections 75 and 76 of the Child Care and Protection Act | |
| | Law Reform (Miscellaneous Amendments) Restorative Justice | To provide restorative justice procedures as an option in the criminal justice system |

# Chapter 10

# Evidential Matters in a Case

## Summary

This chapter examines how to receive the evidence of particular witnesses in the course of a trial. It also reinforces points of law regarding problematic areas such as chain of custody. The Clerk of the Courts must ensure that the evidence is properly led, that all requisite foundation is laid, and that the law surrounding the issue is correctly utilized. So stylistically, Clerks of the Courts may differ in how they try a case, but the information presented here is the basic manner in which they should proceed.

## Terms

Chain of Custody

Witnesses:
- Eyewitnesses (Examination in Chief)
- Eyewitnesses (Cross Examination)
- Witness – Doctor who conducted the post-mortem
- Witness – Identification of a Body
- A Police Witness – Tender a Caution Statement

Statements:
- Putting in Statements into Evidence using the Evidence Act

Establish Possession
- In dangerous drugs cases

Tendering Items into Evidence

Exhibits

Caution Statements and Question and Answers

Dangerous Drugs

Vehicles

Marked for Identity

Medicals

Cross Examination of Accused

Witnesses for Accused

## Chain of Custody[1]

- If at all possible, items that are possible exhibits are not to be opened in the absence of the accused.

  Ensure that, where relevant, the accused and the item are together until they both reach the police station where the item is to be duly labelled and sealed in the accused's presence and then handed over to the storekeeper for safekeeping. The labelling and sealing of an item should consist of the following at minimum: the accused's name, the officer's name, rank, regulation number, and the offences if any.

  For large or bulky items, these details must be recorded somewhere conspicuous on the items. It is this labelling, especially, that will ensure that it gets into evidence, and it is critical that the correct procedures are followed.

  Where computer-generated evidence is to be received, the Evidence Act dictates the manner in which this is to be done.[2]

## Witnesses

### Eyewitnesses – Examination in Chief

The witness goes into the witness box and is sworn or affirmed.

Establish who the witness is by asking for name, occupation, (rank if necessary), and area where the witness lives (vulnerable witnesses need just state that s/he lives in St Elizabeth, for example).

- **Establish that the witness knew the complainant/deceased:**
  - » How did you come to know him (relative of witness, friend, was present at incident etc)?
  - » Do you know where he lived?

- **Establish the circumstances under which the witness knows the accused if necessary by asking questions such as:**
  - » Do you see him here today? (Here, ensure the witness clearly indicates the accused whether by pointing to him in the dock, or by describing his clothes, etc. Ensure the Court records the identification. This is crucial if there are multiple accused.)
  - » How long have you known him?
  - » What do you call him? (Here, if the accused has an alias that the witness knows him as, it would give the witness the opportunity to tell this to the Court)
  - » How often do you speak to him?

Identification of accused per *R v Turnbull* [1976] 3 All ER 54

- **Establish the date and time of the incident**
  To do this you usually:
  - » Ask the witness if he recalls a particular date and time.
  - » Ask the witness what if anything happened.

---

1. For further information on chain of custody, see chapters 5 and 6.
2. See the Evidence Act on computer generated evidence.

- **Establish location of the witness in relation to the accused by asking:**
  - » How far away were you from the accused?
  - » What if anything was blocking your view?
  - » What if anything did you notice about the accused?
  - » Describe what you noticed about the accused (e.g., he had a gun, a knife, etc.).
  - » If there are multiple accused ask about each accused.

- **Establish the lighting conditions to help in the identification of the accused by asking:**
  - » Could you see the accused?
  - » What part of the accused did you see? The usual response is 'face'. Sometimes witnesses say all of him, his whole body, in which case the Clerk of the Courts must re-direct their attention to the face.
  - » For how long did you see him?
  - » For how long did you see his face? This is only asked after the witness states s/he saw the accused's face.
  - » Was there anything that prevented you from seeing his face clearly?
  - » What if anything did you do after you saw the accused?

- **Establish what the accused did by asking:**
  - » Can you show what he did?
  - » Can you show what he did with what he had?
  - » What if anything happened after the incident (the shooting, the stabbing, the stone throwing, etc.)?
  - » Where if anywhere did the accused go?
  - » What did you do at this time?

- **Establish the situation with the complainant/deceased:**
  - » Tell us about the complainant/deceased at this time.
  - » Describe him (gunshots, stab wound, crying, etc.).
  - » Have you seen him since? (crucial for an eyewitness to a killing)
  - » Was there a funeral service
  - » Did you go?
  - » Did you see the body being buried?

- **Establish information about accused subsequent to the incident:**
  - » Have you seen the accused since the incident (this is crucial if there was an identification parade that the witness attended).
  - » Did you go anywhere?
  - » Tell us about that. Where was the parade? What did you do?
  - » Do you see the person you identified on that day here today?

**Eyewitnesses – Cross Examination by the Defence**

An idea of the defence being put forward can be gleaned hereto.

- If necessary, the Crown must address any gaps that might be created on its case (need for additional statements or for deeper probing of witnesses to come)
- Be alert for contradictions in the Crown's case.
- Look out for areas for re-examination.

**Witness – Identification of a Body**

This person is often called the 'id body witness'. This is the person who would have attended the post mortem (most persons call this colloquially 'cut' on the deceased).

- **Establishing this Witness's Particulars**

    To establish the witness's particulars the following information is needed:

    » Name

    » Address

    » If the witness knew the deceased

    » If a relationship exists, the nature of that relationship – how do you know the deceased: was the deceased a relative, friend, etc.?

    » The last time the witness saw the deceased alive.

    » If the witness remembers the date of the post-mortem?

    » What the witness remembers about the date of the post-mortem. If the witness does not remember, refresh his memory after laying adequate foundation.

    » Whether the witness did anything or was asked anything at the post-mortem.

    » Where the post-mortem was done.

    » Who was there (need not name everyone but important to say himself/herself, the doctor).

    » The name of the doctor who conducted the post-mortem.

    » Who was it done on?

    » Age of deceased at time of death.

**Witness – Doctor Who Conducted the Post-Mortem**

- **Establishing the Doctor's Credentials**

    To establish a doctor's (expert's) credential, you should get the expert to do the following:

    » State his or her name.

    » State whether or not the s/he is a registered medical practitioner in the island of Jamaica.

    » State how long the s/he has been so registered.

    » State if s/he is a pathologist.

    » State how long s/he has been a pathologist?

» State where s/he was trained as a pathologist and medical doctor.

» State his or her duties as a pathologist.

- **Establish the particular circumstances of this post-mortem by asking:**

    » Do you recall? State the date of the post-mortem.

    » Did you perform a post-mortem on a male, Tom Strokes, on that date

    » Did you make notes?

    » Can you recall your findings? Seek the permission of the Court for the witness to refresh himself from the notes he made.

    » Where was the post-mortem done?

    » Who identified the body?

    » What were the main external features on the body?

    » What were the main internal features on the body?

    » Describe the injuries on the body?

    » What would have caused such injuries?

    » What in your opinion was the cause of death?

    » Did you prepare any document in relation to the post examination that you conducted on this particular body?

    » What did you do with the document you prepared?

- **Tender the Post-mortem Report**

    The post-mortem should be tendered into evidence through the police officer who received it from the doctor.

**A Police Witness – Tender a Caution Statement**

- **Examine the physical circumstances of when the statement was taken by asking:**

    » Who were the persons present at the time – police, justice of the peace, attorney-at-law, etc.?

    » Where were these persons?

    » For a description of the room.

    » For a description of the accused in the room.

    » For a description of the paper on which the information was written.

- **To examine the caution's administration, keep these things in mind:**

    » The content of the caution.

    » That the caution was read over and read by the accused.

    » That the caution is explained to accused.

    » That the accused understood (if counsel or someone else is there with the accused, s/he can further explain the caution to the accused).

    » That the caution is written on a blank piece of paper.

» That there was no threat, force, or promise made to the accused.

» That the accused was seated comfortably.

» That the accused gave the statement of his or her free will.

» Who wrote the statement.

» Who signed it at the end.

» Who witnessed it at the end.

» What certificates of truth were written on it.

## Statements

- **Putting in Statements into Evidence using the Evidence Act[3]**

To put a statement into evidence, the appropriate limb of section 31D of the Evidence Act must be utilized. To do otherwise would mean that the statement cannot be put into evidence as the test has not been met.

Also, all efforts to contact a witness must be recorded. As such, letters to institutions must be written seeking information on the witness. The most common institutions written to are hospitals, morgues, prisons, immigration authorities, as well as the Registrar General's Department. The investigating officer should ensure that the letters are delivered and the necessary follow-up done to get early responses to the queries.

When the responses are received such that the Crown is ready to proceed, a notice of intention must be prepared and served on the defendant. If the witness is dead,[4] then a copy of the post-mortem report as well as the investigating or other officer or persons' statement to that effect as well as a copy of the dead witness's statement is to be served on the defendant within the requisite time period. It is also useful to serve on the defence, a copy of all the responses obtained in the efforts to locate the witness previously.

Lay the foundation through the relevant officer (usually the investigating officer) as to all the efforts made to locate the witness or provide the proof of the death of the witness. Special care should be taken where a witness is dead so that there is no prejudice to the accused, especially in circumstances where the witness died violently.

Having laid this foundation, the officer then speaks to the circumstances under which the statement of the witness was taken. This would include the date, the time, place, name of the person, how the officer knew it was the correct person, that the statement was handwritten in his handwriting and/or typed and signed by the witness and the officer, that the witness and his certificate of truth are on the statement.

Having laid this foundation, the officer is then asked if he would be able to recognize this statement again and how. After he has indicated how, the Clerk of the Courts is to ask that the witness be shown the item. This application by the Crown can be refused or allowed. Therefore, it is crucial that the appropriate foundation is laid. After the officer identifies the item, apply to have it tendered through the officer at this time.

---

3. Section 31D of the Evidence Act requires that the Crown passes the threshold for the particular limb that it is seeking to have a statement admitted.
4. Remember that where a witness is dead, only the bare fact of his death should be led in the evidence so as to remove or reduce any speculation that the accused was somehow involved in that death.

## Establishing possession in dangerous drugs cases

» Did you speak to accused?

» Where was the accused at the time the item was found?

» Where premises are searched.

» What address was searched?

- What did you do on arriving at premises?

- Did you have anything with you?

- Give brief details of any search warrant that was read to accused.

- Tender search warrant through the appropriate police officer.

- If the accused gave permission to search.

» What link is there to accused with item

- Whether the accused owns the premises and has exclusive control of it.

- Whether the accused operates the premises and has exclusive control of it.

- Whether the accused is travelling with items (such as suitcases or boxes).

- Whether the accused name and other details are on such items (such as tags, labels, receipts, airway bills).

- Whether the accused said he packed his own luggage (for airport cases).

- Whether the accused was driving vehicle with contraband.

» Where contraband was found on the accused

- Establish where exactly it was found, for example, place on clothes, in hands, shoes, etc.

- What was said to the accused after caution? NB, officers ought to caution suspects.

- Was item shown to the accused?

- Was accused told that item resembled a dangerous drug, for example, vegetable resembling ganja (VMRG)?

» What was done with item after it was shown?

- Whether the accused and item taken together, for example, in one vehicle to station.

- Whether the item was sealed and labelled in accused's presence with information about the case.

- Whether the item was locked away securely in good condition (securely sealed).

- Whether the item was retrieved in good condition.

- Whether the item was taken to Government Forensic Laboratory (GFL) for testing by sample or of whole amount.

- Whether the a receipt was issued followed by a forensic certificate.

## Tender items

- **Drugs**
  - » How would you recognize the package that you said you sealed and labelled (by case details, name of officer and regulation number, and handwriting of officer)?

- **Forensic Certificate (FC) – the information is on the top of the FC**
  - » By case details, Forensic Lab (FL) number, name of officer, and regulation number.

## Exhibits

- These can vary from the mundane to the exotic.

- Proper foundation must be laid before any item can be tendered and admitted into evidence as exhibits. The chain of custody where relevant must be established before the item can be admitted as an exhibit. Therefore, be careful to ensure that you have ascertained through whom it is most appropriate to tender an item.

- Unless it is tendered and admitted into evidence, the Court cannot view an item.

- In most situations, persons cannot speak to an item unless it is tendered and admitted into evidence.

- Remember the principle in *R v Peter Blake* (16 JLR 61) which provides that a witness can be shown an item.[5] This is usually utilized by the defence counsel.

- The Clerk of the Courts can indicate to the defence which items s/he will seek to have tendered. If there is an objection raised, one must be able to rebut such objections.

- Some potential exhibits can cause particular problems and so must be dealt with carefully. Of particular note are the following documents:

## Caution Statements and Question and Answers

The Clerk of the Courts must ensure that the witness through whom they wish to admit the potential exhibit can speak to: the persons present, the paper written on, the physical circumstances of the defendant during the statement taking, if there was any threat, fear or inducement visited upon the defendant, the way in which the witness would be able to identify the document, and that the defendant was told of the possibility of the document being admitted into evidence against him.

Regarding documents that are not the original, the Clerk of the Courts must lay the proper foundation to account for what became of the originals. This must be done before copies can be put into evidence.

## Dangerous Drugs

It is usual to tender the actual drugs first and then to tender the forensic certificate. The drugs should be tendered through the person who found it or the person nearest in the chain, to maintain the chain of custody. The forensic certificate should be tendered through the person who took the drugs to the government forensic laboratory and obtained the receipt indicating when the officer should return for the drugs and the forensic certificate.

---

5. *R v Peter Blake* (1977) 16 JLR 61. Counsel was entitled in cross-examination to confront a witness with a document regardless of its admissibility and without disclosing its contents, to elicit a response from the witness that might be favourable to the facts which the cross examiner is seeking to establish or damaging to the credit of the witness being cross-examined as a result of questions which may subsequently be asked.

The forensic certificate is *prima facie* evidence of the tests carried out on the item.[6] If the defendant seeks to challenge the certificate then apply to have the forensic analyst called to testify. This is per section 52 of the Evidence Act.

Where there is need for the Court to leave the precincts of the court building for drugs to be tendered and admitted into evidence, the necessary arrangements must be made. Therefore, the relevant storeroom keeper must be apprised of the intention of the Crown. The Court police officers must also be aware of the need to have officers go with the Court, secure the accused, and that they must open/re-open the Court at the venue and close it at the end.

At the venue, have the items tendered and admitted into evidence.

If there are also samples of the drugs as well as the actual items, also seek to have the samples tendered.

Read the forensic certificate carefully to ensure that the person through whom you seek to tender it is the correct person. The person to tender it is the person who received it from the lab. This person's name is usually at the top of the document. If it was merely collected by someone that person must come to give evidence as to the chain of custody to the point where it was handed over to the person now tendering it in court.

## Vehicles

Where vehicles are to be tendered and admitted into evidence, an application must be made for the Court to go to the venue where the vehicle is being kept. If some party has the vehicle in his possession (such as on a bond), then s/he must be instructed to bring the vehicle on the requisite day. Where such vehicles were used as conveyances, etc., and there is provision for forfeiture, this is to be applied for if the accused has been found guilty and is being sentenced.

## 'Marked "A" for Identity'

This is where an item is really noted as being ready to be tendered later by another more appropriate party (such as the maker of the document). In such circumstances, consider if you will need to recall any earlier witnesses to look at the item when it has been tendered. If this is the case, make the application to the Court when the person is finished giving his evidence.

If possible, store exhibits in the vault of the Court. If there is none, ask that the investigating officer keep it in safe custody at the station's storeroom.

## Medicals

These must be written on the appropriate form. They are to be signed by the doctor before a Justice of the Peace. The information of the Clerk or deputy Clerk is also to be completed. These must be done before the medical is served on the defence.

## Accused – Cross-Examination

The accused can exercise any of the three options open to him or her. Where the accused gives sworn evidence, test the story by probing into what was said in his or her evidence in chief.

---

6.   The forensic certificate as per section 27 of the Dangerous Drugs Act is *prima facie* evidence of the tests carried out on the item.

Careful notes must be taken. After the accused's evidence has been tested, the Clerk puts the case according to the case theory, the evidence of the witnesses, and with the use of the exhibits, if necessary. The Crown's case is put to the accused so that s/he can rebut or agree with the prosecution's version of the incident. Whatever the Crown's witnesses have said or shown to underpin the offences must be put to the accused.

## Witnesses for the Accused

Persons who give evidence for the accused must swear or affirm. They take the stand after the accused has exercised his or her option. Their evidence is marshalled by defence counsel and the Clerk of the Courts cross-examines them. Witnesses for the accused can speak to the accused's character, they can be alibi witnesses, or witnesses as to fact. Therefore, in a case where self-defence is live, such a witness might speak to the complainant only being armed. These are issues to which the Clerk of the Courts must be able to adequately and properly respond as the evidence unfolds.

# Chapter 11

# Fingerprintable Offences

## Summary

The Fingerprint Act outlines and defines what offences are deemed fingerprintable and gives the Court the authority to order that the fingerprints and photograph be taken of any one charged for a particular offence.[1]

The Court here refers to the Circuit Court, the Traffic Court, Children's Court, Family Court, or a Parish Court.

## Terms

Authorized Officer

Who is an Authorized Officer for the Purposes of the Act

When Fingerprints and/or Photographs Can be Taken without a Suspect's Consent

Minors, Fingerprints, and Photographs

Convictions Abroad

Offences that Carry Fingerprint Orders

## An 'Authorized Officer'

The fingerprinting and/or photographing of an offender or suspect is a sensitive matter and so only the 'authorized officer', as defined in the Fingerprint Act, can take someone's fingerprints or pictures.[2]

## Who is an Authorized Officer for the Purposes of the Act

According to sections 3A and 3B of the Act, this authorized officer must be an officer or subofficer of the Jamaica Constabulary Force (JCF), or any correctional officer appointed as such by the Minister of Justice.[3]

Specifically, the authorized officer must not be below the rank of superintendent or the subofficer in charge of a police station.[4]

---

1. Under section 3(1) of the Fingerprint Act, where any person is charged before a Circuit Court, the Traffic Court, Children's Court, Family Court, or a Parish Court with any offence specified in the First Schedule, the Court may order that the fingerprints and photograph of such person be taken.
2. The legislators deemed it sufficiently important that there be strictures on who can take fingerprints. That only the Court can give the order to take a fingerprint curbs any possibility of abuses of justice.
3. Section 3 of the Fingerprint Act shows the wide jurisdiction the court has to order the taking of prints.
4. Fingerprinting and photographing persons who are in custody is examined in section 3A and 3B. Section 3A covers persons who are in custody on reasonable suspicion of having committed a crime. Before being fingerprinted or photographed, the person is to be informed of his or her right to refuse having these done. Also, the person should be informed that consent should be formally recorded in the presence of a Justice of the Peace or an attorney-at-law where one is on the record. This is a safeguard that the Act stipulates. The section further states that it is to be made clear to the suspect that there are specific circumstances

However, the Minister of Justice may authorize any officer or subofficer of the JCF to take a suspect's fingerprints or photographs for the purposes of section 6.

## When Fingerprints and/or Photographs Can be Taken without a Suspect's Consent

Section 3A(4) of the Fingerprint Act stipulates that fingerprints and photographs may be taken without a suspect's consent and without a court order on the written authorization of an authorized officer not below the rank of a superintendent if:

a.  that person is diagnosed by a medical practitioner as suffering from a mental disorder and is thereby incapable of giving consent and a certificate signed by the medical practitioner is received by the authorized officer; or

b.  the authorized officer has reasonable grounds to suspect that the person has been involved in the commission of an offence specified in the Second Schedule and the taking of his fingerprints and photograph will help to confirm or disprove his involvement; or

c.  that person has given an inaccurate identity.

## Minors, Fingerprints, and Photographs

According to section 3A(2), if the person taken into custody is between the ages of 12 and 18 years, a parent or guardian has to consent to the taking of the minor's fingerprint and photograph.

In the absence of such consent, because the parent or guardian cannot be located, a children's advocate or an appropriate person nominated by the Children's Advocate can consent.

A prescribed consent form must be signed by the parent, guardian, children's advocate, or a nominee, in the presence of a Justice of the Peace. If the minor is represented by an attorney-at-law, such signing is to be done in the attorney's presence.

If, however, consent is not obtained, an application should be made to the Children's Court or Family Court for an order authorizing the taking of the minor's fingerprints and photograph. Importantly, there is no authorized officer who can order the taking of such fingerprints and picture of minors; only the Court can authorize it. This is in place to protect minors who are alleged to have committed offences.

## Convictions Abroad

Where a person has been convicted abroad of an offence similar to an offence specified in the First or Second Schedule and is the subject of a deportation order, his or her fingerprints and photograph may be taken by an authorized officer when that person arrives in Jamaica. The consent of the person is requested, and it is recorded on the prescribed form. A Justice of the Peace has to witness that the person consents to the fingerprinting and photographing. If the person is represented by an attorney-at-law, then it is to be done in the presence of the attorney-at-law.[5]

---

in which the fingerprints and photograph may be taken without permission and without an order being made by the Court in the circumstances set out in section 3(A)(4). Where a person is taken into custody on reasonable suspicion of having committed an offence, the fingerprints and photograph of that person may be taken, without his consent and without a court order, on the written authorization of an authorized officer not below the rank of a superintendent in particular circumstances.

5.  Section 3B of the Act focuses on persons who have been deported, who have convictions abroad for offences such as breaches of the Dangerous Drugs Act, breaches of the Firearms Act (First Schedule), murder (Second Schedule), and offences under the Sexual Offences Act (Second Schedule).

Table 11.1        The Offences that Carry Fingerprint Orders[6]

| Schedule | Relevant Reference Section of the Fingerprint Act | Offence under Particular Acts |
|---|---|---|
| **FIRST SCHEDULE** | Sections 3, 3B, 4, 4A, 7 and 9 | Criminal Justice (Administration) Act: Section 46, Part II: after a second conviction of a crime, powers of taking such offender into custody Section 51: penalty for harbouring thieves Section 52: assaults on police. |
| | | Any offence against section 15 (penalties for breach of orders) of the Deportation (Commonwealth Citizens) Act |
| | | Road Traffic Act: Section 34: driving motor vehicles under influence of drink or drugs Section 34A: driving or being in charge of a vehicle while blood alcohol levels exceeds prescribed limit Section 45: unlawful use of motor vehicle Section 46(a): fraudulently altering or using any licence, licensing, or registration mark or plates |
| | | Any offence under the Unlawful Possession of Property Act. |
| | | Under the Public Order Act: Any offence against section 29: Prohibition of offensive weapon |
| | | Any indictable offence not specified in the Second Schedule |
| **SECOND SCHEDULE** | Sections 3a, 3b, 4, 4a, 4b, 7 and 9 | Specific offences under the Dangerous Drugs Act |
| | | Any offence under the Firearms Act |
| | | Any offence under the Explosives (Control of Manufacture) Act |
| | | Any offence under the Explosives (Sale of Deposited Stores) Act |
| | | Any offence under the Gunpowder and Explosives Act |

---

6. See the First and Second Schedules of the Act.

| Schedule | Relevant Reference Section of the Fingerprint Act | Offence under Particular Acts |
|---|---|---|
| **SECOND SCHEDULE** | Sections 3a, 3b, 4, 4a, 4b, 7 and 9 | Any offence against the following sections of the Offences Against the Person Act: |
| | | Section 2: (capital murder) and (non-capital murder |
| | | Section 8: conspiring or soliciting to commit murder |
| | | Section 9: manslaughter |
| | | Section 11: petit treason |
| | | Section 13: administering poison, or wounding with intent |
| | | Section 15: setting fire to shop, etc., with intent to murder |
| | | Section 16: attempting to administer poison, etc., with intent to murder |
| | | Section 17: by other means attempting to commit murder |
| | | Section 31: endangering passengers on a train |
| | | Section 33: genocide |
| | | Section 70: kidnapping |
| | | Section 79: outrages on decency |
| | | Any offence against any of the following sections of the Sexual Offences Act: |
| | | Section 3: rape |
| | | Section 4: grievous sexual assault |
| | | Section 5: marital rape |
| | | Section 10: sexual intercourse with person under 16 |
| | | Section 15: abduction of child under 16 |
| | | Section 16: violation of person suffering mental disability or disorder |
| | | Section 17: forcible abduction |
| | | Section 20 : abduction of child with intent for sexual intercourse |
| | | Section 21: unlawful detention in premises for sexual intercourse |
| | | Treason |

Notably, all indictable offences that are not specified in the Second Schedule of the Fingerprint Act are fingerprintable. As such, it is useful to know which offences are indictable under the relevant pieces of legislation.[7]

---

7. There is a catchall for offences as one of the provisions in the First Schedule states that any indictable offence not mentioned in the Second Schedule is fingerprintable.

**Table 11.2**      Fingerprinting and Various Offences

| Offence | Act and Section | Fingerprintable Offence |
|---|---|---|
| **SUMMARY** | | |
| Exposing goods for sale | Town and Communities, s. 3(I) | No |
| Taking steps preparatory to export ganja | Dangerous Drugs, s. 7(a)<br><br>There are various exemptions that are now found in the act that must be considered. | Yes |
| Dealing in ganja | Dangerous Drugs, s. 7(B). There are various exemptions that are now found in the act that must be considered. | Yes |
| Using premises for sale of ganja | Dangerous Drugs, s. 7(B).<br><br>There are various exemptions that are now found in the act that must be considered. | Yes |
| Using any conveyance...carrying... selling otherwise dealing in ganja | Dangerous Drugs, s. 7(B) .<br><br>There are various exemptions that are now found in the act that must be considered. | Yes |
| Possession of ganja over the prescribed amount or for prescribed purposes | Dangerous Drugs, s. 7(C).<br><br>There are various exemptions that are now found in the act that must be considered. | Yes |
| Possession of pipes or other utensils...smoking ganja | Dangerous Drugs, s. 7(D).<br><br>There are various exemptions that are now found in the act that must be considered. | Yes |
| Sale of ganja on premises | Dangerous Drugs, s. 7(B).<br><br>There are various exemptions that are now found in the act that must be considered. | Yes |
| Attempting to import ganja | Dangerous Drugs, s. 7(a) | Yes |
| | | Yes |
| Dealing in cocaine | Dangerous Drugs, s. 8(a) | Yes |
| Possession of cocaine | Dangerous Drugs, s. 8(b) | Yes |
| Attempting to import cocaine | Dangerous Drugs, s. 8(a) | Yes |
| Breach of Corruption Prevention Act by public servant | Corruption Prevention, s. 15 | No |
| Being in possession of excisable goods | Excise Duty | No |
| Breach of copyright | Copyright, s. 46(1) | No |
| Breach of trademark | Trademark, s. 69 | No |
| Possession of illegal drop pan tickets | Betting, Gaming and Lotteries | No |
| Depositing noxious liquid in a public place | National Solid Waste Management | No |
| Trespassing on works of National Water Commission | National Water Commission | No |

| Offence | Act and Section | Fingerprintable Offence |
|---|---|---|
| Breach of Rent Restriction Act | Rent Restriction Act, s. 27(1) | No |
| Absconding bail | Bail Act, s. 14 | No |
| False declarations contrary to Bail Act | Bail Act, s. 17(9) | No |
| Possession of offensive weapon | Offensive Weapons, s. 3 | No |
| Discharging weapon within 40 yards of a public place | Firearms Act | Yes |
| Operating sound system without a permit | Noise Abatement | No |
| Failing to leave airport | Airport Authority | No |
| **INDICTABLE** | | |
| Simple larceny | Larceny, s. 5 | Yes |
| Praedial larceny | Larceny, s. 13 | Yes |
| Abstracting electricity | Larceny, s. 15 | Yes |
| Larceny as a servant | Larceny, s. 18(1) | Yes |
| Larceny from person | Larceny, s. 19 | Yes |
| Embezzlement | Larceny, s. 22 | Yes |
| Fraudulent conversion | Larceny, s. 24 | Yes |
| Robbery with aggravation | Larceny, s. 37(1)(a) | Yes |
| Robbery with violence | Larceny, s. 37(1)(b) | Yes |
| Receiving stolen property | Larceny, s. 46(1) | Yes |
| Indecent assault | Offences Against the Person | Yes |
| Unlawful wounding | Offences Against the Person, s. 22 | Yes |
| Assault occasioning bodily harm | Offences Against the Person, s. 43 | Yes |
| Conspiracy | All conspiracies are contrary to common law | Yes |
| Forgery | Forgery | Yes |
| Uttering forged documents | Forgery | Yes |
| Forgery of passport | Forgery | Yes |
| Uttering counterfeit note | Forgery | Yes |
| False declaration | Forgery | Yes |
| Obtaining money by false pretences | Forgery | Yes |
| **COMMITTAL PROCEEDINGS** | | |
| Sexual intercourse with someone under 16 | Sexual Offences Act | Yes |
| Rape | Sexual Offences Act | Yes |
| Murder | Offences Against the Person Act | Yes |
| Attempted murder | Offences Against the Person Act | Yes |
| Incest | Sexual Offences Act | Yes |

| Offence | Act and Section | Fingerprintable Offence |
|---|---|---|
| Kidnapping | Sexual Offences Act | Yes |
| Buggery | Offences Against the Person Act | Yes |
| Abduction | Sexual Offences Act | Yes |
| Wounding with intent | Offences Against the Person Act, s. 20 | Yes |
| Burglary | Larceny, s. 39 | Yes |
| Extortion | Larceny, s. 43A | Yes |
| **HEARING** | | |
| Unlawful Possession of Property | Unlawful Possession of Property, s. 5 | Yes |
| Unlawful Possession of Property | Unlawful Possession of Property, ss. 8 and 10 | Yes |
| **LAY MAGISTRATE COURT** | | No |
| Threat | | No |
| Abusive language | | No |
| Resisting arrest | | No |
| Indecent exposure | | No |
| Indecent language | | No |
| Assault | | No |

1. All conspiracies must have a substantive offence.

2. All offences that are contrary to common law are indictable and, therefore, fingerprintable.

# Chapter 12

# Forfeiture[1]

## Summary

On a successful application of the Crown, a Parish Court Judge has the power to make forfeiture orders upon a conviction to seize any asset that may have been used in a crime or acquired as a result of a crime.

Specific Acts provide that anyone with an interest in recovering an item to be forfeited may appear in court to demonstrate why the forfeiture should not be granted. An applicant can pray in aid, for example, that forfeiting an item would cause him great hardship; and/or a lack of knowledge of the activities for which the property was used; and /or of having given permission for only specific use of his property.

## Terms

Forfeiture Proceedings

Forfeiture under the Cybercrimes Act

Offences and Forfeiture

## Forfeiture Proceedings

Where forfeiture orders were granted without any objection from any interested party, an application for court orders may still be made at a later date for a hearing on the matter.[2] The Criminal Justice (Reform) Act provides that any claimant, within six months after the determination of the matter, can seek to have the court restore a forfeited item to him. However, such a claimant must prove that he is the lawful owner of the property and that he did not know that the property would be unlawfully used or did not consent to the offender so having possession.[3]

The Act also provides that where a person is convicted of an offence and punishable on indictment with imprisonment for a term of two years or more, forfeiture can be applied for in certain situations.[4] This Act, therefore, captures indictable offences for which there is no forfeiture provision in a particular enactment, but the Crown is of the view that forfeiture would be fit and proper in all the surrounding circumstances.

---

1. Generally speaking, where forfeiture has been ordered, any person with an interest in the item can file an application for court orders to revoke such forfeiture order. By affidavit, the person should indicate the reasons why the order should be revoked. Forfeiture applications are grounded under the relevant sections of the particular statute granting forfeiture.
2. Section 18 of the Criminal Justice (Reform) Act.
3. See section 24(6) of the Dangerous Drugs Act that indicates the procedure regarding such applications by innocent third parties. *Bertram Sears v Director of Public Prosecutions*, RMCA delivered December 18, 2006, is instructive. It examines the test that the Parish Court Judge should apply in a hearing where an application is seeking return of a conveyance.
4. Section 18(4) of the Criminal Justice (Reform) Act.

Under this same Act, if the Court before which the person was convicted is satisfied that any property which was in the accused's possession or under his control at the time of his apprehension,

    (a) has been used for the purpose of committing or facilitating the commission of the offence; or

    (b) was intended by him to be used for that purpose,

the Court may make an order of forfeiture of that property to the Crown.

## Forfeiture under the Cybercrimes Act

Section 20(1)–(10) of the Cybercrimes Act focuses on forfeiture. Upon the conviction of an accused, where a person owns computer material used in the commission of an offence; where an owner permits his computer material to be used in the commission of an offence; or where the circumstances are just, forfeiture can be granted by the Judge of the Parish Court on the requisite application by the prosecution.

**Table 12.1**      Offences and Forfeiture

| Offence | Act and Section | Forfeiture Order Can be Made | Discussion |
|---|---|---|---|
| Using a conveyance in a drug offence | Contrary to sections 7(B) and 8(B)(1)(c) Dangerous Drugs Act<br><br>Note that especially as regards s. 7B there are exceptions under the Act. | Yes | Section 24 of the Dangerous Drugs Act allows applications for forfeiture by the Crown in appropriate cases.<br><br>The Act also makes provisions for the hearing of any objections by a person who can show cause as to why the order should not be granted by the Court per subsection 6. |
| Unlawful Gaming | Contrary to sections 16, 17, 38 or 48 of the Betting Gaming and Lotteries Act | Yes | Section 60(2)(a) of the Betting Gaming and Lotteries Act.[5] |
| Breaches of the Copyright Act | Contrary to section 46 of the Copyright Act | Yes | Section 48 regarding criminal proceedings discusses the circumstances under which the Court may order that infringing articles be delivered to any person as ordered by the Court. This is subject to sections 137 and 138 of the said Act.[6] |

---

5.    Section 60(2)(a) of the Betting Gaming and Lotteries Act dictates that any document, money, or valuable thing, instrument, or any other thing whatsoever belonging to the convicted person which the court believes was used or intended to be used can be forfeited.

6.    Regarding section 46 of the Copyright Act, section 48 states that subject to subsection (2), the court before which proceedings are brought against a person for an offence under section 46 may, if it is satisfied that at the time of his arrest or charge, (a) he had in his possession, custody, or control in the course of a business an infringing copy of a protected work; or (b) he had in his possession, custody, or control an article specifically designed or adapted for making copies of a particular protected work knowing or having reason to believe that it had been or was to be used to make infringing copies, order that the infringing copy or article be delivered up to the copyright owner or to such other person as the court may direct. Under subsection (2), an order may be made by the Court of its own motion or on the application of the prosecution and may be made whether or not the person is convicted of the offence, so, however, that the court shall not make an order: (a) after the time specified in section

| Offence | Act and Section | Forfeiture Order Can be Made | Discussion |
|---|---|---|---|
| Breaches of the Trademark Act | Contrary to s. 69 of the Trademarks Act | Yes | The unauthorized use of a trademark has several broad categories.[7] |
| Acts of Corruption (regarding public servants) | Contrary to s. 14 of the Corruption Prevention Act | Yes | Corruption Prevention Act, s. 15(3).[8] |
| Breaches of the Proceeds of Crime Act (POCA) | Property[9] is defined as all property wherever located, and includes money, all forms of real or personal property and things in action and other intangibles.[10]<br><br>Contrary to Part II of the Proceeds of Crime Act, in particular, ss. 5–9 examine forfeiture orders and pecuniary penalty orders.<br><br>Forfeiture as regards cash seized is also permissible under POCA. | Yes | Section 9 of the Proceeds of Crime Act details the effect of the forfeiture order per ss. 5–8.[11] |

138; or (b), if it appears to the Court unlikely that any order will be made under section 137. It is also important to recognize that any person to whom an infringing copy or other article is delivered up in pursuance of an order, under this section, shall retain it pending the making of an order or the decision not to make an order by the Court. As such, that person must keep it in the same condition as at the time of the accused's arrest or charge. The Court may release these items on a bond to such a person.

7. Under section 72 of the Trademark Act, forfeiture of infringing articles is permissible. Where the Judge of the Parish Court is satisfied that a relevant offence was committed in relation to items which are representative of the infringing items, the Judge of the Parish Court may accede to the forfeiture application. The infringing articles can be destroyed or they can be released to a particular person.

8. Subject to section 15(3) of the Corruption Prevention Act, where the offence involves the deliberate nondisclosure of a public servant's property, the Court may, subject to determining the beneficial interest of innocent third parties, impose a fine or term of imprisonment or both. If the property involved is situated within the island, the Court may order that it be forfeited to the Crown. Section 15 is the penalty section in the Corruption Prevention Act while section 14 speaks to the offences under the statute.

9. Under section 2 of the Proceeds of Crime Act, in the interpretation section, the definition of property is quite wide. Under the Proceeds of Crime Act, where a defendant is convicted of any offence in proceedings before the Court or committed to the Court, a Judge of the Parish Court shall determine if the defendant has a criminal lifestyle and has benefited from his general criminal conduct. If the Court determines that the defendant has benefited from criminal conduct, the property that represents said benefit shall be identified and an order for forfeiture to the Crown made.

10. Cash found on a person or at a location can be detained and subsequently be made the subject of a forfeiture order.

11. Such detention must follow the strictures of sections 72–76 of the Proceeds of Crime Act (POCA). Detained cash can be released upon an application by the person from whom it was seized. Forfeiture is permissible under section 79. Any appeal against the said forfeiture order can be made in accordance with section 80. An innocent third party claiming the cash to be his and untainted can apply under section 82 for the release of such cash to him. Section 84 illustrates that property obtained through unlawful conduct is recoverable property. Importantly, however, if the property was passed to a party who obtained it in good faith, for valuable consideration and without notice that the said property was recoverable property, only then will the property cease to be recoverable. This is indicated by sections 85–88.

| Offence | Act and Section | Forfeiture Order Can be Made | Discussion |
|---|---|---|---|
| Breach of the Fisheries Act | The offences range from Fishing in the Fisheries Waters without a licence (s.25) to Possession of Fish in contravention of the provisions of the Fisheries Act (s.89). | Yes | Section 84 of the Fisheries Act grounds a forfeiture application where it is that the defendant has been found guilty of an offence under the Act.[12] |
| Aquaculture, Inland and Marine Products and By-Products (Licencing and Export) Act | Sections 24–32 outline the various offences which include exporting aquaculture without the requisite licence (s. 24) and harvesting fish in unapproved areas (s. 26). | Yes | Section 34 allows for the seizure and detention of aquaculture or equipment such as vessels and storage containers that are being used or has been used in the commission of an offence against the Act.<br><br>Section 35 concentrates on the procedure regarding applications for forfeiture under the Act.[13] |
| Standards Act | | Yes | Section 12 of the Standards Act |
| Jamaica Constabulary Force Act | Section 44 of the Jamaica Constabulary Force Act | Yes | Section 44 speaks to the powers of detention and disposition of property alleged to be stolen and in the custody of the police.<br><br>Section 45 authorizes the Commissioner of Police to order the sale of such property after the expiration of three months and such proceeds to be paid to the Accountant General. |

---

12. Under s. 84 (1)(a)(b) of the Fisheries Act where a person is convicted of an offence, the Court may in addition to any other penalty, order the forfeiture of any of the following: (a) a vessel, item or thing used or involved in the commission of the offence; (b) where any fish or other item of a perishable nature has been sold, the proceeds of sale. *Hervey Ander Phillips Wood and Shown Hervie Phillips Thompson v DPP* [2012] JMCA Misc 1. Misc. App 1/2011. Delivered December 14 and 15, 2011; and March 9, 2012 is a good guide on how to approach forfeiture under the Fisheries Act and the Aquaculture Inland and Marine Products and By Products (Licencing and Export) Act.

    The Fisheries Act, unlike other statutes such as the Dangerous Drugs Act, is silent on the procedure for the application for forfeiture. That is:

    - who can make the application – whether the Clerk of the Courts or the DPP
    - how notice is to be given
    - the procedure for abandoned vessels/items
    - applications to the Court to revoke its order.

    Consequently, it is incumbent on the prosecutor to indicate its position from as early as possible.

13. Section 35 of the Aquaculture Act above states that: (1) Where the director of public prosecutions proposes to apply to the Court for an order of forfeiture under subsection (2) of section 34, the Director of Public Prosecutions shall, notify in writing, any owner and or other person with an interest in the particular equipment of the proposed application. Such owner or other person so notified may appear before the Court at the hearing of the application and show cause why the specified equipment should not be forfeited. Importantly, notice shall not be required if the seizure or detention of the specified equipment was made in the presence of the owner or person having an interest in the specified equipment. See too, *Hervey Ander Phillips Wood and Shown Hervie Phillips Thompson v DPP*.

Chapter 13

# Relationship with the Office of the Director of Public Prosecutions (DPP)

## Summary

Section 94 of the Jamaica Constitution created a Director of Public Prosecutions (DPP) whose office should be a public office. A person is not qualified to hold or act in the office of DPP unless s/he is qualified to be appointed as a Judge of the Supreme Court (s.94(2)).

The DPP has power to do a variety of actions; namely to:

a. institute and undertake criminal proceedings against any person before any court other than a court-martial in respect of any offence against the law of Jamaica;

b. take over and continue any such criminal proceedings that may have been instituted by any other person or authority; and

c. discontinue at any stage before judgment is delivered any such criminal proceedings instituted or undertaken by himself or any other person or authority.

The DPP's powers may be exercised personally or through other persons acting under and in accordance with the general or special instructions given by the DPP. In this regard, the various officers (senior deputies, deputies, assistant directors and crown counsel) at the Office of the Director of Public Prosecutions assist in the functions of the office.

These various powers of the DPP ground the manner of all interactions between the Clerks of the Courts and the Office of the DPP.

There is a pending proposal to place the Clerks of the Courts under the direct supervision of the Office of the DPP. However, no significant change in the nature of the interaction between the Clerks of the Courts and the DPP is expected.

## Terms

General Advice

Nolle Prosequi

DPP Prosecuting in the Matter

Extraditions

Fiats

Section 31D of the Evidence Act

Units at the Office of the Director of Public Prosecutions

## General Advice

The DPP or a designate is generally available for advice and counsel. The Clerk of the Courts can make either formal or informal contact with the DPP. If the Clerk seeks general advice, it is not necessary to be formal. However, if the advice sought is in relation to a specific case before the court, then it is most useful to put the request for information in writing. It is best to send a copy of the entire case file upon which advice/an opinion is being sought. This ensures that the advice can be specific to the allegations at hand. In the correspondence, briefly outline the allegations, the law, any peculiarities of the case (such as witness availability), and also to offer an overall opinion. Request the advice of the DPP on the proferred opinion or course of action.

### Nolle Prosequi – 'the Nolle'[1]

There are occasions when a *nolle prosequi* is requested by the Clerk of the Courts. (Section 94 of the Constitution and section 2 of the Criminal Justice (Administration) Act outline the DPP's power in this regard.) *Nolles* can be conditional or unconditional. Section 4 of the Criminal Justice (Administration) Act prescribes that at any stage before the court renders judgment, the DPP may discontinue criminal proceedings in any court by entering a *nolle prosequi*.[2]

- **For a Guilty Plea in the Circuit Court**

  One common instance of a *nolle prosequi* being granted is where an accused indicates that s/he wishes to plead guilty in a matter set down for commital proceedings. As the Judge of the Parish Court has no jurisdiction to take such a plea, the Clerk of the Courts must write to the DPP and ask that a *nolle prosequi* be entered. The DPP also requires that defence counsel should write a letter stating the accused's intention to plead guilty. This letter should be submitted along with the request.

  A copy of the entire file along with a cover letter is to be sent to the offices of the DPP. The proper course is that the Clerk of the Courts should outline the allegations and indicate that the accused wishes to plead guilty and that in the circumstances a *nolle prosequi* is being requested to discontinue the matter in the Parish Court. If the DPP grants the *nolle prosequi*, it is proffered in the Parish Court. This *nolle prosequi* essentially discontinues the proceedings in the Parish Court and begin them afresh in the Circuit Court on a voluntary bill of indictment for the plea. It is the *nolle prosequi* that gives the authority for the accused to be taken directly to that jurisdiction without the committal proceedings being held or completed.

  The DPP may decide to take a matter directly to the Circuit Court without a committal proceeding or before a proceeding ends. The procedure is the same as if the Clerk of the Courts had initiated the proceedings via a request.

A *nolle prosequi* is also required when the Crown no longer intends to proceed against an accused person. Along with the copy file, send a letter to the DPP. In the letter, outline the allegations and indicate the reason for the suggestion for the decision to discontinue. If the Director agrees, the *nolle prosequi* is sent to the Parish Court.

The Clerk of the Courts should ensure that the Director's decision is awaited in every instance where advice is sought.

---

1. The *nolle prosequi* is a document that can only be entered at the instance of the Director of Public Prosecutions or the appropriate designate.
2. *R v Lloydell Richards* (1992) 29 JLR 321.

**Figure 13.1**     Letter of Request for *Nolle Prosequi*

---

Director of Public Prosecutions
Office of the Director of Public Prosecutions
King Street
Kingston


October 2, 20–

Dear Madame Director

RE: Regina v John Brown

For: Murder

Inf#: CA20–/CR0001

---

Please find enclosed a case file which includes statements relating to the above captioned matter. The accused is represented by Mr. Tim Counsels who, after consultation with his client, advised the court that the defendant wished to pursue a course which would obviate committal proceedings in the Parish Court's jurisdiction.

Consequently, I am hereby requesting that a nolle prosequi be entered and that a voluntary bill of indictment to be proferred against the accused, to appear for his trial at the Home Circuit Court.

The matter is next set for the 25th day of July 20-- and your earliest response is anticipated.


*Tom Jones*
Tom Jones

Clerk of the Courts
Corporate Area Parish Court

Figure 13.2     *Nolle Prosequi – Transfer of Matter*

---

IN THE PARISH COURT FOR THE PARISH OF ST. THOMAS

HOLDEN AT  MORANT BAY   ON THE  31ST  DAY OF  JANUARY, 20 - -

INF. NOS. ST20--CR0001

THE QUEEN

VS.

RON SMITH

FOR:

MURDER

In exercise of the powers conferred upon me by virtue of the provisions of section 94 of the Constitution, section 4 of the Criminal Justice (Administration) Act, and every other power thereunto enabling, I hereby inform you accused Ron Smith on the above-mentioned charge that the matter be transferred to the St. Thomas Circuit Court.

DATED THIS 30TH DAY OF JANUARY 20- -

*Deeny Bowes*

DEENY BOWES, Q.C.
DIRECTOR OF PUBLIC PROSECUTIONS

Note: The Crown No Longer Intends to Proceed

To:  Clerk of the Courts
     St Thomas

---

**Figure 13.3**    *Nolle Prosequi* – **Discontinuation of Matter**

---

IN THE PARISH COURT FOR THE PARISH OF ST. THOMAS

HOLDEN AT  MORANT BAY  ON THE  31ST  DAY OF  JANUARY, 20 - -

INF. NOS. ST20--CR0001

THE QUEEN

VS.

RON SMITH

FOR:

UNLAWFUL POSSESSION OF PROPERTY

In exercise of the powers conferred upon me by virtue of the provisions of section 94 of the Constitution, section 4 of the Criminal Justice (Administration) Act, and every other power thereunto enabling, I hereby inform you that the Crown does not intend to continue the proceedings against the accused Ron Smith on the above-mentioned charge.

DATED THIS 30TH DAY OF JANUARY 20- -

*Deeny Bowes*

DEENY BOWES, Q.C.

DIRECTOR OF PUBLIC PROSECUTIONS

Note:    This *nolle prosequi* is entered because the accused is serving a lengthy prison term for the offence of Rape

To:    Clerk of the Courts
St Thomas

---

## DPP Prosecuting a Matter in the Parish Court

There will be instances where the DPP may be the prosecutor in a matter that is before the Parish Court. In such a situation, the DPP or a designate marshals the evidence and Clerk of the Courts assumes a largely administrative role, such as to liaise with the relevant officer from the DPP on the matter. The Clerk signs the indictment if the matter is indictable, labels the exhibits and is the custodian of all the exhibits. The Clerk sets dates for the matter in the face of the court, ensures that subpoenas are processed and that court orders are carried out by the relevant court personnel or police officers.

## Extraditions[3]

When a person is being requested for extradition by another country, the Office of the DPP is involved in the matter. That person is not called an accused, but rather the 'subject'. The Parish Court usually has only the bare minimum of information on the subject as the file remains with the DPP. However, it is useful for the Clerk of the Courts to fully understand how to proceed should it become necessary.

If a subject for extradition has local charges, those charges and case files usually travel with the extradition proceedings for administrative efficiency. It is also the practice to dispose of the local charges before a subject is extradited.

The Judge of the Parish Court who signed the arrest warrant for a subject can adjudicate in the hearing. The procedure begins by ensuring that there is an authenticated bundle on the file, which outlines the basis on which the subject is to be extradited.

The matter is started by announcing: 'This is the matter re *the extradition of the subject John Doe. He is represented by Miss Tuana Jones, of Counsel and I'm Abbia Banes from the DPP, for the Requesting State, the USA.*'

The authority to proceed, the extradition foreign states order, and the Jamaica Gazette with the extradition treaty between Jamaica and the relevant foreign state are put into evidence by counsel for the requesting state under the public documents exception.

The witnesses give their evidence and are then tendered for cross-examination by the subject's attorney or the subject him/herself if there is no representation. The matter is in this respect, therefore, similar to a trial.

At the end of each person's evidence, the deposition extradition papers are read over to the person by the Judge of the Parish Court and then signed by both.

The exhibits of an extradition case should be put into evidence through the relevant witnesses who have direct knowledge of them. The authenticated documents are put into evidence through the relevant officer from the Ministry of Foreign Affairs and Foreign Trade. The prosecutor would necessarily have laid adequate foundation to ensure that that the item can be properly put in through this officer from the ministry. The related warrant and picture of the subject are put into evidence through the relevant police officer who would have received these items as part of his duties to execute the warrant on the subject and as such could identify them.

Copies of all the exhibits in evidence submitted by the prosecutor should be sent up to the Court for perusal. The defence counsel would have had his or her copies previously. All depositions and paper exhibits are kept on the file. When all the depositions have been taken, the Crown closes the case for the requesting state.

---

3.  See the Extradition Act generally.

The defence counsel usually makes a no case submission at this juncture, and the Crown responds on behalf of the requesting state to the no case submission. The Judge might delay the ruling or hand it down immediately. If the subject is to be extradited, the Judge signs a warrant of committal, which will essentially authorize that the subject be taken to the requesting state's jurisdiction.

### The Extradition File

There are particular documents that should be present on an extradition file with which the prosecutor must become familiar. The list below is not exhaustive but outlines the the key documents.

- Diplomatic Note d/d 20th January 20 - - from Requesting State to Ministry of Foreign Affairs and Foreign Trade, Jamaica.

- Letter from Ministry of Justice (MOJ) with Diplomatic Note and copies to the DPP.

- Provisional warrant of arrest (with picture of subject attached) signed by a Judge of the Parish Court (per Art. X of Extradition Treaty between Jamaica and Requestor State, for example) dated as appropriate (several copies signed and sealed).

- Information to ground request for named subject for the offences within the requestor state. Being the Information of Constable Allison Barnes, #456 taken on oath this day... sworn to by Cons. Allison Barnes before Judge of the Parish Court, Her Honour Justia Smith (several copies signed and sealed).

- Report to the Fact of the Issue of a Provisional Warrant of Arrest under section 9 of the Extradition Act (done in acc. with section 9(4) Extradition Act) directed to Minister of Justice and signed by a Judge of the Parish Court (several copies signed and sealed).

- Letter with an original report to the fact signed by Judge of the Parish Court and an original of the Information to Ground Request sent to the Ministry of Justice from the Office of the DPP.

- Consent to Extradition forms signed by subject after his right to a hearing is explained to him and he insists on proceeding to Requesting State without said hearing.

- The Judge of the Parish Court also signs the warrant of committal. This is signed per section 17(2) of the Extradition Act, in relation to the consent to being extradited on the same day as the consent.

- As soon as subject has been taken before the Parish Court, a letter from the DPP is usually sent to the MOJ indicating the court date and that the expiration for the receipt of the authenticated is set to expire in 60 days.

**Figure 13.4**     **Prosecutor's Sample Response to a No Case Submission for Extradition**

What is the test upon which the Learned Court must rely to decide if the subject should be extradited to the United States? We submit that it is only necessary to find that there is a prima facie case established by the prosecution on behalf of the Requesting State. According to Chief Justice, Lord Widgery, in *Union of India v Narang* [1977] 2 All ER 348 at 359 the prima facie case is really 'A test…to see whether it is fair and reasonable to order a suspect to be returned.'

We submit that through the evidence put forward thus far this *prima facie* case is established as follows:

1.  The jurisdiction of this Court to hear the matter is established through the Authority to Proceed per section 8 of the Extradition Act (Exh. 1).

2.  The identity of the subject, Tom Strokes, was established through Exh. 8 – warrant and photo of subject.

3.  The allegations state that from at least November 20--to Feb 20--, the subject, a Jamaican, was the leader of a criminal group (page one of the affidavit of a confidential informant at number four 4) and was involved in conspiracy to import and importing marijuana into the US from Jamaica and conspiring to distribute same in the US.

4.  The affidavits of the witnesses establish that there is a prima facie case and that the elements of the offences are clear.

5.  The offences that are charged are conspiracy and possession. The indictment charges the subject with conspiracy to import, conspiracy to export and possession with intent to distribute. These are at page 2 of the affidavit of the confidential informant at number seven 7 indicates the offences in the indictment.

6.  In the United States, at page 3 of the affidavit of the confidential informant, numbers 13, 14 and 15, conspiracy is defined as an agreement to violate criminal statutes. The law on possession with intent is detailed at page four, number 17 of the affidavit of the confidential informant.

7.  In Jamaica we have similar offences, under the Common Law for conspiracy and in the Dangerous Drugs Act for possession and as such the requirement that the alleged conduct amounts to a crime in the both the requesting and requested state is fulfilled. This is the dual criminality of the offences

8.  The burden of proof regarding the three counts on the indictment lies on the prosecutor and through numbers 18 to 24 of the affidavit of the confidential informant, these will be established.

9.  Exhibits 5 through 10, in the authenticated documents, all support the application of the requesting state and give credence to the submission that a prima facie case has been established to which the subject should be made to answer in a trial court in the requesting state. Namely 5 – the affidavit of Agent John Doe who monitored calls with the subject and went on the drug operations, 6 – the affidavit of DEA agent John Doe 2 who met the subject in Jamaica and recorded conversations re the drugs, 7 – the affidavit of Confidential informant, who is in prison and who knew the subject personally for many years, 8 – affidavit of another informant, who did boat runs for the 418 pounds of ganja and 10 –

the affidavit of the Chemist John Doe 3 that he tested the item and that it was marijuana under the US law. Note well: The Court of Appeal has said that even if the requesting state's definition of ganja is different from ours, it is ganja according to their laws and as such that is no basis upon which to refuse the extradition.

10. The requesting state used a confidential informant in the operations as well as others involved previously with the subject. Whether or not this confidential informant was an agent provactuer is a triable issue to be distilled at the apt time at trial.

11. Whether or not the agent John Doe or any of them was actually in Jamaica, is another triable issue to be distilled at trial and does not affect whether or not a prima facie case has been established.

12. Are the correspondence between the Ministry of Justice (MOJ) and the Ministry of Foreign Affairs (MOFA) relevant and therefore admissible in these proceedings as regards instant case?

13. We are submitting that these docs do not form part of the authenticated documents per section 14 (1A) of the Extradition Act, It states that:

14. A document, duly authenticated, which purports to set out testimony given on oath in an approved State shall be admissible as evidence of the matters stated therein.

15. Nothing in this section shall prevent the proof of any matter, or the admission in evidence of any document, in accordance with any other law in Jamaica.

16. This current request has been supplemented by documents, statement of the facts, copies of warrants, all such evidence that would justify committal because these all tend to show that the offence had been committed in the Requesting State.

17. Several items were sent by the Requestor State to the MOJ at their request to help ground the allegations. These are in evidence and there is no need to look behind it. I humbly submit that to look beyond is irrelevant to these proceedings

18. Regarding any documents covered by Legal Professional Privilege in these proceedings, I would request that the Court consider *R v DPP, Ex parte Thom* The Times Law R 21.12.1994

19. Finally, in this matter, the Office of the DPP in extradition proceedings acts not as a prosecutor but as a representative of a foreign government. This is not a trial on the merits, that's for the trial court in the Requesting State.

## Fiats[4]

The Director of Public Prosecutions often gives written authorization to a party, usually an attorney-at-law to 'associate' with the prosecution in a matter. In such a scenario, the Clerk of the Courts may still marshal the evidence. The attorney with the fiat may wish to offer advice and information if the Clerk marshals the evidence. The attorney may also marshal the evidence himself as the prosecutor by virtue of the authority conferred by the DPP's fiat.

When an attorney with a fiat marshals the evidence, the Clerk of the Courts still has to ensure that s/he is present to take all evidence and notes of the proceedings. This is crucial in the event that the fiat is determined for one reason or another. Where the fiat is determined, the Clerk of the Courts or the DPP may need to continue prosecuting the matter.

## Section 31D(a–e) of the Evidence Act

A case file in the Parish Court may necessitate the use of section 31D of the Evidence Act. Depending on the section, guidance from the DPP may be necessary but section 31D generally addresses:

 (a) death of a witness;

 (b) mental incapacity;

 (c) witnesses outside of the jurisdcition;

 (d) admissibility of a witness statement when a witness cannot be found; and

 (e) fear on the part of the witness.[5]

There is also case law that can be accessed regarding the procedure and practice to prosecute section 31D matters.

## Units at the DPP

There are several legal units at the DPP, including mutual legal assistance, human rights-intellectual property, sexual offences, extradition, corruption prevention, digital evidence, and labour relations. These units are always available to assist the Clerk of the Courts.

---

4. Associating with the prosecution through a fiat in a criminal matter is the purview of the Director of Public Prosecutions.
5. See *Nyron Smith v R* SCCA 241/2001 Jud del 11/4/2003.

**Figure 13.5**     **Example of a Fiat**

ANY REPLY OR SUBSEQUENT REFERENCE TO THIS COMMUNICATION SHOULD BE ADDRESSED TO THE DIRECTOR OF PUBLIC PROSECUTIONS AND NOT TO ANY OFFICER BY NAME AND THE FOLLOWING REFERENCE QUOTED:-

OFFICE OF THE DIRECTOR OF PUBLIC PROSECUTIONS

REF. NO. 100/00/000                    March 1, 20--

Mrs Pamela Boody
Attorney-at-Law
1000 Internet Road
Kingston 40

Dear Mrs. Boody:
Re: Regina vs. Jay Marker
    Breaches of The Rent Restriction Act

With reference to your request for a fiat, I have no objection to you actively associating yourself with the Clerk of the Courts, in the abovementioned matter set for hearing in the St. Catherine Parish Court, holden at Spanish Town on March 10, 20--.

Yours Sincerely,

*Deeny Bowes*

DEENY BOWES, Q.C.
DIRECTOR OF PUBLIC PROSECUTIONS

# Chapter 14

# Bail

## Summary

Bail is governed by the Bail Act, the Jamaica Constabulary Force Act, and the Justices of the Peace Jurisdiction Act. Bail can be offered at a police station, 'station bail' under section 24 of the Jamaica Constabulary Force Act. Sections 15 and 41 of the Justices of the Peace Jurisdiction Act also examine bail by a Justice of the Peace as well as the Judge of the Parish Court in committal proceedings.

When an accused has not been offered station bail, a bail application can be made at the first court appearance. If a defendant is represented, his or her counsel makes the bail application. *Huey Gowdie v R* [2012] JMCA Crim 56 offers guidance on the principles the courts should consider as it hears an application for bail. The unrepresented accused sometimes makes his or her own application. Dependent on the circumstances of the case, the Judge of the Parish Court might offer the accused bail even if no application has been made.[1] The Bail Regulations offer extensive guidance on the manner in which bail applications should be processed in the court.

There is little uniformity in the administrative processing of bail offers across the Parish Court system. This chapter offers the best practice to be utilized by the court administration to ensure that bail is streamlined across the system.

## Terms

Section 4 of the Bail Act

Offers of Bail

Recording Offers of Bail

Refusal of Bail and the Right of Appeal

Administrative Bail Procedures

Escheating Bonds

Warrants of *Distingas* and *Capias*

Bail Process Books

Sureties

Collateral and Suggested Treatment in the Administrative Bail Procedures

Processing Bail Documents and Suggested Treatment at the Bail Desk

Bail Variations

Bail after Conviction

---

1. The Bail Act stipulates at section 6(2) that the Court can require of any accused granted bail that s/he provide a surety to secure his or her surrender into custody. Such a surety must present the relevant documentation to convince the court of the ability to stand as surety.

## Section 4 of the Bail Act

The Clerk of the Courts should know the stipulations in section 4(1) of the Bail Act that outline the specific circumstances that may prevent an accused from being admitted to bail when charged with an imprisonable offence.

- **Further Investigations Needed**

  If the police need to conduct further investigations, or require the accused for further questioning, or if the instant offence was committed while on bail for another offences, the Clerk of the Courts may advance these against the accused being admitted to bail.[2]

  The Clerk of the Courts must have credible information in support from the relevant police personnel in the matter to enable the Parish Court Judge to make an informed ruling on the bail application.

- **Identification Parade Pending**

  If an accused has or could have an identification hearing pending, bail can be denied for logistical reasons. In this case, the accused would not appear before the Court until the parade has been held. The intention to hold the parade as well as the date the parade is to take place should be clearly endorsed on the file.

- **Considerations by the Judge of the Parish Court**

  A Judge of the Parish Court has the discretion to deny an accused bail under section 4(2) of the Bail Act[3] and takes into consideration several factors including the nature and seriousness of the offence and the strength of the evidence against the accused as having committed the offence.

  *Hurnam v State of Mauritius*[4] is a good example of this circumstance.

- **Examination of the Accused Himself by the Court**

  To determine if bail is to be granted, the Judge of the Parish Court must also examine the defendant's character, antecedents, associations, and community ties. Thus, the presence of exemplary behaviour

---

2. Section 4(1) of the Bail Act states that if an offence or one of the offences with which the defendant is charged or convicted is punishable with imprisonment, bail may be denied to that defendant in some prescribed circumstances:
   - Where the Court, a Justice of the Peace, or police officer is satisfied that there are substantial grounds for believing that the defendant, if released on bail would:
     - (i) fail to surrender to custody;
     - (ii) commit an offence while on bail; or
     - (iii) interfere with witnesses or otherwise obstruct the course of justice, whether in relation to himself or any other person;
   - Where the defendant is in custody in pursuance of the sentence of a Court or any authority acting under the Defence Act;
   - Where the Court is satisfied that it has not been practicable to obtain sufficient information for the purpose of taking the decisions required by this section for want of time since the institution of the proceedings against the defendant;
   - Where the defendant, having been released on bail in or in connection with the proceedings for the offence, is arrested in pursuance of section 14 (absconding by person released on bail);
   - Where the defendant is charged with an offence alleged to have been committed while he released on bail;
   - Where the defendant's case is adjourned for inquiries or a report and it appears to the Court that it would be impracticable to complete the inquiries or make the report without keeping the defendant in custody.
3. Under section 4(2) of the Bail Act, there is assistance to the Parish Court Judge to examine if bail should be given to an accused charged with an imprisonable offence.
4. *Hurnam v State of Mauritius Privy Council* delivered December 15, 2005.

on the part of the accused and positive accomplishments are useful for the defence attorney to highlight to the Court.

If the accused has a previous grant of bail, the Court can examine the previous fulfilment of bail obligations to determine whether bail should be granted or denied. Accused persons who did not fulfil their previous bail obligations are not often re-admitted to bail. However, if the accused's current allegations differ from the previous ones, the defence attorney can bring that to the Court's attention to argue for bail being granted.

Any other factor that appears relevant, including the accused's health profile, any glaring inconsistencies on the Crown's case, or the paucity or otherwise of identification evidence as required by *R v Turnbull*,[5] can all be put before the Court to assist in the decision.

Bail may be denied to an accused who is charged with or convicted of an offence punishable with imprisonment if the Court is satisfied that the accused should be kept in custody for his own protection or where the accused is a child or young person.[6]

Under section 4(4) of the Bail Act, an accused may be denied bail even if s/he is in custody for an offence not punishable by a term of imprisonment if all or any of the following factors are present:

» the accused did not surrender to custody on a previous grant of bail;

» there are reasonable grounds to suggest that the accused may fail to surrender in the instant case; or

» the accused is a possible flight risk. To secure bail in such a case, defence counsel may offer to surrender the accused's passport and suggest that the Court place a stop order at all ports to minimize the accused fleeing the country.

The Clerk of the Courts must be prepared to respond to these and any other offers by the defence.

## Offers of Bail

Bail can be offered with or without conditions by the Judge of the Parish Court. The prosecution or the police, via the investigating officer, can also ask the Court to stipulate certain conditions when bail is granted. These conditions are varied as the Judge has wide powers regarding conditions attached to bail. Section 6(2) of the Bail Act outlines these conditions, which include that the Judge can require a surety to secure the accused's surrender to custody or payment of such sum deemed appropriate.

Furthermore, the Court can impose any condition which is deemed necessary to ensure that the person surrenders to custody. Any person granted bail shall surrender to custody[7] and the conditions imposed help to ensure that he does not commit an offence, interfere with witnesses or otherwise obstruct the course of justice.[8]

Other conditions attached to a bail offer may include reporting to a particular police station, reporting on particular days at the specified time, not contacting complainants or witnesses, adhering to particular residence requirements, stop orders, surrendering travel documents, and obeying curfew orders.[9]

---

5.   *R v Turnbull* [1977] QB 224.
6.   Section 4(3) of the Bail Act.
7.   Section 6(1) of the Bail Act.
8.   Section 6(3) of the Bail Act.
9.   Ibid.

**Figure 14.1     Bail Conditions Written on the Number One Information**

On January 15, 20--

Bail offered in the sum of $100,000 with one or two sureties

Surrender travel documents

Stop order made

Report to Mandeville Police Station every

Mon, Wed and Sat between 7 a.m. and 7 p.m.

_____

Judge of the Parish Court, Manchester

Section 6(6) of the Bail Act recognizes that various conditions, or none at all, may be attached to a bail offer and also stipulates that any condition imposed may be varied by the Parish Court Judge on an application by the prosecution or the defence. Therefore, the accused must be advised of the great responsibility to adhere to the bail conditions to prevent an early return to court seeking a variation to all or some of the conditions. The Clerk of the Courts can properly object to any variation, especially if there is little or no basis for the application.

## Recording of Offers of Bail

The Clerk of the Courts writes the details (called the endorsement) of the bail offer on the number one information. The endorsement can be sent up to the Judge of the Parish Court for his or her signature under the conditions. This is not a requirement, however, it is a regular practice of some of Parish Court Judges.

While Clerks record the details of bail offers on the number one information, the Judge writes the offer in the court sheet. Regardless of whether the bail offer is only on the number one information or in the court sheet, a record of the bail decision must be kept as is required under section 7 of the Bail Act.

## Refusal of Bail and Right of Appeal

If bail is refused by the Court, conditions imposed or varied, it should be immediately recorded, preferably on the number one information and in the court sheet and the accused or defence counsel provided with a copy of same within 24 hours.[10] This protects the accused's right to liberty and allows him or her to make an application to a Judge of the Supreme Court if so desired.

The unrepresented accused should immediately be advised by the Parish Court Judge of his or her right to appeal to a Judge in chambers where bail has been denied. Section 9 of the Bail Act stipulates that such an accused is to be informed of this right conferred upon him by section 10 of the Bail Act.

---

10. Section 8(2) of the Bail Act.

## Administrative Bail Procedures

- ### Case File to Court Office

    The Clerk of the Courts usually conducts the interview with the potential surety and must ensure that all documentation presented have been duly authenticated and meet the requirements of the Bail Act and attendant Bail Regulations. The Clerk must, therefore, in his discretion, be satisfied that the necessary safeguards of the Bail Act and Bail Regulations are in place to secure the bail bond.

    The Clerk of the Courts should send the case file as soon as possible to the court office as there are various administrative details required by the bail regulations before the accused can actually take up the offer of bail.

    A member of the administrative staff or an assistant Clerk who is assigned to the 'bail desk' in the court's office usually receives the case file advising that bail has been offered. As such, it becomes even more important to endorse the bail offer on the number information as the Clerk of the Courts will be unable to leave the courtroom before any adjournment to instruct the staff. Notably too, the court sheet is inaccessible during the sitting of the court as the Judge will be writing in it as necessary. The endorsement essentially alerts the staff to the type of documents required to begin the process to include the surety interview and document verification.

- ### Documents Processed

    The accused is returned to the holding area/facility until after the surety has completed the entire bail process. After this, the accused is taken back to the court's office to sign the relevant documents along with the surety (ies). This can be done within the same court day or some days later.

- ### Sureties

    A surety is a person who takes responsibility for an accused and ensures that s/he surrenders to custody on every court date until the matter is determined. Bail may be offered with sureties or to the accused in his own surety. Section 17 of the Bail Act applies to a person granted bail in criminal court proceedings with the condition imposed that s/he provides adequate surety. When deciding whether someone is fit to be a surety, the Court considers the person's profession, occupation, trade or business, character, and his or her proximity to the accused.

    This proximity means the relationship between the surety and the accused whether filial or blood. The Recognizance and Surety Act, and section 6(2) and section 17 of the Bail Act guide the administrative process as it examines persons who offer themselves as fit and proper to be sureties.

    Sureties are required to get a recommendation from one of the following:[11] a Justice of the Peace, a member of the Jamaica Constabulary Force not below the rank of Sergeant, a minister of religion, or a principal of an educational institution other than a pre-primary school. The referee is required to state his or her personal knowledge of the surety's address and good character to establish whether the surety is a fit and proper person. The declaration by the particular referee has the force of law and carries the requisite ramifications if subsequently discovered to have been misleading in some material fact.

    Section 21 of the Bail Act deems the surety to be an integral part of the bail proceedings and stipulates that a potential surety should not be refused unless s/he is exempt pursuant to regulations made under

---

11. Section 17(3) of the Bail Act.

**Figure 14.2**      **Sample Bail Interview Form for Sureties**

## BAIL INTERVIEW FORM

Name of Accused: John Doe

Address of Accused: 2 Swallow Road, Manor Park, Kingston 19

Occupation: Doctor.

Relationship to Accused: Sister

Name of Surety: Jane Doe

Address of Surety: 2 Swallow Road, Manor Park, Kingston 19

Occupation: Nurse.

I.D. Used: Jamaican Passport # A123456789

Collateral Used: Dwelling House located at 2 Swallow Road, Kingston 19

Bail Amount: $2 Million Jamaican Dollars

Conditions: Report to the Duhaney Pen Police Station Daily between 10am
and 6pm

Next Court Date: October 29, 20--..

Surety Accepted by :   *James Earles*

Clerk of the Courts

**Figure 14.3**     **Sample Statutory Declaration by Surety**

---

**The Bail Act 2000**
SCHEDULE
(Section 17)
Statutory Declaration to be made by a Surety or Sureties

CORPORATE AREA

I, ....... Jane Doe ....... the undersigned of ....... 2 Swallow Road, Manor Park, Kingston 19 .......

....... do solemnly and sincerely declare as follows:-

I/~~We~~ have agreed to offer myself/~~Ourselves~~ as surety for ....... John Doe .......

of 2 Swallow Road, Manor Park, Kingston 19 ..... defendant in the case:

R. vs John Doe .......
For    Murder .......
Inf.#  1000/20– .......

In this regard I/~~We~~ acknowledge to owe the Crown the sum of ....... $2 million Jamaican Dollars .......

(TWO MILLION JAMAICAN DOLLARS ) ..... to be levied on my/

~~our~~ several movable or immovalable property if the said ....... John Doe .......

fails in the condition of the recognizance to be entered before ....... Her Hon Edna Noble .......

....... Judge of the Parish Court/~~Justice of the Peace~~

(State property and Value The

Dwelling House Vaulued at $10 million Jamaican Dollars .......

.......

I/~~We~~ hereby declare that no criminal charge is pending against me/~~us.~~

Signed: *Jane Doe* .......

Declarant/Declarants

        I/~~We~~ make this declaration conscientiously believing the same to be true and according to the voluntary Declarations Act; and I/~~we~~ am/~~are~~ aware that if there is any statement in this declaration which is false in fact which I/we know or believe to be false or do not believe to be true, I/~~we~~ am/~~are~~ liable to fine not exceeding ONE MILLION DOLLARS or to imprisonment not exceeding TWO YEARS or both.

Signed: *Jane Doe* .......

Declared before me this ..... 3rd ..... day of ..... OCTOBER ..... 20..........

Signed: *James Earles* .......

~~Judge of the Parish Court, Justice of the Peace~~
Clerk of the Courts, ~~Registrar~~

---

the section or is unsuitable to become a surety in the opinion of the Court. The surety interview and verification process helps the Court to determine objectively whether or not the surety is fit and proper.

All persons who wish to stand as a surety must sign the declaration form provided for in section 17(2)(b) of the Bail Act. This form requires that the potential surety sign that s/he solemnly and sincerely declares and agrees to offer surety for the particular defendant in the case in the Court. This potential surety must further declare that, in this regard, s/he acknowledges owing to the Crown the particular sum stated as the bail sum against both movable and immovable property if the said defendant fails in the condition of the recognizance to be entered into.

Anyone who knowingly makes a false statement in a material particular for the purposes of bail is guilty of an offence and liable, on summary conviction before a Parish Court Judge to a fine not exceeding $3,000,000 or to imprisonment for a term not exceeding two years or both.[12] False declaration, the production of false identification cards or false property ownership documents are some of the punishable offences that persons have been charged for in the bail process.

## Escheating the Bond

Bonds are usually escheated when an accused fails to appear in court. Therefore, sureties are required to prove, to the satisfaction of the court, that they are worth the dollar value of the bond sum as the surety's assets – monetary and physical – are levied to cover the sum. If the accused fails to surrender to the jurisdiction of the court at the appropriate times, the surety will have to pay the bond sum as s/he now owes the Crown.

Therefore, where a surety has provided a security to secure a person's surrender to custody and that person fails to attend court, the Court may order the forfeiture of the security so that the bonds be escheated.[13] This means that the surety forfeits the bail sum that was pledged for the accused.

Where the Court orders the forfeiture of the security, the surety must be prepared to pay the entire bail sum until the Court orders otherwise. The Judge of the Parish Court, at his or her discretion, can accept a sum that is less than the full value of the security.[14] The Court might allow the surety time to pay the whole or part of the sum, along with the bailiff's fee. The sum of money is therefore accounted for and paid into the Court in the same way that a fine would be paid into the Court.[15] The bailiff's fee is a set percentage of the bail bond sum.[16]

## Warrant of *Distingas* and *Capias* (D&C)

A warrant of *distingas* and *capias* or as it is commonly referred to, 'D&C', is the warrant issued for a surety when the accused fails to attend court on his court date and a warrant has been ordered for him. The Judge then excheats the bonds and orders a warranty for the surety. This warrant is prepared and signed by the Clerk of the Courts.[17]

---

12. Section 17(9) of the Bail Act.
13. Section 18(1) of the Bail Act.
14. Section 18(2) of the Bail Act.
15. Section 18(3) of the Bail Act.
16. Section 3 of the Recognizance and Sureties Act indicates that the bailiff shall be entitled to retain as a fee, the costs recovered under any such warrant.
17. Section 2 of the Recognizance and Sureties Act states that a warrant shall be ordered by the terms specified in the form in Schedule A that orders that the surety pays the sums.

**Figure 14.4**     **Sample D & C**

---

**Form of Warrant of Distingas and Capias**

ELIZABETH II, By the Grace of God
of Jamaica and of Her other Realms
and Territories Queen, Head of the
Commonwealth.

To the Bailiff of the St Catherine Parish Court for the parish of St Catherine (holden at Spanish Town) You are hereby required and commanded to levy the sum of $2 million Jamaican Dollars

Upon the goods and chattels of Jane Doe of the parish of St Catherine and make payment of the money so levied to the Clerk of the Courts for the parish of St Catherine. And if you cannot levy the sum of $2 million Jamaican Dollars by reason of there being no goods and chattels to be found belonging to the said Jane Doe then that you take the body of the said Jane Doe and lodge him/-her in the Allways Correctional Prison to await the decision of the said St Catherine Parish Court at the next sitting thereof unless the said Jane Doe shall give sufficient security for his appearance at such St Catherine Parish Court. And have you then and there this Warrant.

for the parish of St Catherine at Spanish Town the 3rd day of October 20-

*James Earles*
..............................
Clerk of the Courts

---

If the surety is in court, the warrant can be executed on him or her by a court police officer. If the surety is not in court, the bailiff collects the D&C and when the surety is found, the warrant is executed. The bailiff then brings the surety to court and the surety is taken into custody. The matter is listed as a warrant of *distingas* and *capias* in the court sheet. The relevant court sheet regarding the information about the bond being escheated is also given to the Judge of the Parish Court to show the basis of the warrant.

The Clerk of the Courts has the substantive case file with the bail documents regarding the accused and surety when the matter is called on the court list. The Clerk should update the case file to show when the bonds were ordered escheated. When a bond is escheated, the surety is questioned, either personally or through a lawyer, about the whereabouts of the accused. Explanations of the accused's absence can include that the accused is in custody elsewhere, hospitalized, or dead. If no satisfactory explanation is proffered, the Court may, in its discretion, order what sum of the security is to be paid.

The warrant is thereafter kept by the accounts department. The receipt number(s) regarding payment(s) is usually written on the case file or in the court sheet. This will prove that the surety has fulfilled his or her obligation regarding the sum that was ordered paid by the Court. This is crucial because unless the Judge of the Parish Court ordered otherwise, such a surety remains in custody until the money is paid.

The case file should be perused to ensure that the warrant for the accused has not been vacated previously. The Clerk of the Courts needs to ensure the notations are made as the escheating of a bond carries significant obligations for a surety.

Figure 14.5    Sample Bailiff Process Book

| Date of Bail | Accused Name | Accused Address | Bail Amount | Offence | NCD | Name of Surety | Address of Surety | Collateral | ID Type | Court Officer's Signature |
|---|---|---|---|---|---|---|---|---|---|---|
|  |  |  |  |  |  |  |  |  |  |  |

## Bailiff Process Book

Under section 4 of the Recognizance and Sureties Act, all sureties are given a written notice, signed by the Clerk of the Courts, which is fully explained to both the accused and surety in each other's presence. It indicates the bail sum. It also indicates that if the accused fails to appear on all subsequent court dates, the surety will have to pay the bond sum. If the surety cannot pay the fee, s/he may be imprisoned for a period not exceeding six months.[18]

Therefore, every recognizance must mention the names in full, the profession, trade, or occupation, and the parish or place of residence of the accused and surety and these details are written in the bailiff process book. This allows a quick perusal of the persons who have been accepted as surety for accused persons.

- **Release of Surety[19]**

  When someone has stood as surety s/he may be released from that obligation in the following circumstances:

  - » where the Court grants such release upon an application by the surety using the requisite prescribed forms;
  - » where the Court makes a no order;
  - » where a *nolle prosequi* is entered in relation to the defendant;
  - » where the matter is adjourned *sine die* or dismissed; or
  - » where the defendant concerned is acquitted or convicted.

  The surety's release frees him or her from any further responsibility for the accused and s/he is free to use his property or the sum previously pledged, as s/he wishes.

Any surety who wishes to be released from his or her obligations can apply in writing to the Court in which the recognizance was taken and do so before the matter has ended.[20] A release request is usually done on the accused's court date, so the relevant notations can be made by the Judge while dealing with the substantive matter. A request for release is detailed above. A request release is usually done on the accused's court date, so the relevant notations can be made by the Judge of the Parish Court while dealing with the substantive matter.

Sometimes the Judge asks for a reason for the surety's release request and records the answer. However, there is nothing in law that requires that any particular reason be given and so the Judge will usually accede

---

18. Section 4 of the Recognizance and Sureties Act and the relevant form is in Schedule B.
19. Section 19(1) of the Bail Act.
20. Section 19(2) of the Bail Act and Bail Regulation 10 and Forms 4 and 5.

to the surety's request. In fact, the Judge usually just advises the surety that there are prescribed forms to be completed to secure a release. The information related to the release of the surety should also be endorsed on the number one information, which the Judge of the Parish Court will sign The fact that the surety has been released is also noted on the notice of recognizance.

When a surety has been released, the accused is to be immediately formally notified of this development.[21] Such a release means that the accused may be taken into custody until he provides a new surety or sureties as is required or is offered own surety (dependent on the allegations and offence). Often, the accused is taken back into custody and must make provisions to obtain new sureties. The Clerk of the Courts must also ensure that the accurate notations about the accused's status *vis-à-vis* bail are recorded on the number one information.

- **Number of Sureties**

  The Judge of the Parish Court indicates the number of sureties. The usual number ranges between one and four. One surety means that a single person must post the entire bail sum. If there are more than one sureties, they can all join together to post the entire sum. There is no legal stipulation as to how the sum is apportioned among the sureties. The Bail Act prohibits certain groups acting as sureties. An attorney-at-law, on record for the accused, is one such prohibition.[22]

- **Accepting Persons as Surety in the Face of the Court**

  Section 6(5) of the Bail Act allows the Judge of the Parish Court to accept persons as sureties for minors. In the Court's discretion, a parent or another relative is acceptable as surety. The surety has to levy assets up to a maximum of $50,000 for minors. When a relative is accepted, the Clerk of the Courts should endorse the number one information accordingly. The surety should give the court administrative staff a copy of a valid national picture identification, which is to be placed on the accused's file. The statutory declaration form per section 17(2)(b) of the Bail Act is also completed.[23] The Clerk of the Courts notes pertinent contact details for the surety on the file.

- **Own Surety**

  Where the accused is offered bail in his own surety, the bail desk staff processes this by having the accused complete and sign the requisite bail documents. These are namely, the recognizance and the statutory declaration. Such a situation usually obtains for minor offences with no custodial sentence as the punishment upon any guilty plea or guilty verdict.

## Collateral

The main items that can be used as collateral are registered title to land, motor vehicle ownership documents, and other financial instruments or cash.[24] Receipts, per Regulation 2 of the Bail Act Regulations, are to be generated for the latter. Notably, personal effects such as furniture and machinery are not usually accepted as collateral.

---

21. Ibid.
22. Regulation 7 of the Bail Act Regulations indicates that several groups are exempt from providing surety for the purpose of securing the release on bail of any person charged with an offence. These include a Judge of the Parish Court who had had any conduct of the said matter relating to bail; anyone jointly charged with the accused; anyone with a pending criminal matter, and a person not resident in Jamaica.
23. Section 17(2)(b) of the Bail Act.
24. Section 6(2)(b) of the Bail Act and Regulation 2 of the Bail Act Regulations.

**Figure 14.6**      Sample Application by Surety for Release

---

### APPLICATION BY SURETY FOR RELEASE

Name of Defendant: John Doe

Address: 2 Swallow Road, Manor Park, Kingston 19

Offence (s): Murder

Name of Surety: Jane Doe

Address: 2 Swallow Road, Manor Park, Kingston 19

Telephone No.: 876 123 4567

Application is made, under section 19 of the Bail Act to the St. Elizabeth Parish Court, at Black River being the Court before which recognizance was taken by the abovementioned surety for said surety to be released from his obligations under the recognizance entered into by him on: August 3, 20-

Grounds for application: selling the property

Signature of surety: *Jane Doe*

Date: October 1, 20–

---

**Figure 14.7**      Notice of Recognizance (new surety replacing old surety)

---

In the Parish Court at May Pen for the parish of Clarendon

Take Notice- That you John Doe and Tom Strokes (Jane Doe) of 2 Swallow Road, Manor Park, Kingston 19 is bound in the sum of $2million Jamaican Dollars and Tom Strokes of 3 Swallow Road, Manor Park, Kingston 19 in the sum of $2million Jamaican Dollars each to appear at the Clarendon Parish Court to be holden at May Pen on the 3rd day of October—

Now next, and at every time and place to which the proceedings may from time to time be adjourned, and unless you personally make your appearance accordingly, the recognizance entered into by yourself and sureties will be forfeited and the amount thereof levied on you, goods and chattels and in default of sufficient goods and chattels that you and each of you may be imprisoned for such period as the Court may think just not exceeding six months.

Dated the 1st day of October 20--

Prisoner: *John Doe*

Surety: *Tom Strokes*

James Earles

Clerk of the Courts

CONDITIONS IF ANY: Report daily to the Duhaney Police Station between 10am and 6 pm

### Registered Title to Land

- **Ownership Issues for Real Property**

  The certificate of title must be in the name of the surety. Where other names appear on the title these persons' consent is required on the prescribed form provided by the court.[25]

  A. **Mortgages**

  Where a mortgage is registered on the title but has been paid up, then supporting documents must be provided. Where there is a current mortgage, the mortgagee must provide a letter addressed to the Court detailing the broad terms of the mortgage. Specific mention must be made of the sum borrowed, payments to date, and the balance. The mortgagee must also clearly state if there is any objection to the use of the property for bail purposes.

  B. **Certified Copy of Title**

  A recent certified copy of the registered title must be obtained from the National Land Agency and presented along with the duplicate title in the surety's possession if available.

### Motor Vehicles

The following documents are needed for a motor vehicle to be used as collateral:

- title in the name of the surety;
- valid certificate of registration;
- valid certificate of fitness; and
- valid proof of insurance, to wit the cover note or insurance certificate.

  All the figures relating to the chassis and engine of the vehicle must be the same on all the documents. If this is not so, the surety will be required to have this rectified before the process can be completed.

  A. **Ownership**

  The title must be in the name of the surety. If other names appear on the title, these persons must give their written consent on the prescribed form provided.

  B. **Liens**

  The title must usually be free from a lien. If a lien is registered on the title but has been paid up, then supporting documents must be provided.

### Accounts at Financial Institutions

#### Bank Statements

A recent bank statement from a commercial bank, addressed to the Court, which shows where the sums are deposited and delineates the activity of the account and account holders, is usually sufficient.

#### Statement of Account

A recent statement of account from other types of financial institutions, addressed to the Court, which shows the account's details is adequate. The passbook for an account is insufficient. The information provided by the institution should show the transaction history of the account holder(s).

---

25. Prescribed form for joint holders to complete giving permission for the item to be used as the bond sum.

### Account Holders

The account must be in the name of the surety. Where other names appear on the account, their consent must be obtained on the prescribed form.

### Hypothecation

If the sum in the account is for the sole purpose of securing bail, then the surety might be asked to hypothecate or pledge these funds. The Clerk of the Courts or designate can write a letter addressed to the institution to make this request, and the institution will then send back a hypothecation letter addressed to the Court, indicating that the request has been granted. The account holder can have no dealings with the funds until a letter of release is obtained from the relevant court. Hypothecation is not actually required under the Bail Act or its attendant regulations, but is a practice that has developed to safeguard the process.

## Processing Bail Documents at the Bail Desk

### General Information to Sureties

Potential sureties are given instructions about how to process the bail, per requirements of the Bail Act, Recognizance and Sureties Act, and the Bail Act Regulations as set out above.

As such, the Clerk of the Courts or a designate will advise that sureties supply proof of the ownership or the permission of any joint holder of the property intended to be used as collateral. The Court will also advise sureties to bring these proof and a valid national identification and two passport-sized pictures of themselves.

- **Surety Recommendation**

   The potential surety is also given the requisite court form, namely a Form 2.[26] This form recommends a surety and must be signed by either a Justice of the Peace, member of the Jamaica Constabulary Force not below the rank of sergeant, minister of religion, or a principal of an educational institution. The surety is to be recommended by only one of these declarants as a fit and proper person to be accepted as a surety by the Court. As such, that declarant must indicate how s/he knows the surety and can therefore attest to him or her being fit and proper.

   The said declarant is also to certify two passport-sized photographs supplied by the surety.

- **Stop Order on Accused**

   When a stop order has been made regarding the accused, the court gives the potential surety a signed letter, sealed with the Court's stamp to take to the Passport Immigration and Citizenship Agency (PICA). This letter details that the defendant has a matter before the Court and the Court's order regarding travel.

---

26. Form 2 per Bail Act Regulation 6(2) and emanating from section 17(3) of the Bail Act.

**Figure 14.8**        **Sample Letter to PICA**

---

October 12, 20–

The Chief Immigration Officer

Passport, Immigration and Citizenship Office (PICA)

25c Constant Spring Road

Kingston 10

> Re:  Regina vs John Doe
> For: Murder.
> Inf. No.: 1000/20–

The above-mentioned accused came before the Court on the 3rd day of October 20--

S/he was offered bail in the sum of $2million Jamaican Dollars ($2,000,000) pending trial.

The Court is requesting that a 'STOP ORDER' be placed at all ports for same accused.

 Please see photocopy of CR 12 for your information.

*James Earles*

Clerk of of the Courts

---

The CR 12 form – the form completed by a police officer regarding the background of the accused, which includes parents' names, address, and physical description – is copied from the case file and enclosed with the stop-order letter as well as with a copy of the defendant's birth certificate.[27]

The surety is then given a letter from PICA to take back to the Court. This letter must indicate that the stop order has been put in place and will not be lifted until the Court sends a formal letter stating that the stop order has ended or is being temporarily lifted.

---

27.  See Figure 8.4 - Sample CR 12 on page 58.

### Accused to Surrender Travel Documents

If the accused's travel documents are to be surrendered, they are deposited with the accounts section of the court which generates a receipt, to be retained by the surety.[28]

Sometimes the investigating police officer has the travel documents. In these instances, the Clerk of the Courts or another designated officer needs to secure them. The police usually keep a list of the various passports they seize, so a request can be made to the police station for the list to be forwarded to the Court.

### Verification of Documents Presented by the Surety

The Clerk of the Courts should verify all documents submitted. Correspondence, with the relevant institutions as well as the authorized officer on any collateral and identification, whether formally in writing or by phone, should be noted on the documents once verification is given.

Originals of evidence of property, identification, and other documents are returned to the surety after the bail desk officer makes copies. It is good practice to make a notation on the court's copies of documents such as 'originals seen and verified' or 'certified copy seen and verified.'

The only exception to this is where the sureties bring documents such as letters directed to the court's office regarding the bail processing. Such letters are retained on the case file.

Only after these documents have been authenticated should the bail process continue so as to meet the requirement that the suitability of the surety be determined to the satisfaction of the Court.[29] Finally, the Clerk of the Courts or another designated court officer interviews the surety.

### The Accused is Brought for His Bail

Once a surety has been accepted, s/he is given a form to take to the detention facility.[30] This form is colloquially known as the 'send for' and alerts the detention facility that the accused is to be taken to the court's administration office as his bail has been successfully processed.

To expedite the bail process in particular circumstances, for example, for a minor or someone with a medical condition, the Clerk can call the correctional facility or police station where the accused is being held and request that the accused be brought. A 'send for' should be given to the accompanying officer who collects the notice of requirement to attend the bail centre and any other relevant record related to the accused. The notice of requirement to attend the bail centre contains the name of the accused, the offence, and the various details of the bail reporting conditions. It also has a place for a picture of the accused, and it indicates that the Court should be notified within 24 hours should the accused fail to attend on any reporting day.

*Dean Palmer v R* [2017] JMCA Crim 26 is an instructive case about the conditions of the bail register at the police station where an accused reports. It illustrates the manner in which bail information is recorded when the accused reports as part of his bail conditions and how the police should report on the accused when s/he arrives at the station as part of the conditions of bail.

---

28. This is per section 6(3)(a) of the Bail Act.
29. Regulation 6 of the Bail Act Regulations and pursuant to section 17 of the Bail Act.
30. Regulation 8(2) of the Bail Act Regulations stipulates that where attendance at a bail centre is a condition of bail, a notice in Form 3 as well as a copy of the decision regarding bail should be sent to such a bail centre. The bail centre is usually a police station and is provided for by section 6(3)(e) of the Bail Act.

Figure 14.9      Sample "Send For"

---

TO:   THE SUB-OFFICER

      HALF WAY TREE LOCK-UPS/REMAND CENTRE

DATE:   October 2, 20--

Please escort the following accused to the Criminal Division Corporate Area Parish Court's Office for bail.

NAME OF ACCUSED John Doe

ADDRESS OF ACCUSED 2 Swallow Road, Manor Park, Kingston 19

NEXT COURT DATE October 20, 20--

NAME OF SURETY Jane Doe

ADRESS OF SURETY 2 Swallow Road, Manor Park, Kingston 19

BAIL AMOUNT Two Million Jamaican Dollars. ($2,000,000)

I.D. TYPE & NO Jamaican Passport #A 1234567

    RECOMMENDED BY Supt Abel Deetz, Manor Park Police Station

   APPROVED BY James Earles

ACCEPTED BY *James Earles*
CLERK OF THE COURTS, CORPORATE AREA PARISH COURT (CRIMINAL DIVISION)

---

**Figure 14.10**      Sample Bail Centre Attendance Requirement Notice

---

**FORM 3**

**(Regulation 8 (2))**

### NOTICE OF REQUIREMENT TO ATTEND BAIL CENTRE

Notice is hereby given that          John Doe

                                       (name of accused)

of      2 Swallow Road, Manor Park, Kingston 19

                                       (address)

is required to attend at Hunts Bay Police Station

                                       (name of bail centre)

during the period     every Monday between 9am and 5 pm

                                   (time and frequency of attendance)

**Particulars of accused:**

Offence: Forgery

Inf. No. 1000/20–

> photograph
> of accused
> \*\*\*

BAIL GRANTED BY THE CORPORATE AREA PARISH COURT (CRIMINAL DIVISION, HALF WAY TREE).

You are required to inform this Court within twenty-four (24) hours if the accused fails to attend at this bail centre.

\*\*\*Accused is to submit a passport sized and quality photograph signed by an Attorney-at-Law, Justice of the Peace, Police Officer not below the rank of Sergeant, Minister of Religion or a Principal of an educational institution other than a pre-primary school.

---

If the surety has presented the form requesting that the accused be brought to the court, the authorized officer will indicate to the surety when the defendant will be taken by the officers to the court's office to complete the process. The surety must then return to the court's office at that time. When the defendant is brought to the court's office, the defendant and the surety both sign the bail bonds in the presence of each other.

The surety and the defendant both sign the bail bonds in the presence of the Clerk of the Courts or another authorized court administrative officer, who also signs the bail bonds. The police officer who accompanied the accused also signs the bonds. The statutory declaration is also completed at this time by the surety.[31]

---

31. Section 17(2)(b) of the Bail Act.

**Figure 14.11        Sample Bail Bond**

---

**15**
**PETTY SESSIONS FORM R-BAIL BOND**

JAMAICA SS.

BE IT REMEMBERED, that on the ........ 3rd ........ day of ........ October 20—

John Doe, 2 Swallow Road, Manor Park, Kingston 19 of the parish of Kingston  and  Tom Strokes

of the same place,                                                           personally came, before the undersigned

one of Her Majesty's Justices of the Peace in and for the said parish of ........ St Mary ........

and severally acknowledged themselves to owe to our Sovereign Lady the Queen the sum of

$100,000 Jamaican Dollars ........ each of good and lawful money of this Island.

To be made and levied of their several Goods and Chattels, Land and Tenements, respectively, to the use of our said

Lady the Queen, Her Heirs and Successors, if he, the said ........ John Doe ........

shall fail in the following condition.

THE CONDITION of the above written Recognizance is such, that if the said ........ John Doe ........

shall personally appear on the ........ 5th ........ day of ........ October 20—

at ten o'clock in the forenoon, at the Court House at ........ Port Maria ........

in the parish of ........ St Mary ........ before such Justices of the Peace for the said parish as

may then be there, and at every time and place to which the proceedings may from time to time be adjourned, to

answer further to the information of ........ Cons John Strokes ........ exhibited against the said John Doe and

to be further dealt with according to Law, the said Recognizance to be void, or else to stand in full force and virtue.

Taken and acknowledged the day and year first abovementioned, at the parish of before me.

Prisoner John Doe                    Sub Officer in Charge  *Supt. Alec McGuiness*

Surety Tom Strokes                   Station Name ........

Date  October 1, 20—

---

The bail conditions are usually explained to both the defendant and surety on the completion of the bail process. The Clerk of the Courts should ensure that both the surety and defendant fully understand the conditions of the bail, especially attending court on subsequent occasions and any reporting conditions, as well as the consequences of any failure to adhere to these conditions.

## Bail Variations

If there is a problem of any kind with the bail conditions, the defence attorney or the unrepresented defendant can ask the Court to revisit the bail conditions. The prosecution can also make such a request.

The matter is to be listed in the court sheet under the heading 'Application to Vary Bail Conditions'. The relevant case file and the accused should be in court, and although the surety is not required at this hearing, some Judges of the Parish Court call for the surety to attend this hearing to determine whethe s/he wishes to remain as surety under the varied bail conditions. Usual variations made to the bail conditions include reporting conditions, travel, return of bail sums, and replacing sureties. The variations are endorsed on the face of the accused's bail bond after the necessary steps have been put in place, such as new surety verified, travel documents submitted, or the like.

If the defendant, for example, indicates that his or her travel documents are lost and a report was filed, the relevant statements from the police and immigration authorities to that effect must be provided. If these cannot be provided for some reason, the defendant should be requested to give a statement to the police. These arrangements, undertaken by the defence attorney and not the Clerk of the Courts, can be made with the investigating officer or an appropriate police officer in the police station regarding the circumstances of the loss.

Variation might also be sought by a defence attorney where a particular condition is proving difficult to fulfil (such as accounting for a lost passport). The accused should be willing to accept other appropriate conditions that the Parish Court Judge may impose to secure attendance at court. If a variation of the bail is sought and obtained, the Clerk is to endorse it on the number one information on the case file and then send it to the Judge of the Parish Court for signing. The Judge will also enter the variation in the court sheet.

When the Court's orders regarding variations are disobeyed (whether by an agent of the State of other party) the Parish Court Judge need not be involved initially. The Clerk of the Courts is expected to rectify the situation and should notify the offending party that s/he is required to comply with the Court's orders. For example, if the Court orders that an accused's passport, which is in the possession of the investigating police officer, be surrendered as a bail condition and that officer fails to submit the passport to the court's administration office, bail cannot be processed. The defence attorney should then alert the Clerk of the Courts who in turn must advise the investigating officer (whether formally or informally) to comply with the Court's orders.

### Treatment of Popular Variations

If reporting conditions are varied, the amendment is made on three additional copies of the bail bond. These are again signed by the accused and surety and then duly signed and sealed by the Clerk of the Courts. The initial documents should never be defaced in any way. Nor should they be destroyed. They form part of the permanent record on the case file. The previous bonds should be copied, the old conditions deleted and the 'new' copy endorsed with the variations.

### Variations about Travel Documents

An accused may apply to the Court for permission to travel and for the release of his travel documents for the purposes of travel.[32]

To do this, a letter is sent to the PICA indicating the variation order of the Court to lift and replace a stop order on travel. Formal supporting evidence of the travel details should be presented by the accused, such as an affidavit and other documentation, to assist the Court in making a determination if such a variation should be granted.[33]

The Clerk of the Courts should examine these documents prior to the matter being heard in court to assist the Court regarding any questions and/or issues that are brought up.

---

32. Regulation 3 (1) of the Bail Act Regulations.
33. Regulation 3(2) of the Bail Act Regulations.

Figure 14.12        Sample Notice of Application to Vary Terms of Bail

---

**NOTICE OF APPLICATION TO VARY THE TERMS OF BAIL**

IN THE PARISH COURT
FOR THE CORPORATE AREA PARISH COURT (CRIMINAL DIVISION)
HOLDEN AT HALF WAY TREE


Regina v. John Doe


  The Defendant, John Doe , hereby makes a formal application
for the variation of the terms of Bail in this matter for reasons which are more
particularly described in the Affidavit in Support of this Application herein.


Dated the   2nd   day of   October, 20–


*John Brown*

ATTORNEY-AT-LAW FOR THE APPLICANT


Filed by JOHN BROWN Attorney-at-Law of No. 2 Corner Street, Kingston for
and on behalf of the Applicant herein.  Telephone No. 876 123 4567

## AFFIDAVIT OF JOHN DOE

IN THE PARISH COURT

FOR THE CORPORATE AREA PARISH COURT (CRIMINAL DIVISION)

HOLDEN AT HALF WAY TREE

Regina v. JOHN DOE

I, JOHN DOE, being duly sworn make oath and say as follows:

1. That my address for the purpose of this Affidavit is that of my Attorney's No. 2 Corner Street in the parish of Kingston. Where the matters are not within my own knowledge, the information is based upon the sources referred to herein as true to the best of my knowledge, information and belief.

2. That I was charged with the breach of Section 30(1)(a)(i) of the Consumer Protection Act.

3. That as a condition of my bail I was required to deliver my travel documents, that is, my passport to the Fraud Squad and that I duly delivered said Passport to Detective John Lue of that body.

4. That I have been to court in accordance with the times scheduled for so doing.

5. That I am a Businessman, in that, I own and operate a clothing store which sells men, women and children clothing.

6. That I purchase my goods in China; however, since the aforementioned charges have been brought against me I am unable to travel as part of my bail condition is to surrender my travel documents.

7. That having surrendered my Passport I am unable to travel overseas to conduct business.

8. That I humbly request of the court that my bail be varied to return my Passport to me to allow me to travel between the 17th day of April 20-- to the 4h of May 20---. I exhibit hereto marked "SS1" a copy of my itinerary for identification.

9. That I pledge to return to the Island at the aforementioned date.

| | |
|---|---|
| SWORN to at 2 Half Way Tree Road | ) |
| in the Parish of St Andrew | ) |
| this 2nd day of October 20– | ) |

*John Doe*

JOHN DOE

Before me: -

SEAL OF JUSTICE OF THE PEACE

*Willis Wilk*

JUSTICE OF THE PEACE FOR THE

PARISH OF: St. Andrew

Filed by JOHN BROWN of No. 2 Corner Street, Kingston, Attorney-at-Law for and on behalf of the Applicant herein. Telephone No. 876 900 0000 or 876 123 4567.

---

**EXHIBIT "SS1"**

COPY ITINERARY REFERRED TO IN PARAGRAPH 8 OF AFFIDAVIT SWORN
TO ON THE                     DAY                          , 20--.


_____          _____

JUSTICE OF THE PEACE FOR THE                    JOHN DOE

PARISH OF: -

---

### New Sureties

New Sureties must complete all of the documentation as if the accused was being bailed for the first time.

## Bail after Conviction

An accused who has been convicted may have his or her bail extended until the day of sentencing. An accused person who was granted bail prior to the determination of his or her matter, upon conviction, can apply for bail pending appeal. The accused may apply to the Judge of the Parish Court who handed down the conviction. If it refused, there is recourse to a Judge of the Court of Appeal for bail pending the determination of the appeal.[34]

### Future of Bail and the Bail Act

There is some discussion of possible amendments to the Bail Act to allow for the bond system currently used in the United States of America. The current system is quite workable if there is increased resources, increased due diligence on the part of the legal and administrative court staff, as well as the adoption of greater technology in the process utilized in the system.

---

34. Section 13 of the Bail Act.

# Chapter 15

# When a Matter Starts

## Summary

There is much to be gleaned from case law regarding the point at which a matter is considered started. An instructive case is *R v The Resident Magistrate For Saint Andrew And The Director Of Public Prosecutions Ex Parte Basil Black Tyrone Chen George Chai And Edmund Thomas* (1975) 24 WIR 388.

## Terms _____

Trials

Committal Proceedings

Summary Trial

Indictable Trials

Hearings

_____

### Trials

There are wide and varied powers vested in the Clerk of the Courts.[1] Regarding trial matters, the Clerk of the Courts marshals the evidence in a summary trial and takes the notes of evidence.[2]

It is the Judge of the Parish Court who takes the notes of evidence in the trial of all offences on indictments.[3] For practical purposes however, the Clerk of the Courts also records the evidence, tenders exhibits, and marshals the trial generally. As such, the notes of the Judge are duly signed and sealed by the Clerk as a true copy if and when the need arises. These shall be admitted at all times in all courts.[4]

### Committal Proceedings

In committal proceedings, the Judge of the Parish Court should take all the necessary and requisite depositions on charges or informations for indictable offences triable in the Circuit Court.[5] The Clerk of the Courts is also required to certify copies of entries made per sections 38 and 39 of the Judicature (Parish Courts) Act.

---

1. Section 16 of the Judicature (Parish Courts) Act speaks of the Clerk of the Courts' myriad functions under the appointment of clerks of the courts
2. Section 27(1) of the Judicature (Parish Courts) Act. Clerks, in particular, must ensure that they are familiar with mode of trial of offences. See *Regina v David Griffiths* RMCA 178/1970 (January 12, 1971) where a summary matter was tried onnindictment thus rendering the entire trial a nullity.
3. Section 27(1) of the Judicature (Parish Courts) Act.
4. Ibid.
5. Section 64 of the Judicature (Parish Courts) Act.

## Summary Trial

For a summary trial, the Clerk of the Courts should have already completed file preparation in anticipation of the start of the matter. Both the Clerk of the Courts and defence counsel should be familiar with the mode of trial of offences. See *Regina v David Griffiths RMCA 178/1970* (January 12, 1971) where there is a useful discussion about a summary matter that was tried on indictment, thus rendering the entire trial a nullity.

At the appropriate time, the Clerk of the Courts should indicate to the Judge of the Parish Court that the matter is set for trial and that witnesses have been procured to attend, are present, and ready to give evidence.[6] In essence, everything must be in place on the Crown's case, and all appropriate disclosure must have been effected on the defence.

It is the duty of the Clerk of the Courts to ensure that the witnesses to give evidence have been refreshed from their statements beforehand. This ensures that the salient ingredients to prove the offences can be established through relevant witnesses.

The Crown does not apply for an order for indictment since this is a summary trial that is to be preceded on using the number one information. Save and except for this area, the format followed is that delineated regarding an indictable trial.[7]

### The Plea

The Clerk of the Courts calls the accused to the dock as follows: 'The Queen against John Brown'. When the accused goes into the dock, the Clerk of the Courts should ask the Court, 'Might he be pleaded, Your Honour?' The Judge of the Parish Court then replies in the affirmative.

It is the Clerk of the Courts who then pleads the accused by reading out the allegations on all the number one informations that are summary, which the Crown (after the requisite due diligence has been done) will be proceeding on at that juncture.

The accused is pleaded on each and every charge separately. The plea is to ascertain if the accused confesses guilt to any and/or all charges. For every charge, the Judge enters the plea, whether guilty or not guilty. The Judge will record the pleas regarding all the summary matters in the court sheet and also in the Judge's notebook. The Clerk should record the plea for every charge at the appropriate section on the number one information to which it refers.

Where the plea is not guilty, the trial should commence, unless there is good cause shown to the contrary by a party.[8] In such a scenario, an adjournment may be granted and a new trial date fixed.

### Joinder of Types of Offences

Only one type of offence can be tried at a time. Section 22 of the Criminal Justice (Administration) Act discusses the issue of joinder of summary matters. *Regina v Traille* (1969) 15 WIR 139; *Regina v Fenwick Tucker* (1971)16 WIR 535 and *Regina v Richard King and Leo Cox* (1992) 29 JLR 334 are also important cases that examine the matter in detail.

---

6. Section 281 of the Judicature (Parish Courts) Act illustrates that it is the duty of the Clerk of the Courts to prepare cases for hearing on the day so fixed by the Parish Court Judge for the trial thereof. The act speaks of indictable cases; however, practically speaking, the preparation will extend to all other matters that are heard substantively in the Parish Courts.
7. Section 275 of the Judicature (Parish Courts) Act examines the procedure regarding the trial of persons charged with indictable offences but it is followed in the main also for summary trials.
8. Ibid.

Therefore, the Clerk of the Courts should never plead an accused to both a summary and an indictable offence at the start of a trial. See *Steven, Bryan and Searchwell, Smith v Regina* SCCA 187 and 188/2001 (December 20, 2002) on trying summary and indictable matters together and whether it renders a trial a nullity. Contrast that case with *Regina v Rudolph Brown* (1970) 12 JLR 139 on the same point that the Court in *Searchwell* did not follow but did not overrule. Indictable matters should be noted at the end of the summary trial and the necessary actions should be taken for a subsequent trial on indictment.

### Multiple Accused

Care must be taken where there are multiple accused, but not all are charged with every offence. In such a scenario, it is crucial for the Clerk of the Courts to plead the correct accused persons.

After all pleas have been taken (and for the purposes of the chapter it is assumed to be 'not guilty' pleas) the accused should sit in the dock. The Clerk of the Courts then calls the first witness. All witnesses are either sworn or affirmed.[9] The examination in chief is marshalled by the Clerk of the Courts who takes the witness through giving evidence (previously reduced to a statement and served on all accused and/or the Attorneys).

### Exhibits

Any exhibits are to be tendered through the relevant witness, as necessary, the Clerk of the Courts having laid adequate foundations. The Clerk of the Courts, for ease of reference, can write up an exhibit list in his or her evidence notebook. This is quite useful where there are many exhibits in a matter.

### Discussions in the Absence of a Witness Currently in the Witness Box

If there are points of law that require discussion in the absence of the witness, the Clerk of the Courts must apply to the Court for the witness to step outside of the presence and hearing of the court's proceedings. Such a witness properly could be accompanied by a police officer or court staff to ensure the witness is not contaminated or approached, even inadvertently, by anyone. After the point of law has been settled, the witness should return, advised that s/he is still under oath, and the examination continues. At the end of the examination in chief, the Clerk of the Courts offers the witness for cross-examination by defence.

When the witness has finished giving evidence, if the witness is no longer required to attend court then the Clerk of the Courts may apply to the Judge for the person to be released by the Court.

### Adjournments of Trials

If the matter is not finished in one day, it becomes 'part heard' and adjourned until a further date.[10] This notation is to be written on the file for all the subsequent dates for which the matter is set. Thus, it becomes a part heard trial or part heard hearing (PHT or PHH).

At the end of the matter on each day, the Judge, indicates the volume and folio number in the evidence notebook where the matter is being written as evidence is given. The Clerk of the Courts should write this information in his or her notebook and on the section marked 'vol' and 'folio' on the indictment, for indictable matters. The Clerk should make a notation on the number one for summary matters.

---

9.   *R v Hines and King* 17 WIR 326 and *Leroy Lowe* RMCA 2/2005 delivered May 25, 2005.

10.  Section 278 of the Judicature (Parish Courts) Act examines the Judge of the Parish Court's power to direct a trial to be adjourned or recommenced from any point where such a direction appears proper in the interest of either the prosecution or the accused.

## Case for the Crown

The Crown's witnesses testify in examination in chief and then are cross-examined by the accused or his attorney. If the accused is unrepresented, the Judge should assist the accused in cross-examination to the extent permissible. When all the witnesses have been examined and cross-examined, the Clerk closes the case for the Crown as follows: 'That is the case for the Crown, Your Honour.' This means that all the evidence that the Crown will be seeking to rely on to prove the case has been heard.

## No Case Submission

The attorney-at-law for the accused may make a no case submission at the end of the Crown's case. Every attorney representing an accused in a multiple accused matter has the right to make a no case submission. The Clerk of the Courts should be prepared to meet each and every no case submission, being mindful of the Crown's case against each accused. It is useful to have a copy of *Lord Parker's Practice Note* and *R v Galbraith* on hand.[11]

The Practice Note, by Lord Parker, indicated that such a submission may properly be made and upheld if no evidence exists that would prove a key ingredient of the alleged offence that took place. Such a submission can also be upheld where the evidence put forward by the prosecution has been so discredited under cross-examination that it would be unsafe for a reasonable tribunal to convict on such evidence. The submission can also be upheld where the evidence presented is so manifestly unreliable that a reasonable tribunal cannot safely return a guilty verdict.

Lord Parker's Practice Note further states that 'apart from these two situations a tribunal should not in general be called on to reach a decision as to conviction or acquittal until the whole of the evidence which either side wishes to tender has been placed before it.'[12]

Apart from these scenarios, if a submission is made that there is no case to answer, the decision must depend more on if a reasonable tribunal might convict on the evidence so far laid before it. If the tribunal is of this view, then there is a case to answer.

Therefore, it is not so much on whether the adjudicating tribunal (if compelled to do so) would, at that stage, convict or acquit but on whether the evidence is such that a reasonable tribunal might convict.

The response to the no case submission should not speak to the prosecution's witnesses as 'witnesses of truth' as that would suggest that the Judge of the Parish Court need not hear from the defence and should essentially, automatically, believe the prosecution. Rather, the Clerk of the Courts should indicate per *Galbraith's* limbs: (1) that the witnesses have not been so discredited by cross, (2) that the offence is made out on the allegations, and (3) everything that arose out of the evidence of the witnesses called and the exhibits tendered supported the Crown's case.[13]

The defence counsel may also elect not to make a submission if, for example, the material issues might actually turn on credibility and the like.

## No Case Submission when Accused Unrepresented

If the accused is unrepresented, there is not usually a no case submission. It is, however, quite permissible for the Judge of the Parish Court to ask the Clerk of the Courts to indicate why the accused should be called

---

11. [1962] 1 All ER 448 Lord Parker's Practice Note on submission of no case to answer and *R v Galbraith* [1981] 2 ALL ER 1060.
12. [1962] 1 All ER 448 Lord Parker's Practice Note on submission of no case, 448.
13. *R v Galbraith* [1981] 2 ALL ER 1060.

upon to answer the charges. So the Clerk of the Courts must be prepared to respond, even if the accused is unrepresented.

### The Court's Decision on the No Case Submission

If the Court finds that the Crown's case fails on material points, the *prima facie* case is not established. The Judge will indicate to the accused that s/he is free to go.

The Clerk should write 'case dismissed' on the relevant number one informations for the Judge to sign.

If the no case submission fails, where none is made or the Judge of the Parish Court merely indicates 'case to answer'[14] at this juncture, the defendant then chooses his or her specific option.

### Defence's Case

At the end of the case for the defence, the Judge of the Parish Court hears closing arguments (if the accused is represented) from both sides. After the closings, the Judge may pronounce the verdict immediately or may set another date for verdict. Whenever the verdict is announced, it should be written on the number one informations by the Clerk who must take particular care that where the verdict is not guilty, on some or all charges, this is written on the relevant number one informations.

### Guilty Verdict

For a guilty verdict, the antecedents and a social enquiry report of the accused are often requested by the Judge of the Parish Court and another date is set for sentencing. It is improper to sentence an accused without these two documents when they were specifically requested by the Court to assist in a proper sentence. The Clerk of the Courts must, therefore, ensure that the relevant arrangements are made for the police to do the antecedent report and for the probation officers to conduct the social enquiry and prepare the report. On the day of sentencing, the Clerk of the Courts writes the sentence of the Court, on all the relevant number one information. This is critical, especially if there are several charges against the accused. The Judge of the Parish Court signs all the relevant, number one information after sentence has been imposed and recorded.

### Summary Matters Not Proceeded on at Trial

The Clerk of the Courts, at the end of the trial, must again peruse all the number one informations carefully. If there was no evidence led on a particular summary count and the Crown does not intend to do so in the future, the proper course now (if it was not done not before) is to indicate to the Judge of the Parish Court that no evidence is being offered or whatever is appropriate. After hearing from the Clerk of the Courts, the order is endorsed on the particular number one information, and the Judge of the Parish Court should sign the order. This is critical for the completion of a matter.

### Custodial Sentence

If a custodial sentence is imposed, the court police officers are to receive the original CR form for the accused. It will form part of the record at the facility where s/he will serve the sentence.

---

14. When the Judge of the Parish Court is to rule on a no case submission there is no need to do more than indicate that there is a case to answer or alternatively that there is no case to answer.

## Indictable Trials

The procedure before the Judge of the Parish Court at the trial of any indictable offence shall be the same, or as near as may be as in the case of offences which are summary in nature.[15]

### The Accused is Pleaded in an Indictable Trial

As for a summary trial, the Clerk of the Courts calls the accused as follows: 'The Queen against John Brown.' When the accused goes into the dock, the Clerk of the Courts asks the Judge if the accused might be pleaded.

The Clerk of the Courts pleads the accused by reading out the allegations on all the counts on the indictment that is been proceeded on by the Crown. The accused is to be pleaded on each and every count on the indictment.[16] The Judge will record the pleas in the court sheet and in the Judge's notebook.

### Open to the Allegations

Where the Clerk of the Courts opens to the allegation, very briefly indicate to the Court the basis of the counts on the indictment. One significant reason for an opening to the allegations is to establish the jurisdiction of the Parish Court in the matter.[17] At this stage, the Clerk of the Courts should ask the Judge of the Parish Court for an order on indictment to be signed.[18] The Judge should sign the indictment order in the appropriate place on the number one information.

The indictment form should have been previously prepared with all the counts being proceeded on. The Clerk of the Courts must sign the indictment order form and record the not guilty plea of the accused in the appropriate space.

The section on the indictment form relating to any sentence handed down by the Judge of the Parish Court cannot be completed, as the case has not proceeded that far. The accused sits in the dock and the trial proceeds as for a summary trial.

The Judge may make an enquiry of the Clerk of the Courts as the allegations are being opened and s/he may also add any count to an indictment which is so revealed from the allegations by the Crown. This is so even if such offences were not previously contained in any number one information.[19]

---

15. Section 282 of the Judicature (Parish Courts) Act dictates that unless otherwise stipulated, procedure for the indictable trial and summary trial should be the same or 'as near as may be.'
16. Section 275 of the Judicature (Parish Courts) Act. Note that according to section 287, of the act, the forms set out in Schedule E are applicable regarding the form of the indictment. Schedule E of the Act also states that after the commencement of the indictment which indicates that the proceedings are in the Parish Court for the relevant parish, the subsequent format follows that of the Indictment Act as are applicable for the Parish Court and should so proceed accordingly. Section 4 of the Indictment Act says that the indictment is sufficient if it contains a statement of the offences and with enough particularity for the accused to meet the nature of the charge(s) therein. Per section 3 of the Indictment Act, the rules regarding the format of an indictment are found in the Schedule.
17. Section 272 of the Judicature (Parish Courts) Act.
18. Ibid. See too *Regina v Monica Stewart* (1971) 17 WIR 381, where the Court of Appeal held that the provisions of section 272 of the then Judicature (Resident Magistrates) Law, Cap 179, which required the resident magistrate, as s/he was then styled, to hold an inquiry to ascertain whether the offence charged in the information against an accused person is within the Court's jurisdiction, to make an order for trial to be endorsed on the information and to sign the order, must be strictly complied with and non-compliance with any of those provisions renders any trial on indictment relating to the charge laid in the information a nullity.
19. Section 273 of the Judicature (Parish Courts) Act.

**Power of the Judge of the Parish Court in the Indictable Trial to Vacate Indictable Trial Proceedings**

As the indictable trial proceeds and the evidence unfold, at any time, prior to calling on the accused for his or her defence, the Judge of the Parish Court has a very important power.[20] If it appears on the evidence that the accused ought to have been charged with a more serious offence than that on the indictment, but that particular offence is beyond the jurisdiction of the Parish Court, the Judge should declare the order for the indictable trial vacated. This declaration brings the trial to an end.

At that point, the Clerk of the Courts is to make an endorsement on the particular number one information. This endorsement is in the form of an order and is to state that the order for an indictable trial is vacated. Thus, the indictable trial has ended as there is a matter for committal proceedings revealed on the evidence elicited. This order is to be signed by the Judge. After this procedure, the Judge should deal with the matter according the requirements for committal proceedings.[21]

It is also within the powers of the Judge of the Parish Court to determine if a case cannot be dealt in the Parish Court under two other circumstances. The two prescribed circumstances are: (1) having regard to the antecedents of the accused and (2) having regard to the nature and circumstances of the crime alleged. The Judge can then vacate the order for the indictable trial of the accused person (even without hearing any evidence at all), thereby ending the trial and proceeding to treat and deal with the case as one for committal proceedings to be tried in the Circuit Court.[22] The appropriate endorsement is written on the number one information by the Clerk and signed by the Judge of the Parish Court.

**Determining Committal Proceedings and Ordering Indictable Trial**

It is also permissible that where the Judge of the Parish Court signed an order for committal proceedings for a case (in appropriate circumstances) and it has begun and such depositions are being taken, the order may be vacated and the matter dealt with as an indictable trial.[23] The Judge of the Parish Court may vacate the committal proceedings when the alleged offence is not made out on any statements and/or depositions being taken, but there is evidence of a lesser offence that is triable in the Parish Court.

The Judge of the Parish Court has to determine if the offence that could be charged is within the Court's jurisdiction.[24] If it is, then it is lawful for the Judge of the Parish Court to vacate the order for the committal proceedings. Immediately afterwards, an order for an indictable trial is to be endorsed on the number one information and signed by the said Judge of the Parish Court.[25]

The order is to the effect that the committal proceedings (to the extent under the Committal Proceedings Act) are determined and that the accused is to be tried in the Parish Court, if the accused consents immediately or within seven days after the date of the order.

In such circumstances, any deposition hitherto taken (or any statements being relied on) before the Judge of the Parish Court signed the indictment order, need not be taken again.[26] However, it is the accused's right to require that witnesses be recalled for cross-examination or further cross-examination.[27]

---

20. Section 275 of the Judicature (Parish Courts) Act.
21. Ibid.
22. Ibid.
23. Section 276 of the Judicature (Parish Courts) Act.
24. Ibid.
25. Ibid.
26. Ibid.
27. Ibid.

**Office of the Director of Public Prosecutions**

The Director of Public Prosecutions may also make a requisition of the Judge of the Parish Court that a matter be dealt with as committal proceedings or be adjourned. The Judge of the Parish Court then deals with the case accordingly.[28] This, of course, must be before the defendant has stated his or her defence.

**Amending Indictments**

At any stage before sentencing in a trial for an indictable offence, the indictment can be amended or altered on the evidence as it arises.[29] Such amendment or alteration would occur where the indictment is defective in a material particular.[30]

Thus, the Court shall make such order to amend the indictment as the Court thinks necessary to meet the circumstances of the case. Notably, however, the Judge of the Parish Court may deny the Clerk of the Courts' application to amend the said indictment.[31] If, having regard to the merits of the case, the required amendments would cause injustice, embarrassment, or prejudice to the accused, it will not be granted.[32] An order for such new counts can, however, be granted for separate trial on indictments. Furthermore, the Court may make such order as it deems fit for the payment of any costs incurred owing to the amendment sought.[33] Where an amendment has been sought and granted, the trial may be adjourned until a later date to give the prosecution and defence an opportunity to meet the amendment.[34] The Judge of the Parish Court may also order that the matter be essentially recommenced. In such a scenario, the accused is re-pleaded to the amended indictment, and the matter progresses as if that was the original indictment.[35]

The case of *Oneil Hamilton v R* [2014] JMCA Crim 50 perfectly delineates the proper treatment of an application to amend an indictment in the trial.

The Judge of the Parish Court can adjourn the trial as previously noted and may also remand the accused or take other requisite safeguards to ensure the continued attendance of the accused by continuing bail and the participation of any witnesses necessary (through subpoenas).[36]

**Crown Case Ends and the Defence Case Begins**

At the end of the Crown's case, the accused is entitled to state his or her defence and to call witnesses on his or her own behalf. For an unrepresented accused, the Judge of the Parish Court should ask if there are witnesses who s/he wishes to be called, based on the evidence or unsworn statement of the accused or otherwise.[37] The Judge then asks the accused if s/he wishes such persons summoned, if they are absent, and where the accused answers positively, the order is made to secure such attendance using the same steps for securing prosecution witnesses. The Judge should also adjourn the matter to allow these witnesses to attend on the Court if they appear to be material to the accused's case.[38]

---

28. Section 277 of the Judicature (Parish Courts) Act.
29. Section 278 of the Judicature (Parish Courts) Act. The Indictment Act also indicates the position as regards amendments and alterations to indictments. At section 7(2) of the Act, it states that the procedures related to the indictment affect those preferred in the Supreme Court. The Supreme Court has inherent jurisdiction over the Parish Court.
30. Section 278 of the Judicature (Parish Courts) Act. Section 6(1) of the Indictment Act also provides further guidance.
31. Section 278 of the Judicature (Parish Courts) Act. Section 6(3) of the Indictment Act is also useful.
32. Ibid.
33. Section 278 of the Judicature (Parish Courts) Act and section 6(4) of the Indictment Act.
34. Section 278 of the Judicature (Parish Courts) Act.
35. Section 278 of the Judicature (Parish Courts) Act and also section 6(2) of the Indictment Act.
36. Section 279 of the Judicature (Parish Courts) Act.
37. Section 280(1) of the Judicature (Parish Courts) Act.
38. Ibid.

Where the accused has counsel, the Judge of the Parish Court, at the close of the case for the prosecution, should ask the counsel for each and every accused person on the indictment if they intend to adduce evidence in support of their case.[39]

If there is no such evidence to be elicited, then the Clerk of the Courts addresses the Court first. This closing argument essentially sums up the evidence against the accused.[40] The defence attorney should then address the Court to indicate the lack of sufficient evidence to make the tribunal feel sure of the guilt of the accused.

## Findings of Fact

The Judge of the Parish Court, after hearing all arguments, delivers the verdict of guilty or not guilty in the findings of fact.[41]

### Figure 15.1        Example of a Findings of Fact

Having heard the evidence of how the statement came into existence and the salient parts thereof I am satisfied that on being cross-examined on his statement to the police, Mr. Brown adopted and confirmed in the witness box, the content of his statement which underpins the charge before the court. The evidence, for the avoidance of doubt, was that he gave Mr. Doe "the blue car". According to the theory of the prosecution, this "blue car" is the same car accepted by Mr. Doe. I am satisfied that this blue car is the said blue car referred to in Exhibit 1 by Sgt. Harry....

## Hearing

This is expressedly for matters under legislation such as the Unlawful Possession of Property Act. The Crown proceeds as above regarding the plea and taking evidence from witnesses. When the Crown closes its case, the Judge of the Parish Court rules on whether or not the defendant should account for the items on the Crown's case that are in evidence.

If the accused is called upon to account, an order must be signed by the Judge of the Parish Court (see chapter on court orders) to that effect. If the accused is not called upon to account, then s/he is free to go.

If the accused is called upon and his or her account is unsatisfactory, another order is signed by the Judge of the Parish Court. If s/he is found guilty, the sentence might be passed immediately or postponed.

As matters proceeds in a Parish Court, there may be evidential issues that the bench or bar might be persuaded to think require a *voir dire*. The trial within a trial is appropriate only in cases tried before a Judge sitting with a jury.[42]

Judges of the Parish Court must be mindful of this as they carry out their functions.[43]

---

39. Section 280(2) of the Judicature (Parish Courts) Act.
40 Ibid.
41. Section 280(2) of the Judicature (Parish Courts) Act.
42. *R v Cargill and Roberts* 24 JLR 217.
43. *Hylton and Parsingh v R* RMCA 32/2005 delivered February 10, 2006.

# Chapter 16

# Verdict and Sentencing

## Summary

At the verdict, the Parish Court Judge is expected to do the findings of fact.[1] Indeed, the Parish Court Judge ought to demonstrate how the various issues in a case is dealt with,[2] especially in a case where the verdict is one of guilty. Having recorded the notes of evidence, the Judge reduces it to a findings of facts in summary form, to show the basis upon which the particular verdict has been reached.[3]

This findings of fact is crucial for a guilty verdict as the convicted offender might wish to appeal. However, even if the verdict is not guilty, it is extremely important for the Parish Court Judge to show his or her examination of the legal principles present in the case.

Inscrutable silence is decried as it does not lend itself to examination, per JA Rowe:

> The language therefore in which the findings are couched should demonstrate an awareness of the legal principles which are involved in the case. If he must warn himself, the findings should show he has done so....[4]

In fact, the case of *R v Vince Stewart*, (1990) 27 JLR 19, at page 23, is also quite instructive in the guidance it offers:[5]

> ... the Judicature Resident Magistrate's Act (as it then was) requires that the Resident Magistrate (as s/he then was) gives a brief summary of the facts found. It does not require otherwise, but the authorities indicate that where the decision of the tribunal is governed by the application of settled legal principles, e.g., the desirability of corroboration, it must appear that the tribunal's mind was averted to it – *R v Donaldson* (supra). Even if there is a presumption that the judge knows the law, there is no presumption as to its application 'he must demonstrate in language that does not require to be construed that in coming to the conclusion adverse to the accused person he acted with the requisite caution in mind,' per Wright, J.A., in *R v George Cameron* S.C.C.A. 77/88 (unreported) dated November 30, 1989.

There are standard areas that the Parish Court Judge should keep in mind.[6] At the end of the findings and just before the actual verdict, the Judge should ask the prosecution and defence if there is any area that they think should be discussed or that should have been discussed.

---

1. Section 291 of the Judicature (Parish Courts) Act speaks to the issue.
2. *R v Lloyd Chuck* (1991) 28 JLR 422.
3. Section 291 of the Judicature (Parish Courts) Act.
4. *R v George Cameron* [1985] Supreme Court Criminal Appeal 77/88. Notably too, in *R v Lloyd Chuck* (1991) 28 JLR 422 at 433.
5. *R v Vince Stewart* (1990) 27 JLR 19, 23.
6. See p. 170 'Considerations for the Parish Court Judge in Arriving at a Verdict'.

## Terms

## Not Guilty Verdict

If the defendant is found not guilty, the Court tells the defendant that s/he is free to go due to his acquittal of the offence. The not guilty verdict is written on the relevant place on the number one information or the indictment, dependent on the type of trial that took place. This would be the judgment of the Court, and the Parish Court Judge signs once at the end of the record.[7]

## Guilty Verdict

A guilty verdict is also endorsed on the number one information or the indictment, dependent on the type of trial that took place. The sentence that is imposed is also endorsed, and the Parish Court Judge signs accordingly.[8]

For summary proceedings, it is sufficient for the Parish Court Judge or Clerk to record on or in the fold of the information (the adjournments, if any, being noted), the place and day of hearing, the name of the adjudicating Parish Court Judge, and his/her final findings.[9]

The defendant should receive a certificate of acquittal or conviction signed by the Clerk.[10] This is preferably prepared immediately after the verdict by the courts office for ease of administrative efficiency. Section 280(3) of the Judicature Parish Courts) Act states that it is the Judge of the Parish Court who gives the certificate to the accused but in practice and reality it is signed by the Clerk.[11]

## Sentences Generally

There is no scientific scale by which to measure punishment; however, a trial judge must impose a sentence to fit the offender and at the same time to fit the crime. There are four classical principles a trial judge must consider when imposing sentence. These are retribution, deterrence, prosecution, and rehabilitation.[12]

Sentences take two forms dependent on the provisions in the statute(s). These are custodial and non-custodial. There may be provisions for both to be imposed as well, subject, of course, to the relevant legislation.

---

7. Section 291 of the Judicature (Parish Courts) Act.
8. Ibid.
9. Ibid.
10. Section 280(3) of the Judicature (Parish Courts) Act.
11. Ibid.
12. See *R v Sydney Beckford and David Lewis* (1980) 17 JLR 202 at 203.

After the guilty verdict has been delivered and before the sentence is handed down, antecedents are generated for the accused to ascertain if s/he has any previous criminal convictions. Antecedents are generated by the criminal records office of the Jamaica Constabulary Force using information gathered from the accused as well as processing the accused's fingerprints. Such reports are not generated for minors before the Court. They are done before sentencing to assist the Court in determining the type of sentence to impose on an adult offender.

The Parish Court Judge at his or her own volition, at the behest of defence counsel, or upon an explanation of the merits thereof to the unrepresented defendant, may order a social enquiry report into the defendant's social background. Such a report assists in determining the type of sentence best to be handed down in appropriate cases. The character and antecedents of the specific individual who stands before the Court must also, therefore, be assessed.[13]

The probation officer would, therefore, speak to the complainant, the accused, as well as persons in the latter's community.[14] The probation officer then writes a report and makes a formal recommendation regarding the sentence to be given.[15] The report is presented to the Parish Court Judge as well as to the attorney on record or the accused. At the appropriate time, the probation officer can be questioned about the content, and any errors in the report must be corrected on the record.

The Court is always anxious when a minor is to be sentenced, and the case of *A v R* [2018] JMCA Crim 26 offers a comprehensive review (even as it is a case on manslaughter) on all that a Court is to be mindful of regarding such an offender.

## Non-custodial Sentences

### 1. Probation Order

The Court may, in lieu of imposing a sentence of imprisonment, make a probation order where it is deemed expedient to release the offender on probation.[16] However, the offender must agree with the terms and conditions of a probation order, once fully explained by the Parish Court Judge, to be granted probation.[17] The Court has to explain the terms of probation in ordinary language, stating the full effects of the order – the offender's responsibilities and obligations and that, if the offender fails in any respect to comply with any of the stipulated written terms or commits another offence, the offender will be liable to be sentenced for the original offence.[18]

The probation order is of a minimum of one year and a maximum of three years.[19] The Parish Court Judge imposes in the probation order any requirement considered adequate to ensure that the offender is adequately supervised, to promote adherence to the order and a reduction of the possibility of re-offending.[20]

---

13. See *R v Errol Campbell* (1974) 12 JLR 1317.

14. According to section 2 of the Probation of Offenders Act, a probation and after-care officer is someone appointed as such under the Corrections Act.

15. Section 5 of the Probation of Offenders Act stipulate that it is the circumstances, the nature of the offence, the character and home surroundings of the accused that are all to be considered.

16. Ibid.

17. Ibid.

18. Ibid. Notably too, section 9 of the Act speaks of the consequences where the probationer fails to comply with the terms of his probation order.

19. Section 6(1) of the Probation of Offenders Act.

20. Section 8 of the Probation of Offenders Act speaks to the Court's powers where a probationer has re-offended whilst on probation. Section 9 focuses on the supervision of the suspended sentence Order.

**Figure 16.1   Sample Probation Order**

5258

WHEREAS in the PARISH COURT                    }

LAY MAGISTRATE COURT                    }          for the Parish of ___St Ann___

Holden at      St Ann's Bay                    on the ___3ʳᵈ___ day of October 20–

John Doe            of 2 Swallow Road, St Ann's Bay, St Ann

(hereinafter called the offender) was charged for UNLAWFUL WOUNDING that he on the day of ___1ˢᵗ___ day of September 20– at   St Ann's Bay   in the parish of   St Ann   did      unlawfully wound Jane Doe

AND the Court thinks that the charged is proved, but is of opinion that having regard to the circumstances including the nature of the offence and the character and home surroundings of the offender it is expedient to release the offender on Probation, and

a.    the Court having convicted the offender.

b.    the Court without proceeding to conviction and having explained to the offender the effect of the order which it is proposed to make and the offender having expressed his willingness to comply with the provisions of such order.

IT IS HEREBY ORDERED that the offender be discharged subject to the following conditions: -

1.    That the offender shall be of good behaviour for the period of ___three___ years and shall during the same period lead an honest and industrious life.

2.    That the offender shall reside at   2 Swallow Road, St Ann's Bay St Ann   or with _____ for the period of  years.

3.    That during the period of ___three___ years the offender shall be under supervision of the Probation Officer of the Parish in which the offender resides and the offender shall observe the following conditions for securing such supervision, namely: -

   i.    That the offender shall receive at the place where he resides visits from the Probation Officer at such times as the Probation Officer may think fit;

   ii.    That the Offender shall report at the Office of the Probation Officer or at such other place as the Probation Officer shall direct, at times fixed by the Probation Officer;

   iii.    That the offender shall answer truthfully all questions put to him by the Probation Officer with regard to his conduct, associates, employment or residence;

   iv.    That the offender shall report immediately to the Probation Officer any change of his residence or place of employment.

Additional
conditions

                On breach of any of the conditions of this Order or on the conviction of the offender of any offence while this Probation Order is in force, the offender may be brought before the Court (c) to be sentenced, (d) to be convicted and sentenced for the offence for which this Probation Order is made.

N.B.-   (a) and (b) strike out the word which is inapplicable.

        (b) is only applicable where the offender is charged with an offence punishable on Summary Conviction.

N.B.- (c) and (d) strike out the one which is applicable.

**AND THE COURT FURTHER ORDERS** that the Probation Officer shall immediately report to the Court any breach of this Order by the offender, and the Probation Officer shall, in addition, submit a report to this Court at intervals of three months from the date on the behaviour of the offender.

Dated at St Ann's Bay in the parish of St Ann

on the 3rd day of October 20--

*James Earles*
....................................................
Clerk of the Courts for the
Parish of St Ann

Two copies of this Order must be furnished, one for the Probationer and the other for the Probation Officer. The original order must be kept by the Court.

To ensure that the probationer is fully aware of the responsibilities, a copy of the probation order is given to the offender or a parent where appropriate per section 6(3) of the Probation of Offenders Act.

When the probation report is first generated, of the two copies furnished, one is furnished to counsel for the represented accused, to the accused personally if s/he is unrepresented, or to a parent for a minor.[21] Defence Counsel can utilize the said report to urge any mitigating factors on the Parish Court Judge to give the accused the best possible probation order in all the circumstances.

## 2. Fines

Fines must be paid into the accounts section of the court on the day that the defendant is sentenced unless otherwise stipulated. If the fines are not paid by the end of the court day, the defendant is taken into custody and remains there until the fine is paid. However, the Parish Court Judge may allow time for the payment of the said sum.[22] This can be at the urging of counsel, the defendant, or if the Parish Court Judge considers it just in all the circumstances.

The Parish Court Judge, therefore, would direct that payment be made by instalments until the whole of the sum has been paid.[23] If fines are not paid, the court can sentence the accused to an additional term of imprisonment along with the original custodial sentence. The monies are paid into the court's account section.

The defendant may be given time to pay with or without sureties. However, with or without a surety, the

---

21. Section 22 of the Probation of Offenders Act requires that the probation report is given to counsel, the unrepresented accused or the parents for a minor (where counsel is not in the matter). This report assists counsel to urge the necessary mitigating factors on behalf of the accused and to highlight any positive features in the said report.
22. Section 68(1)(a) of the Justices of the Peace Jurisdiction Act.
23. Section 68(1)(b) of the Justices of the Peace Jurisdiction Act. Section 268(3) of the Judicature (Parish Courts) Act discusses the failure of an accused to pay a fine ordered in the Court.

defendant, in effect, agrees to the payment of the sum.[24] Any person acting as a surety, in this instance, would have to meet the provisions in the Recognizance and Sureties of the Peace Act.[25] If there are sureties, those persons have to produce evidence of collateral and complete and sign the bail documents in the same way one would if one was standing as surety for someone who had been in custody and offered bail. If the defendant is granted time to pay in his or her own surety, then the defendant completes and signs the bail documents but need not produce any evidence of collateral.

Once the defendant satisfies the Parish Court Judge that there is no sufficient means to pay and he has a fixed place of abode, unless there are other serious considerations to prevent the granting of the application, the Court should so grant the application.[26]

Pursuant to section 69 of the Justices of the Peace Jurisdiction Act, the Parish Court Judge may order that the accused be searched and any monies found applied to whatever fine has been ordered by the Court. Any surplus is to be returned to the accused.

### 3. Suspended Sentence

According to the Criminal Justice (Reform) Act, a 'suspended sentence' is a sentence which does not take effect unless the offender commits another offence and is convicted.[27] Incarceration follows a violation of this court ruling, and the offender will be imprisoned for the period that was previously stipulated by the Court in addition to any custodial sentence for the current conviction.

A suspended sentence can be for a maximum term of three years for any offence.[28] The Court may order that the sentence be in abeyance for the operational period stipulated.[29] The operational period is a minimum of one year but no more than three years. If, during this time, the offender commits in the island of Jamaica another offence punishable by a custodial sentence of more than six months and is convicted,[30] the original sentence takes effect.

Sometimes a Parish Court deals with an offender in respect of whom a Circuit Court has passed a suspended sentence that is still in operation.[31] In such a matter, the Parish Court Judge should sign a certificate regarding the relevant particulars of the current offence and the sentence for onward transmission to the registrar of the Supreme Court.[32] A Judge of the Supreme Court then makes a determination when the offender is brought before him or her, without prejudice to the subsequent order of the Parish Court Judge. The Judge in the Supreme Court may order that the 'suspended sentence shall take effect with the original term unaltered or with the substitution of a lesser term for the original term.'[33]

The offender who is given a suspended sentence must be told of the terms, in ordinary language, and is required to complete and sign the requisite documentation. The court keeps a copy on the offender's case file, and the defendant receives the other.

---

24. Section 68(1)(c) of the Justices of the Peace Jurisdiction Act.
25. The Recognizance and Sureties of the Peace Act deals with the way in which sureties are to be accepted.
26. Section 68(2) of the Justices of the Peace Jurisdiction Act.
27. Section 2 of the Criminal Justice (Reform) Act. Section 6(1) of the Criminal Justice (Reform) Act. Section 6(3) also provides guidance on when a suspended sentence should be considered.
28. Section 6(1) of the Criminal Justice (Reform) Act.
29. Ibid. Section 7(1) of the Criminal Justice (Reform) Act indicates that upon a subsequent offence if the accused is found guilty during the term of a suspended sentence, the suspended sentence takes effect.
30. Section 7(3) of the Criminal Justice (Reform) Act.
31. Ibid.
32. Ibid.
33. Ibid.

**Figure 16.2   Sample Recognizance**
**(With Condition endorsed where a convicted party is allowed time in Sureties to pay a penalty)**

---

5207

RECONGNIZANCE WITH CONDITION ENDORSED WHERE A CONVICTED PARTY IS
ALLOWED TIME IN SURETIES TO PAY A PENALY

JAMAICA SS.

BE IT REMEMBERED that on the    3rd    day of    October 20–

John Doe, of 2 Swallow Road, Trelawny Street of the parish of Trelawny and Tom Strokes of the same place personally came before the undersigned Clerk of the Courts in and for the said parish and severally acknowledged themselves to owe to Our Sovereign Lady the Queen the sum of $150,000 Jamaican    Dollars each of good and lawful money of this Island to be made and levied of their several goods and chattels lands and tenements respectively to the use of Our said Lady the Queen, Her Heirs and Successors if he the    said John Doe    shall fail in the following condition.

THE CONDITION of the above written recognizance as such that if the said    John Doe    does not pay    $100,000    to    Jane Doe    in three parts by October 30, 20–

John Doe and Tom Strokes    Shall forfeit and pay the sum of $150,000 Jamaican    Dollars as a penalty and a further sum of $50,000 Jamaican Dollars for costs imposed on him by His Honour    John Black    Parish Court Judge for the parish aforesaid for the offence of    Unlawful Wounding

within    27    days from the date hereof then the said recognizance to be void or else to stand in full force and virtue.

Taken and acknowledged the day and year first above written at    Falmouth Parish Court

in the parish of    Trelawny

before me.

*James Earles*
Clerk of the Courts

Parish of Trelawny

---

Figure 16.3   Sample Suspended Sentence

IN THE PARISH COURT JUDGE'S COURT
FOR THE PARISH OF Westmoreland
HOLDEN AT Savanna La Mar


REGINA                                    )

VS                                        )

John Doe .........                        )

                                          )


Tried on the ................. 1st ................. day of ................. October ................. 20--


Sentence that the said John Doe
                      .........
                        (herein after referred to as the offender)


For his/her said offence be imprisoned and kept at Hard Labour for the space of
three years


IT IS FURTHER ORDERED THAT the Sentence be suspended, that is to say that
the Sentence imposed shall not take effect unless during the period of  from the
date thereof, the Offender commits in the Island of Jamaica a subsequent offence
punishable with imprisonment.


OFFENDER: John Doe
           .........


WITNESS:  Tom Strokes
          .........


                                    *Nassia Barnes*
                                    .........................
                                    Clerk of the Courts for the
                                    Parish of Westmoreland

### 4. Admonish and Discharge[34]

The Parish Court Judge indicates in strong terms to the offender that s/he must abstain from participating in any criminal activity, keep the peace and be of good behaviour, noting that a continuation down the path of criminality will have serious consequences. After the Parish Court Judge has warned the accused, s/he is then released.

### 5. Bound over to Keep the Peace

Under the Recognizance and Sureties of the Peace Act, the Parish Court Judge may order that a person enter into a recognizance and find sureties to keep the peace, or to be of good behaviour.[35]

**Figure 16.4   Sample Bail Bond**

---

**BAIL BOND**

JAMAICA SS.

BE IT REMEMBERED that on the      3rd      day of      October 20–

John Doe,                of           2 Swallow Ave, Kingston 2

in the parish of        Kingston        and        Tom Strokes

of 3 Swallow Road, Kingston 2 in the parish of                Kingston

personally came before me the undersigned one of Her Majesty's Justices of the Peace in and for the parish of     Kingston   and severally acknowledged themselves to owe to Our Sovereign Lady the Queen the sum of $100,000 Jamaican Dollars each of good and lawful money of this Island to be made and levied on their several goods and chattels, lands and tenements respectively to the use of Our said Lady the Queen, Her Heirs and Successors if the said John Doe  shall fail in the following condition.

THE CONDITION of the above written Recognizance is such that the said  John Doe shall keep the peace and be of good behaviour towards Her Majesty and all liege people and especially towards John Brown   for the term of  36 months   now next ensuing then the said Recognizance to be void or else to stand in full force and virtue.

Taken and acknowledge the day and year first abovementioned at the parish of before me.

John Doe
Name of Accused

*John Doe*
Signature of Accused

*Paula Harris-Stowes*
Clerk of the Courts
for the Corporate Area

---

34. Section 5 Recognizance and Sureties of the Peace Act.
35. Ibid.

## 6. Community Service

Under section 10 of the Criminal Justice (Reform) Act, the Court may order an accused to undertake community service upon finding him or her guilty of an imprisonable offence.[36] Such an order is, however, not made in murder cases or in cases involving the use of a firearm (or imitation).[37]

### Figure 16.5 Sample Community Service Order Form

---

**Form 4**

(Rule 8)

**COMMUNITY SERVICE ORDER FORM**

In: Corporate Area Parish Court (Criminal Division) ........................................
(name and division of Court)

For the parish of/held at: Corporate Area Parish Court, Maxfield Avenue ........................

Before: Her Hon Miss Thelma Jean ..................................................
(name of Judge)

In the matter of: R. *v.* John Doe ......................................................

For the offence of: Assault ...........................................................

Name of offender: John Doe .........................................................

UPON the offender having been ~~convicted~~/pleaded guilty to the said offences, punishable with imprisonment, and having attained the age of seventeen years, PURSUANT to the provisions of the Criminal Justice (Reform) Act, instead of sentencing the offender to imprisonment, the Court, having been satisfied ---

   a.   That for the duration of this order the offender resides or will reside at the following address:
      2 Swallow Road, Kingston .................................................

   b.   That arrangements can be made in the area in which the offender resides, or will reside, for him to perform work under a community service order and for the proper supervision of that work;

   c.   After considering a report by a probation officer in respect of the offender and his circumstances, that the offender is a suitable person to perform work under a community service order,

**HEREBY ORDERS** that –

1.   The offender perform  100 hours  of unpaid work in accordance with the directions given to him by his probation officer.

2.   In performing unpaid work under this order, the offender shall comply with the directions given to him by-
   a.   His probation officer;
   b.   Any person in charge of supervising the work at the place where the offender is required to perform unpaid work.

3.   The offender shall inform his probation officer of any change in his address.

4.   The offender shall be under the supervision of an authorized officer for the following period:
   one year .................................................................

5.   During the period specified in paragraph 4, the offender shall ---
   a.   keep in touch with the authorized officer in accordance with such instructors as may from time to time be given by that officer; and
   b.   Notify the authorized officer of any change of the offender's place of residence.

---

36. Section 10 (1) of the Criminal Justice (Reform) Act.
37. Section 10(1)(a) and (b) of the Criminal Justice (Reform) Act.

---

**BY ORDER OF THE COURT.**

This ....3rd.... day of ....October.. 20--.

*James Earles*
..........................
~~Registrar~~/Clerk of the Courts

I, John Doe consent to the making of this order and I am aware that if I fail to comply with any of the requirements of this order---

    a.    a warrant may be issued for my arrest or a summons issued requiring me to appear before the Court;

    b.    this order may be revoked; and

    c.    I may be sentenced to imprisonment or dealt with any other manner in which I could have been dealt with for the offence if this order had been made.

Dated this ...3rd... day of ..October. 20--

*John Doe*
..........................
Signature of offender

**\* To be included where a combination community service and supervision order is made pursuant to section 15 of the Act.**

---

A community service order requires the accused to perform unpaid work for not less than 40 and no more than 360 hours. The Court must be satisfied that the circumstances exist for adequate supervision of the accused during the currency of the order.

A curfew order can also be made pursuant to section 12 of the Criminal Justice (Reform) Act. Such an order stipulates curfew times, supervision of the curfew, and the means by which it is to be adhered to.

## Custodial Sentences

Under section 268 of the Judicature (Parish Courts) Act,[38] the Parish Court Judge may impose a custodial sentence of a maximum of three years and a fine of $1,000,000. In particular circumstances, the Parish Court Judge may impose a custodial sentence of five years.[39]

Dependent on the relevant statute, the accused can be sentenced to serve a term of imprisonment at one of the adult correctional facilities for the time imposed by the Parish Court Judge. A commitment form follows the defendant to the facility.[40] All corrections must be initialled. The necessary notations are made in the commitment book that is kept at the court's office. The period of incarceration often determines the facility in which the convicted accused is kept.

## No Conviction Recorded

The Parish Court Judge may order that a conviction should not be recorded on the accused's records. This can be requested by counsel or the unrepresented accused where a non-custodial sentence or a suspended sentence has been handed down. Such an order may also be made at the Parish Court Judge's own volition.

---

38. Section 268 of the Judicature (Parish Courts) Act.
39. Ibid.
40. Section 288 of the Judicature (Parish Courts) Act and Schedule gives the proper format for the commitment that accompanies a person convicted of an offence who has been sentenced to a term of imprisonment when s/he is entering the correctional facility.

For minors, the sentences are not recorded in the Parish Court.

The Court may impose sentences that run concurrently or consecutively. The sentences are to be clearly written on the number one. In *Kirk Mitchell v R*, the Court of Appeal set out clearly the manner in which consecutive and concurrent sentences should be determined.[41]

## Considerations for the Judge of the Parish Court in Arriving at a Verdict

Section 291 of the Judicature (Parish Courts) Act provides that the Parish Court Judge must show that all the live issues in the case at bar have been considered. The following list is not exhaustive but offers a cursory guide on the areas to be considered in the findings of fact. When the Judge has indicated the findings of fact, the Clerk of the Courts can assist the judicial process by advising if there are any proper areas for consideration that were not deliberated on by the tribunal. Every nuance will not need discussion but the Clerk of the Courts must be mindful of possible glaring omissions.

*The Supreme Court of Judicature of Jamaica Criminal Bench Book* (2016) and the *Sentencing Guidelines for Use by Judges of the Supreme Court of Jamaica and the Parish Courts* (2017) offer substantive guidance that every Parish Court Judge as well as the Clerks of the Courts should consult throughout a matter.

These are some of the areas:

- Accused
  - a. Absence from trial
  - b. Evidence, unsworn, silence
- Accepting or Rejecting Witnesses
- Accepting and Rejecting Parts of the Evidence
- Accomplice: See Sections 34, 35, and 41 Criminal Justice (Administration) Act for their treatment.
- Accomplice Warning
- Alibi
- Antecedents
- Assessing Witnesses
- Burden of Proof
- Cautioned Statement
- Character Evidence
- Circumstantial Evidence
- Confession
- Contradictions
- Corroboration – definition
- Corroboration – whether or not there is
- Credibility
- Defence Witness
- Definition of the Offence
- Discrepancies
- Demeanour
- Distance
- Elements of the Offence
- Examples of Discrepancies
- Expert Evidence
- Identification – visual
- Identification – voice
- Identification Parade
- Inconsistencies
- Indictment
- Information
- Inferences
- Intention
- Issue
- Joint Enterprise/Common Design
- Lighting
- Lying Accused

---

41. *Kirk Mitchell v R* [2011] JMCA Crim 1.

- No Extraneous Material
- Omission of Evidence in Summary
- Options Open to Accused
- Plea in Mitigation
- Possible Verdicts
- Prejudice or Sympathy
- Presumption of Innocence
- Probation Report
- Provocation
- Prosecution Witnesses
- Purpose of Cross-examination
- Reasonable Inferences
- Recognition
- Res Gestae

- Self-defence
- Sentencing
- Speculation
- Standard of Proof
- Sworn Evidence of Accused
- Time
- Unsworn Statement
- Warning – children and young persons
- Warning – identification
- Warning – convicting on uncorroborated evidence of young girls
- Warning - Alibi
- Verdict

Chapter 17

# Courtesy, Useful Words, and Phrases in the Courtroom

## Summary

The use of the words 'Your Honour' generally appears at the start and end of nearly every sentence in the Parish Court as the Clerk of the Courts and everyone else addresses the Bench. This is to ensure that there is no appearance of familiarity with the Bench or worse yet, disrespect to the Court.

Collegiality among all attorneys, both prosecuting and defence counsel, is not only civil but the subject of Canon VI of The Legal Profession [Canons of Professional Ethics] Rules which binds all attorneys with a duty to maintain a proper professional attitude towards fellow attorneys. All interactions are to be characterized by courtesy and good faith, and Canon VI (a) goes further to require that attorneys should not permit ill-feelings between clients to affect the relationship with fellow attorneys or his or her demeanour towards the opposing party.

This is especially crucial in a criminal case. The Clerk of the Courts and the defence counsel often approach the case from two divergent planes. The cut and thrust of a criminal trial may well see the trial deteriorate in civility. Therefore, in an effort to maintain the highest level of propriety in the courts, it is useful to have some of the following phrases in hand to utilize.

## Terms

> Some Phrases in Addressing the Parish Court Judge
>
> Some Phrases in Cases Where the Assistance of the Parish Court Judge is Needed
>
> Some Phrases in Outlining the Case for the Crown
>
> Other Useful Phrases

### Some Phrases in Addressing the Judge of the Parish Court

The many phrases listed below are used to address the Court respectfully and prevents the potential faux pas of addressing the Parish Court Judge by name or by some other unsuitable greeting. These phrases are liberally used by both Clerks of the Courts and defence attorneys.

Some of these phrases are:

> 'I crave your Honour's indulgence'
>
> "I crave the Court's indulgence"
>
> "I ask the Court's leave"

If there is need to do something other than pay attention to the Parish Court Judge, e.g., speak with someone in the face of the Court, read something, or check some information in a file, these are useful. The Clerk is never to turn his back on the Court or otherwise ignore the Court. By extension, the Court should never be left alone. The Clerk must always ensure s/he is present (except if there is an emergency for which leave would have been sought to address) or that other attorneys are present or the Court rises briefly.

### 'Subject to the Court's Agreement'

The Clerk of the Courts must never assume that the sitting Judge will simply accede to whatever agreements are made with defence attorneys, witnesses, or investigating officers. The Court is not a rubber stamp, and so whatever course the Clerk proposes (and indeed the defence attorney) it remains a proposal until the Parish Court Judge is satisfied that it has merit. (The caveat being in relation to the full disposition of a matter, which is within the responsibility of the Clerk. Therefore, offering no evidence, proceeding on particular offences, and decisions regarding witnesses and exhibits are the sole purview of the Clerk with conduct of the matter.) The seeking of adjournments and dates for compliance with  orders are common examples of areas needing the Court's agreement.

### 'Your Brother/Sister His/Her Hon. Miss Smith'

In the manner that all attorneys are 'Learned Friends', so too are all Judges 'Brethren' (regardless of the court they sit in). The terms Brother/Sister are generally, however, more in usage.

### Some Phrases in Cases Where the Assistance of the Judge of the Parish Court is Needed

> 'Seek the Court's guidance'
>
> 'Guided Your Honour'
>
> 'Grateful for the information/guidance'

These phrases are appropriate when the Clerk of the Courts asks the Court a question or to determine the manner in which the Court wants to proceed regarding the matter being discussed or regarding another matter.

### Some Phrases in Outlining the Case for the Crown

> 'Your Honour, the allegations are that...'

The Clerk of the Courts must remember that until the Crown has proven its case beyond a reasonable doubt, everything against the accused is an allegation. Therefore, it is beyond inappropriate to say that the 'facts are that...' Those are the facts *according to the Crown*. The accused, no doubt, may have a *different version of facts to air*.

### Other Useful Phrases

> 'The Crown's application today is...'
>
> 'Might he be bound over'
>
> 'The Court instructed that . . .'
>
> 'On a previous occasion'
>
> 'That matter is not before you today'

'Is the Court minded to rise/adjourn/hear the application/witness . . . ?'

'The Crown seeks a five-minute adjournment to . . .'

'We seek the leave of the Court to add the matter of *R v John Brown* to the Court Sheet as it was inadvertently left off.'

'No Returns on file regarding the summons'

'Set this matter for priority, Your Honour?'

'This matter is first before the Court'

'This matter was last before the Court on . . . '

## Some Phrases in a Trial or Hearing

'Might I have the benefit of the Court's note?'

If the Clerk of the Courts did not record or did not hear the evidence just elicited, it is proper to ask the Court for the notes of evidence written down by the Parish Court Judge. These notes are what form the official record, and accuracy is crucial. Where there is a stenographer taking electronic notes, the request can be made of the stenographer, through the Court.

If the Clerk believes that the notes of evidence are inaccurate, it is proper to indicate to the Court, the note that the Clerk made and to ask the witness to repeat his/her answer so that there is accuracy. Therefore, the Clerk should never argue with the Court, especially, in this regard, as it is a matter easily dealt with.

## Some Phrases in Reference to the Accused

'The accused man'

Most legislation refers to 'the accused' and so is proper to do so as well.

'The defendant'

The term 'the defendant' has been increasingly used in case law and is a proper phrase to refer to the accused when addressing the Court about his matter.

'The defendant wishes to shorten proceedings'

The Clerk of the Courts is advising the Court that the defendant wishes to plead guilty to all or some of the offences for which s/he is before the court.

'The accused has not been brought'

Since a matter should not (usually) be heard in the absence of the accused, it is the duty of the Clerk of the Courts to advise the Judge of any general issues related to the accused who are in custody (such as outbreaks of illness at a detention facility). Information regarding if and when accused may be brought from detention facilities should be obtained previously if at all possible. That will help the Court to decide if such a matter should be adjourned to another date, put to the foot of the list, or require enquiries of senior police or correctional officers at the detention facility.

## Some Phrases when Addressing the Accused

'Mr. Tom Brown'

'Mr. Tom Brown, the accused'

Courtesy must always prevail in the court, and so the accused must be addressed as formally as any other party inside (or outside as is required) the courtroom. By extension, it is always proper that the court police officers remove any handcuffs when the accused enters the dock. The Clerk of the Courts should never begin to discuss the accused's matter until this has been done.

Traditionally, the custody officers are experienced and know this duty, but sometimes lapses happen, and it is the duty of the Clerk the Courts to ensure good order throughout the Court.

Indeed, the Clerk of the Courts must never refer to an accused as a 'prisoner' unless s/he is now convicted for the offence before the court. It is prejudicial to the accused for both the Court and witnesses to hear the accused described in this manner.

### Some Phrases in Addressing Defence Attorneys

'Mr Tom Brown is represented by Mr Alfred Smith of counsel'; or '...by Mr John Brown, Queen's Counsel'.

'My Learned Friend'

'Is this a defence application?'

### Other Useful Phrases

'Canvass a date'

The Clerk of the Courts can ask the defence attorney and or other parties to a matter the convenient dates for the matter to heard.

'Interposing'

Matters can be interjected between others for many reasons. For example, a defence attorney may request it of the Court. A witness may need to leave. There are many reasons why this might be necessary.

'On my feet'

When the Clerk of the Courts is addressing the Court on a matter, s/he does so from a standing position while in counsel's bench and never outside it. This shows the proper amount of respect to the dignity of the office of the Judge of the Parish Court. By extension, any address to the Court from an attorney (whether that attorney is the prosecutor, defence, watching proceedings, or merely wishing to greet the court) is to be done from counsel's bench and certainly never from the well of the court.

When others address the Court they can do so whilst standing in position. If it is that evidence is being taken, then clearly this would be done from the witness box. The witness stands. The Clerk of the Courts may ask for the Court's permission for the witness to sit (if there is provision) when s/he is marshalling the witness.

'A delicate matter has arisen'

This phrase is used to alert the Court to areas in a matter requiring sensitivity. All sexual offences matters are held in camera and require sensitivity by the Clerk, the Court and defence counsel.

However, there may be matters, outside of sexual offences, that require some level of sensitivity. At the Court's discretion, the courtroom can be cleared. In some instances, the Clerk can ask for the prosecution and the defence to approach the bench, and if the Parish Court Judge accedes, the information can be relayed fully to the Court. A decision can then be made by the Court as to how to proceed.

The phrase, 'a delicate matter has arisen', is also useful where there is an issue that the Clerk of the Courts might wish to distill (or the defence attorney) surrounding private details related to persons in the case. Furthermore, it is useful as a method of asking the Court for rise momentarily for the Clerk of the Courts (or defence attorney, witness, or accused) to use the restroom. The Court may simply indicate that s/he will remain on the Bench or may rise.

# Chapter 18

# Court Orders

## Summary

The Judge of the Parish Court has the power to make a wide variety of orders regarding matters before the Courts. This power stems mainly from the Judicature (Parish Courts) Act and the Justices of the Peace Jurisdiction Act. Particular statutes make provision for orders that the Judge of the Parish Courts can make.

The prosecution and the defence must both comply with the orders of the Court. The Court's orders are not made in vain. If court orders are disobeyed, the accused's attorney can return to the Court and indicate the position to the Judge of the Parish Court. The accused himself or other parties in the matter can also advise the Court. Therefore, the Clerk of the Courts must ensure that all parties understand the need to comply with court orders. In most cases it is prudent for formal communication of the Court's orders.

Terms _____

      General Orders

      Specific Orders

      _____

## General Orders

As case files come before the Parish Court, certain orders are made as a matter of course. These include:

- the investigating officer is to be bound over (must be present for this to be done)
- the investigating officer is to be subpoenaed
- the witnesses are to be bound over (must be present for this to be done)
- the witnesses are to be subpoenaed
- the witnesses are to be contacted
- the accused are bound over (if brought before the Court via a summons)
- the accused's bail is extended (if brought before the Court via arrest).

These are endorsed on the case file along with any other information regarding the matter on that day.

Persons can only be bound over to attend on a subsequent date if they were present in court. Sometimes witnesses arrive late, after a matter has been disposed of for the day. In such circumstances, the Clerk or defence counsel can seek the leave of the Court to revisit the matter so long as there is no undue disruption to matters currently underway. If the Parish Court Judge agrees, the Clerk and/or defence counsel advise the Court who is present and request that he is bound over for the subsequent court date or whatever else is appropriate for that witness.

## Specific Court Orders

These Orders can be requested by the prosecution, defence, or at the instance of the Court at any time during the life of a matter.

They should be endorsed on the number one information, and they should be sent up to the Court for the Judge of the Parish Court to sign them. However, even if the Judge of the Parish Court does not sign the order, s/he often writes them in the court sheet. It is good practice for the Clerk of the Courts to check that the endorsement on the case file about an order matches what is written in the court sheet. Sometimes the Judge may not have written each order on the court sheet and so it is important that the Clerk of the Courts endorses the order on the number one information for signature by the Judge.

If necessary, ensure that the paperwork required for the order to be carried out is completed. The form of this paperwork may vary depending on the type of order made. Examples include, a results letter, warrant, forfeiture order, application to vary bail, or perhaps a writ to issue. It is the duty of the clerk to ensure that the requisite information is correctly provided.

- **No Order Made**

    **On January 2, 20_**

    **No order made[1]**

    **_Justicia Justis_**

    **Corp Area Parish Court Judge (Criminal Division)**

This is usually made, for example, when the prosecution witnesses or the complainant does not attend court over multiple trial dates. However, the Crown can revive the matter when and if the situation changes. In such an event, the accused should be summoned to return to court and the matter is to be re-listed in the court sheet in a trial court. Evidence of service on the accused must be on the case file before any process can be issued for him or her for disobedience of the summons. If there is no such evidence, the summons can be re-issued.

    **On January 2, 20_**

    **No order made at the instance of the Complainant[2]**

    **_Justicia Justis_**

    **Corporate Area Parish Court Judge (Criminal Division)**

---

1.  No order has been considered in the following: *Michael Feurtado v the Director of Public Prosecutions* [1979] 16 JLR 405 as well as *Grays Justices, ex parte Low* (1989) 2 WLR 984. In essence, where there was no adjudication on the merits on the charges there is no bar to institute fresh proceedings. Notably, in *Feurtado*, the Court did allow the new indictment to proceed. It held that 'to determine whether time is unreasonable, the test must be whether the delay has resulted in prejudice to a party and whether it would be unjust or oppressive to allow the charges to be proceeded with. In the circumstances of this present case, it will be unjust to allow the new indictment to proceed.'

2.  Where the parties have gone to mediation per section 16 of the Criminal Justice (Reform) Act and have reached an amicable settlement, the Court in appropriate circumstances can 'no order' the matter. Notably too, for such a matter, an order for 'no evidence offered' brings an end to the matter forever. This latter order may, therefore, properly be sought instead of the 'no order' by the defence counsel.

On January 2, 20-

**No order made at instance of complainant**

_Jane Doe_

**Complainant**

When a 'no order' has been made at the instance of a complainant, the complainant has decided in the face of the court or through a provided statement that s/he does not wish to proceed. In this case, s/he must sign to this effect on the number one information. This signing ensures that the Court proceedings and all concerned are protected in the event of any later challenge.

Where there are summary and indictable offences on a case file, if the Crown cannot or will not proceed, the Clerk of the Courts must endorse 'no evidence offered' on the summary and 'no order made' on the indictable offences. Indictable offences require that the Judge of the Parish Court make an order to indict the accused on the charge on the application of the Crown. If no such order will be applied for, the correct endorsement is 'no order made'.

- **No Evidence Offered**

    On January 2, 20_

    **No evidence offered by Prosecution**[3]

    _Justicia Justis_

    **St Catherine Parish Court Judge**

This is usually made when the prosecutor has examined a case file and has come to the conclusion that it cannot proceed due to insurmountable evidential hurdles. Where case files are especially old and do not appear to be making progress towards a resolution, the prosecution should examine them carefully to establish whether it is possible to proceed. There may also be cases where the prosecution might offer no evidence of fraud, the accused has repaid all the monies taken from complainants, the prosecution witnesses have resiled from earlier statements, or where it is impossible to ground the offence under the relevant Act.

- **No Further Evidence Offered**

    On January 2, 20_

    **No further evidence offered by the Prosecution**

    _Justicia Justice_

    **Trelawny Parish Court Judge**

This is done only _after_ a trial has begun. It is where the prosecution realizes that it can proceed no further. Usually, if there is an insurmountable hurdle on the Crown's case, then the just and proper course is to offer no further evidence in the case.

---

3.  When the Crown offers no evidence in a matter, it ends there. The accused is pleaded formally in the same way as when the trial is about to start, per the requirement in the Judicature (Parish Courts) Act. (See chapter, 'When a Matter Starts'.) When the plea of not guilty is heard and recorded, the Crown outlines the reasons for the decision.

- **No Case to Answer**

  **On January 2, 20_**

  **No case to answer**

  *Justicia Justis*

  **St Elizabeth Parish Court Judge**

A 'no case to answer' follows a successful no case submission made by the defence attorney. However, the Judge of the Parish Court may also require the Clerk of the Courts to prove that a prima facie case has been established against the accused without hearing from the defence. It is also permissible that the Judge of the Parish Court can simply state 'no case to answer' after the Crown has closed its case. Regardless of which scenario occurs, the defendant is free to go as the Crown has not established a prima facie case for which s/he has to answer. Such a matter cannot be revived at a later date by the Crown.

### Figure 18.1 Sample Bond for an Item

BE IT REMEMBERED that on the ............ 29th ............ day of ............ August, 20–, ............

............ Jane Doe ............ of ............ Lot 1 Hills ............

in the parish of ............ St Andrew ............

came before ............ Her Honour Miss Justicia Justice, ............ one of her Majesty's Justices in the Corporate Area Parish Court (Criminal Division) and severally acknowledged to owe to Our Sovereign Lady the sum of One Hundred and Fifty Thousand Dollars ($150,000.00) of good and lawful money of this island, to be made and levied upon the goods of the said ............ Jane Doe ............ if she shall fail in the following conditions:

THE CONDITION of the above recognizance is that one green 1990 Toyota Tundra Motor Truck, Chassis No.:123456789, Engine No. 987654321, Registration No. 0000 JD, Exhibit in the case of Regina v John Doe, for: Larceny of Motor Vehicle etc., and on Info. Nos. 0001-0012/07 is to be returned to Jane Doe. That no changes be made to the said exhibit without the Court's consent and that it be produced to the Court whenever required until the matter is disposed of.

Taken and acknowledged the day and year first above-mentioned.

*Jane Doe*
............
Jane Doe

*James Earles*
............
Clerk of the Courts

- **Return of Property to a Party on a Bond**

    On January 2, 20 –

    Return of – (vehicle, boat, goods etc) on bond of $150,000.00 to be brought to Court as required by the Court until disposal of matter

    *Justicia Justis*

    St James Parish Court Judge

- **Fingerprint Order Made**

    On January 2, 20_
    Fingerprint order made/ FPO Made

    _____

    *Justicia Justis*

    Westmoreland Parish Court Judge

Under the Fingerprint Act, the Judge of the Parish Court can make fingerprint orders (FPOs) for many offences. The Schedules to the Act indicate the variety of offences that can attract such an order.

- **Adjourned *Sine Die***
    On January 2, 20_

    Adjourned *sine die*

    *Justicia Justis*

    St James Parish Court Judge

Adjourned *Sine Die* means that the matter is adjourned without any subsequent date being set. If at some later stage the prosecution can maintain a possible case against the accused, the accused may be summoned to come to court once again.

- **Defendant not Appearing**

    On January 2, 20_
    Defendant not appearing

    Bench warrant to issue
    Bonds escheated
    *Justicia Justis*
    St Ann Parish Court Judge

The defendant is bailed to appear on each and every occasion that the matter is dealt with in Court unless there is some cogent reason for an absence, which must be conveyed to the Court. If there is none, the Judge of the Parish Court has the power to order that the defendant be taken into custody. As such, where the accused was bailed by a surety, the surety forfeits the bond that was posted for the bail of the accused.

A warrant for the accused is then written up for the signature by the Judge of the Parish Court who ordered it. Warrants should usually be done expeditiously and only a Judge of the Parish Court can sign a warrant. The accused may be taken in by any officer of the Jamaica Constabulary Force who sees him. The warrant is immediately executed on the accused and the execution endorsed on the back.

A warrant of *distingas* and *capias*, commonly called a 'D&C', should also be written up, for the Clerk of the Courts to sign. This warrant is for the forfeiture of the bond amount pledged by the surety. When this warrant is executed if the bond sum is paid into court (at the accounts section) then the surety is released from any obligations to the accused. If the surety is present in court when the warrant is ordered, the surety must make the arrangement for payment by another person or be taken into custody immediately by the assigned court police.

If the 'D&C' is executed subsequently on the surety, there is an additional bailiff's fee to be paid. The bailiff endorses the execution on the back and brings the surety to court. The surety, in the face of the Court, may request or be given time to pay the bond amount.

- **Defendant not Appearing, Warrant of Disobedience to Issue**

  **On January 2, 20_**
  **Defendant not appearing**
  **Warrant of Disobedience to issue**
  *Justicia Justis*
  **St Thomas Parish Court Judge**

This is where the defendant is summoned to court. Before the Clerk of the Courts can apply for this warrant, s/he must ensure that proper service was effected on the defendant. When a defendant is summoned to court there is no surety and so no 'D&C' needs to be issued.

- **Defendant not Appearing, Warrant Issued and Execution Stayed**

  **On January 2, 20_**
  **Defendant not appearing**
  **Bench warrant to issue**
  **Execution stayed until February 28, 20_**
  *Justicia Justis*
  **St Mary Parish Court Judge**

This is where the Judge of the Parish Court stays the execution of the warrant. Stays are granted at the discretion of the Judge. Evidence such as medical reports, surety attending the Court and giving information about the accused, or the attorney indicating the surety's status is useful. Therefore, the warrant will not be prepared until the next court date, at which time, if the defendant does not appear, it will be issued after being signed by the Judge of the Parish Court.

- **Warrant Vacated**

  **On January 2, 20_**
  **Warrant vacated for John Doe**
  *Justicia Justis*
  **Corporate Area Parish Court Judge (Criminal Division)**

If there appears to be a cogent reason why an accused did not attend court on the last date, any warrant previously ordered for him may be vacated. The Judge of the Parish Court who ordered the warrant should vacate it. If that particular Judge is not sitting, another Judge can vacate the warrant. However, the Clerk of the Courts and the court staff must first conduct due diligence to ensure that the warrant is in hand before the Judge vacates it. It is most prudent to have the unexecuted warrant in the hand of the Crown. If it is not, then its whereabouts must be determined. When the warrant is located, the relevant police officer should be notified that the Judge wishes to vacate the warrant.

As such, arrangements should be made to have the unexecuted warrant brought back to the court's office so that it will not be later executed in error.

- **Witness Bound Over, Not Appearing, Warrant of Disobedience**

  **On January 2, 20_**

  **Witness, John Doe bound over for today/summoned for today and not appearing**

  **Warrant of Disobedience to issue**

  *Justicia Justis*

  **Portland Parish Court Judge**

This is often issued for police and/or civilians who were bound over for the particular court date, but did not appear and there is no explanation or an inadequate explanation is proffered for their absence.

- **Investigating Officer not Attending, Warrant to Issue**

  **On January 2, 20_**

  **Investigating Officer, Tom Strokes, not attending**

  **Warrant to issue_**

  *Justicia Jusits*

  **St Mary Parish Court Judge**

When the investigating officer has not attended court in a long time without a reasonable explanation, the Court may issue a warrant for the officer. A warrant can also be ordered if an officer was bound over to attend court but did not.

- **Mediation Ordered**

  **On January 2, 20_**

  **Parties to attend Mediation[4]**

  **At the Dispute Resolution Foundation**

  **and return to Court on February 4, 20_**

  *Justicia Jusits*

  **Hanover Parish Court Judge**

Mediation is provided for in particular circumstances under the Criminal Justice (Reform) Act. The Dispute Resolution Foundation (DRF) offers parties, in matters before the criminal courts, an opportunity to discuss the various issues in a setting outside the court. Parties who go to the DRF still have their legal rights in the

---

4. According to section 16(1) of the Criminal Justice (Reform) Act, parties can be referred to mediation where the offence is one in the Second Schedule and they agree to attend and all the circumstances of the matter are distilled therein.

criminal courts, which is usually explained to them by the Judge of the Parish Court who makes the order.[5] The DRF hears what both parties have to say and sends back letters regarding the outcome to the Judge of the Parish Court. Depending on the outcome of the intervention, the Judge of the Parish Court can make various orders. These orders can include no orders, setting further dates for mediation, or accepting the parties' decisions, after having had the parties advise the Court what their wishes are in the matter.

- **Matter Dismissed after Successful Mediation**

  **On January 8, 20_**

  **Mediation agreement letter presented to Court[6]**

  **Matter dismissed**

  *Justicia Justice*

  **St Elizabeth Parish Court Judge**

The parties, having attended on the mediation centre at the DRF, and agreed to certain things, should return to the Parish Court with a letter. The letter must outline the terms and conditions of the agreement. This agreement becomes binding on the parties. If there are obligations to be fulfilled, the Judge of the Parish Court will ensure they are met by making enquiries of the Clerk of the Courts, the investigator, or the parties themselves. Upon hearing that the obligations have been met, the order for dismissal is made by the Parish Court Judge.

- **Accused Dies While Matter is Before the Court**

  **On January 2, 20_**

  **Detective Sergeant Tom Strokes, having this day, given evidence that on December 20, 20–, he identified in the Public Morgue, the dead body of John Doe, as the accused man in the case *Regina v John Doe*, Information Numbers 0001-0005/20–. It is ordered that the endorsement on the record be as aforesaid and be declared now to be of no legal effect and that the file be closed unless and until the Court, on cause being shown, otherwise orders.[7]**

  *Justicia Justice*

  **Westmoreland Parish Court Judge**

Where an accused has died, this is the notation that is to be placed in the court sheet and endorsed on the number one informations relevant to his charges. Evidence must be brought that the accused is, in fact, dead. The investigating officer or someone who knew the accused should attend the scene of the death and/or the morgue to view the body of the deceased. The investigating officer or other police officer having attended the post-mortem of the deceased accused would then testify regarding what actions were taken, and the evidence is recorded in court.

---

5. Section 16(6)(b) of the Criminal Justice (Reform) Act. This provides for the matter to be tried if mediation is unsuccessful.
6. The Judge of the Parish Court, as per section 16(6)(i) and (ii) of the Criminal Justice (Reform) Act, can dismiss the charge against the accused and also incorporate the terms of the mediation agreement (which may include an agreement for restitution, monetary compensation, non-molestation) or any other such agreement as may be approved by the court.
7. See Archbold 1999, 284.

- **Release of Surety**

  On January 2, 20_

  Surety, John Doe, released[8]

  *Justicia Jusitice*

  **St James Parish Court Judge**

Sometimes, sureties request to be released before the matter is fully disposed of by the Court. In such an event, the surety can attend on the Court at the next court date for the accused. At this time, the surety should indicate this wish to the Court. The surety does not have to explain why s/he wants to be released because a surety cannot be forced to continue as such. A new surety has to be found, and the accused must remain in custody until that new surety is secured.

- **Surety Accepted in Court**

  On January 2, 20_

  Surety, Jane Doe, accepted

  *Justicia Justice*

  **St. Catherine Parish Court Judge**

This occurs when the Judge of the Parish Court decides to accept someone as surety for an accused, in the face of the Court. It is discretionary and sparingly used, such as for certain cases involving minors.

- **Application to Vary Bail Conditions**

  On January 2, 20_

  Application for variation of bail conditions granted.[9]

  Travel documents to be returned to John Doe, Accused, for travel between February 15, 20 — to February 21, 20 —. Travel documents to be returned to Court on or before February 21, 20 —. Stop order lifted between February 15, 20— and February 21, 20—.

  *Justicia Justice*

  **Manchester Parish Court Judge**

Any Judge of the Parish Court may vary the bail conditions of an accused, not solely the Judge who offered the accused bail. Applications to vary bail conditions are usually done orally, but they may also be done in writing. Written applications, where done, should be properly filed into the Parish Court via a notice and an accompanying affidavit in support. The Judge of the Parish Court is then handed the notice and accompanying affidavit in court, when the matter is set down to be heard. The Clerk of the Courts must be able to advise the Court as to the allegations, status of accused in honouring his bond to date, the initial bail conditions, and any objection to the variation. Some Judges of the Parish Court wish that the surety be present to agree or disagree with the variation.

---

8. The Bail Act, section 19.
9. Regulation 3(2) Bail Regulations.

- **Matter Transferred to the Drug Court**

  On January 2, 20_

  Matter transferred to the Drug Court[10]

  *Justicia Justis*

  **Portland Parish Court Judge**

Where an accused before the Court is a drug addict, the Court, in its discretion, may place him before the Drug Court. The Drug Court determines if the accused should be placed on the drug rehabilitation programme. The accused is required to follow the programme for a prescribed period. If the rehabilitation is successful, the matter in the Criminal Court may be dismissed. This is, of course, depends on the nature of the matter.

- *Habeas Corpus* **Application**

  On January 2, 20_

  **John Doe, being held at the Hunt's Bay Police station, since December 2, 20– must be charged by January 5, 20– at or by 4p.m. or is to be otherwise released[11]**

  *Justicia Justice*

  **Corporate Area Parish Court Judge (Criminal Division)**

An application for *habeas corpus* can be made orally or the notice and affidavit of support can be filed beforehand into court. At the hearing of the application, the Judge peruses the documents, if a written notice was filed, or listens to the oral application for *habeas corpus*. In any event, the attorney making the application outlines the circumstances to the Court to assist in the order that may be made.

The Judge of the Parish Court often requests the presence of the police officer in charge of the detention facility where the accused is being held so that the officer can give an update on the accused's status. Alternatively, the Judge may also ask the court inspector to find out where the accused is being held. When the ruling of the Court is made, the relevant officer is expected to convey the ruling to the holding facility.

- **Committal Proceedings**

  On January 2, 20_

  **Let Committal Proceedings be held into the within charge with a view to committing the accused to stand and take his trial at the forthcoming Session of the Circuit Court commencing _____ 20– if a prima facie case is made out against him.[12]**

  *Justicia Justice*

  **Corporate Area Parish Court Judge (Criminal Division)**

Where committal proceedings are going to proceed partially or otherwise on depositions, the Clerk of the Courts may outline the allegations and then apply for the order for committal proceedings to be signed by the Judge of the Parish Court. The order is endorsed on the relevant number one information and signed by the Judge. An order for committal proceedings must be applied for and, more significantly, must be signed and dated by the Judge.

---

10. Drug Offenders Rehabilitation Act.
11. Section 286 of the Judicature (Parish Courts) Act.
12. Justices of the Peace Jurisdiction Act at section 39 and the Committal Proceedings Act.

On January 2, 20_

Prima Facie case having been made out against the accused he is hereby committed to stand and take his trial at the forthcoming session of the Circuit Court commencing _____ 20-.

*Justicia Justice*

**Corporate Area Parish Court Judge  (Criminal Division)**

Where a *prima facie* case has been made out against an accused, the Judge of the Parish Court informs the person at the end of the no case submission. The Judge of the Parish Court then signs the order of committal and the case is committed for the next circuit. The Clerk of the Courts should know when the next circuit commences to ensure that the matter is properly committed.

• **Trial on Indictment**

On January 2, 20_

Indict the accused hereinbefore me this day for the offence of simple larceny contrary to section 5 of the Larceny Act. Add a second count for the offence of robbery with aggravation contrary to section 37(1) of the Larceny Act. Add a third count of —[13]

*Justicia Justice*

**Manchester Parish Court Judge**

Indictments can be for a single count or multiple counts. Even when there are multiple counts, the Judge signs only one order. After the first count, start by stating, 'Add a second count for the offence of....' The Clerk of the Courts should continue doing this until all the relevant counts are recorded and ensure that the order matches the indictment order form on which the accused will be pleaded. If there is an error it might prejudice the accused or the Crown's case, so be careful. The Clerk of the Courts may apply to amend the indictment, but it is much better not to have to so do.[14]

• **Accounting Under the Unlawful Possession of Property Act**

On January 2, 20_

Let the accused account to my satisfaction by what lawful means he came into possession of Exhibit 1 – a cellular phone.

*Justicia Justice*

**Westmoreland Parish Court Judge**

This court order is made when a *prima facie* case has been established against the accused in a hearing under the Unlawful Possession of Property Act. The accused is called upon to 'account', that is, to either give evidence on oath, give an unsworn statement from the dock, or remain silent. This is for offences under section 5 of the Unlawful Possession of Property Act.

On January 2, 20_

The accused having satisfied me by what lawful means he has come into possession of Exhibit 1, Exhibit 2 and Exhibit 3, he is hereby discharged.

*Justicia Justice*

**Westmoreland Parish Court**

---

13. Section 274 of the Judicature (Parish Courts) Act.
14. See the Indictment Act and section 278 of the Judicature (Parish Courts) Act.

If the accused's account satisfies the Judge of the Parish Court, the endorsement above is made. If the accused's explanation only satisfies some of the exhibits, the order is adjusted accordingly. This is for offences under section 5 of the Unlawful Possession of Property Act.

> **On January 2, 20_**
>
> **The accused having failed to account by what lawful means he has come into possession of Exhibit 1, Exhibit 2 and Exhibit 3, he is hereby found guilty as charged.**
>
> *Justicia Justice*
>
> **Westmoreland Parish Court Judge**

This is for offences under section 5 of the Unlawful Possession of Property Act.

> **On January 2, 20_**
>
> **Let the accused account to my satisfaction how Exhibit 1 (black laptop with serial number 12345), Exhibit 2 (black monitor with serial number 67890) and Exhibit 3 (one a multicoloured motorcycle with registration plates 0001 JD) came to be in his house**
>
> *Justicia Justice*
>
> **Westmoreland Parish Court**

This is for offences under section 8 of the Unlawful Possession of Property Act.

- **Writ to Issue**

  > **On January 2, 20_**
  >
  > **Writ to be issued for John Doe**
  >
  > *Jusiticia Justice*
  >
  > **St Catherine Parish Court**

If an accused is in custody but is not brought before the Court, a writ can be ordered for him or her by the Judge of the Parish Court. This writ ensures that, on the next occasion, the accused will be brought from the detention facility. Any Judge of the Parish Court may sign a writ; however, no Clerk of the Courts may sign one.

- **Costs**

  > **On January 2, 20_**
  >
  > **Costs in the sum of $2,000[15]**
  >
  > *Justicia Justice*
  >
  > **St Catherine Parish Court Judge**

---

15. Under section 271 of the Judicature (Parish Courts) Act, the Judge of the Parish Courts can order costs be paid by a defendant in a case where the case could be tried on information by virtue of the special statutory summary jurisdiction of the Court.

# Chapter 19

# Accounts and Related Matters

## Summary

Whenever an order of the Court includes a monetary component, such as a fine, it must be paid into the court's accounts section. Therefore, no administrative or legal officer such as the Clerk of the Courts is authorized to accept any such payments. Upon the relevant payments, the payee is issued a receipt, which can be copied for the specific file, and the original returned to the payee.

## Terms

Fines

Fines Paid at Correctional Facility and Coming to the Court

Collection and Storage of Evidence

Travel Documents of Accused

Warrants of *Distingas* and *Capias*

Payments into Court

## Fines

Where the Court orders an accused to pay fines, these are to be paid into at the accounts section of the court[1] on the day the fines are ordered unless the accused has been granted time to pay.[2]

If the accused is not in custody, s/he is escorted to the accounts section by a court police officer who takes the file endorsed with the sum to be paid by the accused. If the accused is in custody, whoever has undertaken to pay the fine goes to the accounts section and pays the money. The case file can be sent to the accounts section with the assistance of court police officers, administrative staff, or other legal staff members if the court is still sitting. Sometimes the accounts staff may come to the courtroom to take files to do the necessaries themselves. A receipt is obtained by the payer with the details. The case file is then returned to the Clerk of the Courts who should ensure that the payment details have been recorded on the relevant number one information.[3]

The receipt number is written in the court sheet beside the accused's name. This is usually done by the accounts staff. If necessary, this number can be used to trace the status of a matter regarding payment of

---

1. Sections 41A, Section 41B, and section 41C of the Judicature (Parish Courts) Act detail the appointment of court administrators and accountants.
2. Section 63 of the Justices of the Peace Jurisdiction Act.
3. Section 41C(1)(a) of the Judicature (Parish Courts) Act notes that the accountant is to take charge and keep an account of all fines payable or paid into court. Such funds are to be properly accounted for in the manner delineated.

fines. As such, the Clerk of the Courts can also put a copy of the receipt on the file or write the receipt number on the relevant section of the number one information.

It is useful that as the Judge of the Parish Court orders fines, the case files are so endorsed and sent to the accounts section to expedite the disposal of the matters.

## Fines Paid at Correctional Facility and Coming to the Court

Sometimes the court order is a fine or an alternative custodial sentence. In such a case, if the fine is not paid immediately, the accused is taken to the correctional facility. However, as soon the fine is paid into the authorized office at that facility, a sealed letter containing a cheque for the sum of the fine is sent to the specific court where the accused was convicted.

These letters are to be opened in the presence of two authorized (usually court administrative or legal) officers. The sums are then entered in the value book. The Clerk of the Courts can check that the monies correspond with the cheque details. The usual information included is the cheque number, name of payee, sum of money, and date of cheque.

## Collection and Storage of Evidence

From time to time, it is necessary to keep exhibits and potential exhibits at the courthouse and these exhibits should be secured in the court's vault. The accounts staff writes up the details of the items being left in the evidence register, and an accounting staff member signs that the exhibits have been received and dates them. When the Clerk of the Courts goes to retrieve the items, they should be checked again and then s/he signs that the items have been received.

## Travel Documents of Accused

If the Judge of the Parish Court has ordered an accused's travel documents be surrendered, they are surrendered to the court administrative personnel assisting with the matter, and the court usually has several vaults for this purpose. Surrendered documents are usually kept by the accounts section. The passport details are noted, namely the number, name of holder, and the expiry date, on a receipt which is given to the person surrendering the document. The name of the person surrendering the passport and the date are also on the receipt. These travel documents are sent to the Passport Immigration and Citizenship Agency (PICA) for safekeeping under cover of letter, until such time as are required or that the matter is disposed of in the court proceedings.

This receipt is then used to transact whatever other business the accused has within the court system.

## Warrants of *Distingas* and *Capias*

Sureties are brought before the Court on this warrant when the accused absconds. The sum pledged as the bail amount or any portion thereof, in the discretion of the Judge of the Parish Court, must be paid into the accounts section.

## Payments into Court

When virtual complainants are to receive sums of money in a matter that is before the Court but are absent, the money can be paid into the accounts section of the court for collection at a convenient date. A receipt is issued. If the sums are collected in the face of the Court, the person should sign for it on the number one information. The sum collected is noted, and the balance to be paid is also noted. This assists in the quick calculation of sums outstanding.

# Chapter 20

# Important Court Books

## Summary

The administrative arm of the court is critical to the efficiency of the overall structure of the system. Before the day starts in the courtroom and after the day ends there, much has to be done to ensure that the actual court day operates smoothly.

This chapter focuses on the 'behind the scenes' areas that are so vital to the proper administration of the Parish Court system.

## Terms

- Court Sheet
- Court Diaries
- Transfer Books
- Daily Process Book
- Bailiff Book
- Value Book
- Commitment Book
- Straight to Prison
- Appeals Register
- Requests for Letters (Back Desk)

### Court Sheet

Each court has a court sheet when there are multiple courts on a court building. Where there are several types of matters heard by a single Judge of the Parish Court, there may be multiple court sheets. So, for example, there may be a Return Day court sheet, a Traffic court sheet and a Family court sheet.

The court sheet is a book in which the Judge of the Parish Court records all the relevant information regarding all of the matters before the Court. Only a Judge of the Parish Court has the authority to write in, add, or change anything in the allotted section of the court sheet unless there are exceptional circumstances. The various matters are written in before the court day starts by the assistant clerk. The order in the court sheet is determined by the types of case files that are before the Court on that day (see also Return Day Court for a sample court sheet).

Each day, the court sheet must be written up to reflect the date and the name of Judge of the Parish Court sitting in a particular court. If another Judge of the Parish Court sits in the stead of the assigned Judge, the amendment is made, as the court sheet forms part of the official record and so must be accurate.

The matters that are part-heard are usually written first. As offences are classified as summary, indictable, hearing, and committal proceedings – this is how they are written on the court sheet. The way in which they are listed will be determined by whether or not they are for trial, committal proceedings, or sentence.

Private prosecutions are usually listed at the end of the sheet.

The sheet is written up as follows: The type of offence and what is to happen on the day –trial, mention and so on, the information number(s), Regina, the name of the accused person(s), and the charges. There is a section for the Judge of the Parish Court to write in the details about the matter on the day as the matter unfolds. All matters in a particular offence category are listed together. Where accused persons are charged with different types of offences, they must be listed under all the types.

It is usual to list the matters according to their information numbers. This is useful as it indicates immediately how long matters have been before the Court. This can also help in determining which matters ought to begin on a subsequent occasion because of the length of time on the court's list.

It is possible that a matter slated to be heard was inadvertently not listed on the court sheet. This may be brought to the attention of the Clerk of the Courts, for example, by the accused or his attorney. Usually the court has started and the Judge of the Parish Court has the court sheet on the bench. The Clerk of the Courts must respectfully request the permission of the Court to list the matter. The Judge usually then sends the court sheet down to the Clerk of the Courts and s/he should list the matter as expeditiously as possible under the appropriate headings. If there are multiple charges the Clerk of the Courts need not list them all unless the matter will be fully distilled on that day. Therefore, the Clerk of the Courts could simply write information number CA20–CR0001-10 and the name of the accused, for expediency's sake.

Matters might also have been inadvertently put on the court sheet. When it is realized that the matter is not for the day, the Clerk of the Courts can write 'wrongly listed' beside it in the section that the Judge of the Parish Court is to write, if the error is found before the court begins. This is one of the few times that the Clerk of the Courts can properly write in a court sheet. If it is discovered in court that the matter is wrongly listed, the Clerk of the Courts should bring it to the attention of the Judge who will usually make the appropriate notation.

It is also possible that a matter could be accommodated on a particular day but was not slated for that day or even in that court. Such matters include warrants of *distingas* and *capias*, bail applications, *habeas corpus*, executed warrants, and the like. These are listed using the case file if applicable or the other documents that come into court such as the executed warrant or warrant for a surety.

The court sheet's start date must be clearly written on the cover. When a case is finished, the end date must then be written on. The name of the court is also written, for example, 'Court Five'. These help to track the matters heard within the period that the sheet was being used.

Court sheets must be secured at the end of the court day by the Clerk of the Courts and taken to the court's administrative office for action by relevant court staff.

**Figure 20.1   Sample Court Sheet**

| Before Her Hon Justicia Justis | | | |
|---|---|---|---|
| Corporate Area Parish Court (Criminal Division) | | | |
| March 2, 20— | | | |
| **Part Heard Trials (PHTs)** | | | |
| Info # | Accused | Offence(s) | **Judge of the Parish Court Writes Here** |
| CA20--CR0001 | R v John Doe | Assault | *Acc remanded. Virtual complainant to attend court on*<br>*March 3, 20--* |
| CA20--CR0002 | R v Tom Strokes | Breach of DDA | *Evidence of IO taken.*<br>*Mr. Tom Jones (Def. Attorney) to cross examine on March 3, 20--* |
| **Committal Proceedings Mention (M)** | | | |
| Info # | Accused | Offence(s) | *Acc remanded. Representation to be Settled or LAA* |
| CA20--CR0003 | R v Mary Smith | Murder | |
| CA20--CR0004 | R v Tom Doe | Rape | *Case file incomplete. Defence not yet served by prosecution. Service by March 25, 20--* |
| **D&C** | | | |
| Info # | Accused | Offence(s) | *Surety given time to pay – one week from today.* |
| CA20--CR0005 | R v John Smith | Assault with Intent to Rob | |
| CA20--CR0006 | R v Tom Strokes | | *Wrongly listed. Correct date is March 5, 20--* |

## Court Diaries

Each court has a diary. The Clerk of the Courts uses it in court to set matters for subsequent days. It would have dates with matters set from previous court days. When there are enough matters for a particular day, the Clerk of the Courts can write 'closed' at the bottom of the day or at the instruction of the Judge of the Parish Court.

The Clerk of the Courts can either quickly jot the accused's name on the page or s/he can use some kind of a tally system to decide when enough cases have been set for a day (perhaps a sheet indicating how many matters can be set on a day based on what is already set on those days and what they are set down for). In the flow of the court day, it is not usually possible to do more. After the court day ends, the court assistant writes in the full details of matters set down for particular days.

Dates for matters are set in several ways:

- As case files come into the court system they are also listed in the court diary for either the return day (or return court) or petty session, according to the day on which the particular matters are to be heard.

- When case files move to trial courts, they are listed according to the day for which they have been sent from the Return Day.

- Matters can be transferred from other courts.
- Matters might have been previously set in the same court.

The court diary has the matters set for the days on the respective court calendars.

The diary is written up using the information number, the date (if any) on which the matter was last heard, the name of the accused and the name of the offence and what is to take place on the next occasion the matter comes up in the court. Sometimes, it may have the accused status beside his/her name.

Completing the court diary in this manner can help to track a case file and is a quick ready reference for information about the case file.

**Figure 20.2   Sample Court Diary**

| Monday March 2, 20-- | | | | |
|---|---|---|---|---|
| **Info #** | **Accused** | **Offence** | **LCD** | **Purpose** |
| SJ20--CR0008 | R v John Doe (C ) | Rape | February 2, 20-- | Bail appln |
| SJ20--CR0003 | R v Tom Strokes (B ) | Murder | January 7, 20-- | Disclosure |
| SJ20--CR0016 | R v John Brown (B) | Breaches of Airport Authority Act | January 19, 20-- | Trial |
| **DIARY CLOSED FOR THIS DAY** | | | | |

## Transfer Books

Each court has a register that is completed when a case file is transferred to another court. It is called the transfer book. This is another record of the movement of the case file in the court system. A file can be transferred to another court for a variety of reasons. Some of these include if the accused or complainant is known personally by the Judge of the Parish Court or Clerk of the Courts, if the Judge of the Parish Court had tried the accused on a previous occasion, or if another court has agreed to assist with the matter.

**Figure 20.3   Sample Transfer Book**

| **Info #** | **Accused** | **Offence** | **LCD** | **Transferred to** |
|---|---|---|---|---|
| SE20--CR0009 | R v John Doe (B ) | Rape | February 2, 20-- | Transferred to Court 8 |
| SJ20--CR0017 | R v Tom Strokes (C) | Murder | January 7, 20-- | Transferred back to Return Day/Court |
| SJ20--CR0012 | R v John Brown (B) | Breaches of Airport Authority Act | January 19, 20-- | Transferred to Court 6 |

## Daily Process Book

New case files are entered on a daily basis into the daily process book. The details written in this book are: the information number(s) the name of the accused person(s), the charges and the type of offence (hearing, indictable, summary, extradition, petty session, etc.).

Administrative court staffers are responsible for numbering case files which is done as they are entered into the daily process book. The usual information number given to a file is the next available consecutive number in the book with the last two numbers of the current year. Therefore, for example, WL20–CR0001.

Where there are multiple charges, every number one information is to be given a number, even if the accused is the same. This is as each number one information is specific to one offence and one offence only. There is a fairly new numbering protocol for files in the parish court system. It is called 'Case Numbering Protocol for Jamaican Courts' and all Clerks of the Courts and court staff should be familiar with it.

**Figure 20.4  Sample Daily Process Book**

| Info # | Accused | Offence | Type of Offence |
|---|---|---|---|
| SM20--CR0005 | R v John Doe | Rape | Committal Proceedings |
| SM20--CR0019 | R v Tom Strokes | Murder | Committal Proceedings |
| SM20--CR0020 | R v Tom Strokes | Conspiracy to Rob | Indictable Trial |

## Bailiff Books

Sections 42 to 56 of the Judicature (Parish Courts) Act set out clearly the appointment of bailiffs, their duties, and their requirement to keep proper records.

One tool to help bailiffs carry out their tasks is the bailiff book. This book contains information regarding the surety and the accused. The details are entered to ensure that a proper record is kept of persons who offer themselves as surety.

**Figure 20.5  Sample Bailiff Book**

| Info # | Name of Accused | Name of Surety | Address of Surety | Other Information |
|---|---|---|---|---|
| MN20--CR0004 | John Doe | John Smith | 1 Maxfield Avenue, Kingston 10 | Occupation - Tailor |
| MN20--CR0007 | Tom Strokes | Mary Brown | 16 Deanery Avenue, Kingston 10 | Occupation - Nurse |
| MN20--CR0009 | John Brown | Tom Brown | 27 Stony Hill Avenue, Kingston 19 | Occupation - Pastor |

## Value Books

The value book is written up by the accounts staff. Where monies are received into the court system, such as when prisoners pay their fines at the penal institutions, it is sent to the courthouse and must be entered and accurately accounted for in this book.

## Commitment Book

Section 288 of the Judicature (Parish Courts) Act indicates that a commitment is done for each person convicted in the Parish Court. The accused persons, who are sentenced to custodial sentences, must be taken to the particular facility with a 'committal'. The committal is a document that states the name of the accused, the information number(s), offence, and the custodial sentence of the Court. If there is a fine in the alternative this is also noted. The Clerk of the Courts must peruse this document carefully before signing to ensure that it accurately reflects the sentence of the Court. When signing these, it is best to have the court sheet and case file together, especially if there are ambiguities.

Where accused persons are fined and there is an alternative custodial sentence if they do not pay, the committal is still completed. If they were not granted time to pay and do not pay the fine on the day sentenced, then the accused persons must be taken to the facility along with the committal. Whenever the fine is paid, the accused is released forthwith. The correctional facility then forwards the payments to the court.

**Figure 20.6   Sample Commitment Book**

| Info # | Date | Name of Accused | Commitment Number | Offence | Name of Court | Date of Conviction | Sentence | In the Alternative | Court Officer Signature |
|---|---|---|---|---|---|---|---|---|---|
| | | | | | | | | | |
| | | | | | | | | | |
| | | | | | | | | | |

## Straight to Prison

Where an accused has been sentenced to a custodial sentence, a commitment document is completed and taken with the accused to the facility where s/he is to serve the sentence.

## Appeals Register

Appeals from the Parish Courts, per section 293 of the Judicature (Parish Courts) Act, lie in the Court of Appeal. A defendant must file the necessary notice within 14 days of the sentence being passed per section 294 of the Judicature (Parish Courts) Act. This notice must be duly served on the Clerk of the Courts per section 294 of the Judicature (Parish Courts) Act. The details regarding the particular case are noted in the appeals register. The particulars include the name of the accused, the name of the Judge of the Parish Court, the offence, the date the notice was filed, and the name of the court administrative officer receiving the document.

When a notice is received, the court's 'received stamp' is endorsed on all the copies. The defendant gets back some of the copies, and the other copies are kept on the case file. After the appeal has been heard, the outcome of the appeal is forwarded to the Parish Court as well. It is to be entered in the appeals register.

## Requests for Letters from Back Desk

As matters are disposed of in the courts, persons may make requests regarding these cases. Taking note of these requests as well as any information about how these requests were fulfilled is the proper administrative protocol.

# Chapter 21

# Assigned Police Officers in the Court

## Summary

Crucial to the effective administration of justice in the criminal court are the police personnel assigned to the courts. These police officers carry out a range of functions and roles.

Police officers, ranking from inspector to constable, from the Jamaica Constabulary Force are assigned court duties. Inspectors oversee the efficient running of policing duties in the court by assigning various tasks to their staff. Other ranks that are inside the Court include sergeants (who wear three chevrons on the sleeve); corporals (who wear two chevrons on the shoulder); and constables (who have none).

## Terms _____

> Search, Open, and Close Courts
>
> Swear Witnesses
>
> Duties Regarding Accused in Custody
>
> Police Record Book

_____

## Search, Open, and Close Courts

In court, duties for assigned police officers include searching courtrooms before and after court to ensure the safety of all users of the facilities. The court police officers also open the Court on every single morning that the Court sits in a specific ceremonial manner.[1] If there are more than one type of court sitting, then each has to be opened and closed. At the start and end of each court day, the Court is opened and closed by police officers with other specific ceremonious words.[2] The opening invites persons with business in the face of the Court to attend on the Court. The closing indicates that the Court's business has ended and that the Judge of the Parish Court is no longer sitting.

## Swearing of Witnesses

The swearing of witnesses is also done by the court's assigned police officers.[3] This is a crucial task that marks the beginning of evidence being given in a matter. The witness must recognize the solemnity of the

---

1. The court is opened: 'Oyez, Oyez! All manner of persons having anything to do or so at this Her Majesty's Parish Court and Lay Magistrate Court (insert as necessary) to be held here this day (insert date) before (Her/His) Honour (insert name), Judge of the Parish Court for the parish of (insert parish) let them draw near and give their attendance and they shall be heard. Oyez! Oyez! God save the Queen.'
2. The court is closed: 'This Court now stands adjourned until (insert date).'
3. Witnesses are sworn as follows: 'I swear by Almighty God that the evidence that I shall give to this Court, shall be the truth, the whole truth and nothing but the truth.'

occasion and the necessity to be honest. Witnesses, therefore, can also be affirmed.[4] The effect is the same and persons can tell the court their preference.

Interpreters must also take an oath to faithfully interpret for the Court's proceedings.[5]

## Duty Regarding Accused in Custody

Where accused persons are in custody, it is the duty of court-assigned officers to take them into the courtroom from the holding area where they are kept. The accused persons are brought in with their record cards (colloquially called the prisoner card) and all relevant details are recorded thereon by the police officers, such as court orders for medical treatment, the next court dates, and bail offers.

## Police Record Book

The court-assigned officers also have their record book in the courtroom. They insert all the necessary details of all the matters therein so that there is a record of what occurred regarding the accused persons on the specific date.

Court-assigned officers should have a list of the matters that are before the Court for the day's proceedings and should use this list to call the names of accused persons who are on bail as well as relevant witnesses.

When matters have started, the court-assigned officers have additional duties. They stand guard over the accused in the dock. They show items to persons at the request of the Clerk of the Courts or the Judge of the Parish Court, such as exhibits and potential exhibits.

As trial/hearing matters progress, the court-assigned officers prepare the antecedents or criminal record history of accused persons and liaise with their colleagues in the fingerprint and records section. Relevant information is taken from the accused such as his fingerprints (where ordered by the Judge of the Parish Court for certain offences and automatically for other offences). At the end of the matter, if the accused is found guilty or pleads guilty, the antecedent report is generated. It is then presented to the Judge of the Parish Court to aid in the sentencing phase as well as to the defence counsel to assist in plea in mitigation.

---

4. Witnesses are affirmed as follows: 'I (insert name) do solemnly, sincerely, truly declare and affirm that the evidence which I shall give to this Court shall be the truth, the whole truth and nothing but the truth.'
5. Where interpreters are utilized in a case, the oath is as follows: 'I swear by Almighty God that I will well and faithfully interpret any answers made/given from the (insert language) to the (insert language) of all such matters and things as shall be required of me according to the best of my skill and understanding.' See *Archbold* 2001 edition, 316.

# Chapter 22

# Tips for the Clerk of the Courts

## Summary

The Clerk of the Courts receives notebooks to record evidence. It is useful to number the pages in this book to find easily a trial, even after time has passed, by using a table of content or marked tabs. Start each trial on a new page. At the top, write the name of the accused, the representation, the offences, the sections of the Act that is allegedly contravened, the name of the Judge of the Parish Court, and the date that the matter starts. There are several issues to contend with as a matter is heard in the courtroom, and the Clerk must be prepared.

## Terms

Trials

Witnesses

Exhibits

Applications during Examination in Chief

Discussions with Defence

Statements

Particular Witnesses

Questions by the Parish Court Judge

Cross Examination

Re-examination

Closings the Crown's Case

No Case Submission by the Defence

Hearings

Closings

Hearings under the Unlawful Possession of Property Act

## Trials

The Clerk should not be distracted while taking evidence in any type of matter. Many things are happening in court, often all at once, and sometimes persons may seek information as the Clerk is on his feet. It is easy to lose focus, but it is also disrespectful to the Court and the witness to do so. To prevent this, the Clerk should simply indicate to them by a gesture to write a note or return. As the matter starts, the Clerk should already have his notebook, with the initial notations ready to start.

**Figure 22.1   Sample Heading for Each Trial**

*Regina v John Doe*

**Offence: Possession of ganja contrary to section 7c of the Dangerous Drugs Act**

**Judge of the Parish Court: Justicia Justice**

**Date: January 2, 20–**

**Defence Attorney: Tim Counsels, Q.C.**

**Plea: Not guilty**

## Witnesses

It is imperative that witnesses have refreshed their memories from their statements given previously and are made aware of the general procedure. Firstly, they swear or affirm, and the accused remains in the dock. The Clerk will ask questions; the Parish Court Judge can ask questions at any time; and the defence attorney or the accused if unrepresented asks questions. Only a witness who is going in the witness box should be in the court. All other witnesses, for the Crown and defence, in the case, should be outside. This is where a witness list is useful. Simply call the names of the persons expected to be in court or say, 'Anyone who is present to give evidence in the matter of *Regina v John Doe* is asked to stay outside until his or her name is called.'

As witnesses are taken, note should be made of their names and whether they are sworn, affirmed, or gave true answers. Whether it is examination in chief or cross-examination should also be noted and special care taken to accurately record dates, names, and other critical areas on which the case rests.

When a Clerk completes taking the evidence of a witness who has been cross-examined, the Court should be asked if the witness can be released. If an application has been made to recall the witness or if the defence makes the request, the Court may request the witness's return on a subsequent date.

**Figure 22.2   Sample Notation for Each Witness**

| | |
|---|---|
| | **Examination in Chief** |
| Attorney: | Jon Black present |
| Sworn: | Tom Strokes |
| Evidence in chief: | I saw John Brown hit Mark Hall in the head with a brick, I ran to help Mark. John ran away |
| Clerk: | Nothing more, Your Honour. Your witness |
| Cross-examination by Mr Black: | Mark cut at John with a knife, didn't he? |
| Witness: | No, I didn't see Mark take up a knife and cut at John Brown |
| Question by Parish Court Judge: | Do you live in the same yard as John? |
| Witness: | No Ma'am. I live next door and there is a low zinc fence separating the yards them. |
| Question by Parish Court Judge: | Anything from that Mr Black? |
| Defence Attorney Mr Black: | Nothing Your Honour. |
| Cross-examination: | Nothing further Your Honour. |
| Clerk: | Can the witness be released Your Honour? |
| Parish Court Judge: | Yes |
| Clerk: | Sir you can come down and you can leave if you want to do so or sit in the courtroom. |
| Witness released | |

## Exhibits

As the Clerk of the Courts takes evidence, an exhibit list should also be recorded. It need not be elaborate. It should be written in a conspicuous place in the file, such as on the number one information, on the indictment, or a blank page inserted in the case file. The exhibits should also be noted in the Clerk's notebook as they are admitted. This exhibit list is useful if for some reason several Clerks of the Courts take evidence in the matter. A list of the exhibits expected to be admitted and through whom is useful (see chapter on file preparation). The Clerk of the Courts must ensure that potential exhibits are in court on the day needed. If they are not, the Court and the Defence must be advised.

Figure 22.3   Sample Exhibit List

| Number | Description |
| --- | --- |
| Exhibit 1 | 10 transparent bags with vegetable matter resembling ganja (VMRG) |
| Exhibit 2 | 2 original cheques in name John Doe |
| Exhibit 3 | |

The Court cannot view or examine an item, or consider it a part of the case, unless it is properly tendered into evidence.

## Applications during Examination in Chief

As the Clerk of the Courts takes the examination in chief, s/he must remember relevant applications to be made to the Court. Applications are varied and include application to tender and admit items as exhibits, requests for the Court to go to a locus, requests to view a potential exhibit, and the like. The appropriate foundation for each application must be laid so that the Court has a basis on which to make its decision. If a witness needs to be recalled, an application to do so should be made either at the beginning or at the end of that person's evidence.

It is useful to record the application and the Court's ruling on it.

If there are objections and applications by the defence, these should also be noted. Writing such objections and applications is especially useful so that the Clerk can address the concern at a later date if necessary. The Clerk should also write down his/her own response to what defence counsel indicated.

Anything that will affect a matter should be indicated by the Clerk in open court. This will allow the Court to note it and for the defence to state its position. Common examples of issues that may affect a matter include a potential exhibit not being in court, a statement being missing from a file, or an original document is unavailable, and so on.

As evidence proceeds, if there is a need for distances and heights, it is useful to agree them with the defence. If it is not crucial to the Crown's case, estimates are good enough.

The Clerk of the Courts must always bear in mind the theory of the case. This requires getting out the evidence to support the allegations and proving the offences under the statute. The Clerk should mark the relevant sections of evidence related to responding to no case submissions, conducting cross examinations and in closing arguments.

## Discussions with the Defence

It is useful for the Clerk of the Courts to enquire from the defence beforehand if there are potential exhibits or issues to which they might object in the course of taking the evidence. Depending on the answer, a Clerk will know what to lead on as the evidence is taken. The proper foundations must still be laid and the Court advised that the prosecution and the defence have agreed on a particular area as it not being objected. The Evidence Act now provides for several aspects where the prosecution and the defence can agree on various areas.

## Statements

Many statements of witnesses are still handwritten by police officers, who may or may not be involved in the case. The originals of these statements, not copies, should be on hand. If the statements are typed, the Clerk of the Courts must check that they are originally signed and dated, and also ascertain if there was ever a handwritten statement. The defence often asks for the original statement in court to show to witnesses. Therefore, it is critical to know if such original statements exist.

## Particular Witnesses

**Police officers:** These officers swear or affirm themselves (without the court police officer's assistance) when giving evidence. They are required to know the oath or affirmation and so are expected to recite it at the beginning of their testimony. Officers, especially if they are formal witnesses, usually give their evidence with the need for only minimum questions being asked.

When questioning police officers in court, they often need only be lead to the date and they give a narrative of what happened and what they did in the matter. Of course, if it is a particularly complex or involved matter, it is appropriate and expected that the Clerk will ask the relevant questions to ensure that the prosecution's case is clear. Interjections can be made at the appropriate time(s) to tender items as necessary or seek clarifications.

**Expert witnesses:** Formal witnesses such as doctors, accountants, auditors, forensic analysts, and others may need to bring their notebooks and findings as regards the matter on trial, and they should be made aware of this beforehand. If there are formal documents on file from such reports, the foundation can be laid to show that the document is contemporaneous with what they did and that as authors of these documents they have the authority to inform the Court from the documents. The Evidence Act provides that such witnesses' reports can be admitted without their attending on the court to be examined if the necessary provisions are followed.

## Questions by the Judge of the Parish Court

If the Judge of the Parish Court questions the witnesses, the Clerk should record the exchange as it is sometimes in these exchanges that interesting statements are elicited that can be used in arguments or otherwise bolster the prosecution's case.

## Cross-examination

Record the cross-examination of witnesses in a different ink colour, to distinguish it from chief. Listen carefully to the questions to ensure that the inadmissible or the objectionable is not asked. Be prepared to quickly deal with these. All objections and any other submission should be recorded by the Judge.

Counsel should remain alert and ensure that the evidence given so far is not misquoted or misrepresented and the trial's testimony record is protected.

Items that have not been properly tendered in evidence should not be shown to witnesses unless it is under the *Peter Blake* principle (*R v Peter Blake* (1977) 16 JLR 61). Be alert to ensure, however, that this principle is not extended beyond its natural limits.

Ensure that the defence does not misquote the evidence given so far. This means the Clerk must know the evidence given, especially where the trial has been over a period of time and must protect witness(es) and ensure that the case is fair as much as possible by being alert throughout.

Object to items being shown to witnesses that are not in evidence, unless it is under the *Peter Blake* principle.

## Re-examination

As a witness is cross-examined, the Clerk should check for areas where re-examination might be necessary. These can be noted using slips of paper, highlighters, asterisks, and the like and allows for re-examination as soon as the cross-examination is completed.

It is crucial to note any question that the Parish Court Judge asks during examination in chief, cross-examination, or re-examination. Sometimes there are clues as to the legal issues the Court might be grappling with as the evidence unfolds. Sometimes it means that the elements of the offence are still unclear. It is the duty of the Clerk of the Courts to present the evidence that grounds the offence, and also be alert to the questions asked and those not asked by the defence as the matter proceeds for the same reasons of ensuring that the evidence grounds the offence. So, for example, if identification is an issue in a case, the Clerk should consider if all of the *Turnbull* principles have been met on the evidence and bring out that identification evidence accordingly through the witnesses.

## Closing the Crown's Case

When the Crown closes its case, the Clerk of the Courts usually says: 'That is the case for the Crown' or 'That is the case for the prosecution.' The case should be closed only after all the relevant evidence has been taken, all the witnesses have been tendered for cross-examination, and all relevant exhibits admitted into evidence.

Closing the case is a crucial juncture as it is here that the defence may make a no case submission, if appropriate, and so it would be a procedural error for the prosecution to seek to reopen the case after the defence has made its decision based on the evidence to date. Therefore, it is critical that the Clerk of the Courts has put everything relevant into evidence and that the  ingredients that are necessary to prove the offence(s) have been made out on the Crown's case. In the event that the prosecution must re-open the Crown's case, any objection by the defence or queries by the sitting Judge can be properly dealt with in the application to re-open.

## No Case Submission (NCS) by Defence

As the defence makes it NCS, note that it is usually one or both limbs of *R v Galbraith* [1981] 1 WLR 1039. However, sometimes the defence's NCS focuses on something else. The Clerk should focus on what those areas in the NCS are. Some common areas include a lacuna in the Crown's case, identification errors, errors in technical areas such as warrants, or alleged abuses of power.

In response to an NCS, the Clerk of the Courts cannot say that the prosecution witnesses are witnesses of truth. That would mean that the Court should believe the prosecution over the defence, effectively removing the burden the prosecution bears to prove their case beyond reasonable doubt. Instead, the Clerk should indicate that the prosecution witnesses have not been discredited to the point where the jury mind of the Judge could not reach a guilty verdict. As the Judge of the Parish Court sits alone, at this stage, his role is the judge of the law regarding a no case submission and not as the judge of the facts.

## Part-heard Matters

When a matter begins, whether it is a trial, hearing, or committal proceedings, if it is not concluded on the same day, it becomes 'part heard'. This is so for all subsequent occasions that it is dealt with until it is disposed of in the Court. When a matter is part-heard, a notation should be made on the case file of what happened and what is to happen on the next court date on the case file.

**Figure 22.4   Sample Notation When a Trial is Part-heard**

> PH: January 12, 20–
>
> **Evidence in chief of Tom Strokes to continue – Put in potential exhibits (cheques, money)**

## Closings

At this stage, the Clerk of the Courts can ask that the Crown's witnesses be accepted as witnesses as truth.

Significant extracts of the evidence can be used to bolster the case theory, ground the offences, and indicate the inferences the Court is being asked to draw.

**Figure 22.5   Sample Closing by Prosecution**

> *"The Court will remember that that Sergeant Tom Strokes said he searched only the stall of the accused. Yet, the accused stated in his evidence that it was the garbage bin that was some yards away, which he admitted in cross-examination, which was searched. The Court would, therefore, have to believe that there was something that alerted the officer to the garbage bin. Yet, the accused told us of nothing and, indeed, there is no such thing on the Crown's case. Therefore, the Crown submits that this should be rejected and instead urges that the Court should believe that exhibit one, the twenty one pounds of vegetable resembling ganja, and proven to be marijuana by exhibit one, the forensic certificate of Sergeant Roll, was found on the stall of the accused."*

## Hearings under the Unlawful Possession of Property Act

A hearing is not a trial. Therefore, there is no plea by the defendant. The prosecution's witnesses who go into the witness box are sworn or affirmed and give their evidence. Any exhibits that are to be tendered are so tendered. The prosecution then closes its case.

Sometimes, the prosecution is invited to submit on where the 'suspicion' in the case arises. The Judge of the Parish Court, at that point, indicates if the accused should account. If the accused is called on to so account, this means that there is a prima facie case.

It is at this juncture that the order is signed as follows by the Judge of the Parish Court.

> **'Let the accused account to my satisfaction by what lawful means he came to be in possession of Exhibit 1 – a cellular phone.'**

Mary Lee

**Corporate Area Parish Court Judge (Criminal Division)**

The accused at that point has the usual three options and can choose to exercise the one which he so desires.

If the account satisfies the Court, the Judge of the Parish Court indicates that the accused can go.

'**The *accused having satisfied me by what lawful means he has come into possession of Exhibit 1 – a cellular phone, he is here*by discharged**.'

Mary Lee

**Corporate Area Parish Court Judge (Criminal Division)**

If the account is not satisfactory, the Judge of the Parish Court signs the following order.

'***The accused not having account to my satisfaction by what lawful means he came into possession of exhibit 1 – a cellular phone, he is hereby found guilty.***'

Mary Lee

**Corporate Area Parish Court Judge (Criminal Division)**

# Chapter 23

# Accused Persons

## Summary

Accused persons come before the Court by way of arrest or summons as noted earlier. This is important to remember as it can have implications for a variety of issues.

## Terms

Where is the Accused?

Absence of the Accused from Trial

Antecedents

Bail

Certificates

Defendant Not Appearing

Case and Cross Case

Fingerprint

Pleas

Photographing Accused

Prisoner Cards

Social Enquiry Reports

Witnesses

Writs

Medical Examinations

Death of the Accused

## Where is the Accused?

At the first mention of the matter, if the accused was arrested, s/he may still be in custody and so the relevant checks should be made. The Clerk of the Courts should first, check the file for any bail bonds. If there are none, it is quite likely that the accused is still in custody. The Court and the court police officers should be advised of this and the holding area checked to determine if the accused has been brought for the matter.

For persons who are on bail, their bail would have been extended until this current date. On the date in question, unless something arises, the person's bail will usually be extended (even if the matter begins on this date). This will happen until the matter is disposed of in the court. Sometimes, the Court remands the accused in custody once the matter begins or once verdict is passed pending sentence. The correct notation should be made on the case file.

If the accused remains in custody over a period, s/he will be brought to court, on each occasion, by the relevant police officers from the holding facility.

## Absence of Accused from the Trial

Trials can continue where an accused has deliberately absented himself from his trial.[1] However, where there is some mitigating factor, such as illness, or the accused has not been brought from a facility, the Judge of the Parish Court will order that the accused attend on a subsequent day or is to be brought by the relevant police officers. A writ is often issued in the latter circumstance.

## Antecedents

The antecedents are also known as the criminal record. The Court often asks for the results of a criminal records investigation of the accused when an accused has pleaded guilty or when an accused is found guilty at the end of a trial or hearing.

The antecedents are useful in guiding the Court in the current sentencing of the accused. These can also form excellent aides in mitigation for the defendant. The Clerk of the Courts, having received the copies of the antecedents, should provide a copy to the defence counsel if the accused is represented. The unrepresented accused should also receive a copy. If there are no convictions noted on the antecedents for the accused, it means that the accused has no formal criminal past that the Criminal Records Office can find. If there are convictions noted, that information is detailed separately and that document is handed to the Judge of the Parish Court for perusal as well. The defence attorney sees the conviction document after the Judge of the Parish Court and should request that no spent convictions or convictions when the accused was a minor, be considered by the Court.

---

1.    This is per common law.

**Figure 23.1   Sample Antecedents Report**

---

### ANTECEDENTS REPORT OF   JOE DOE   INDICTED IN THE ST ANN PARISH COURT ON A CHARGE OF ROBBERY WITH AGGRAVATION

---

| | |
|---|---|
| Place & Date of Birth: | The accused who is called "Stapler" was born on the 1st day of December 19– at the Vince Hospital. He is the 3rd of 10 children for his mother. |
| Mother: | Miss Jane Pritt of a USA address. |
| Father: | Mr Dan Doe, taxi operator also residing in the United States. |
| Education: | The accused grew up with his mother in Babylon, St Catherine. He started his early childhood education at Zebidian Basic School in Kingston until age 12.  Accused moved to Comforters Primary School. This same year, he was successful in the Common Entrance Examination and went to Ray Hall High School. He continued at this school until he did his CXC Examinations where he was successful in Mathematics and Electrical Installation. He is literate. |
| Employment: | After leaving school he was employed at the Quickstop Distributors Limited as a clerk earning about $600 weekly. He was later employed to Bull Dog Security as a security guard earning about $12,000.00 per fortnight. He was so employed to the time of his arrest. |
| Marital Status: | Accused is single and has a 13-year-old son dependent upon him for support. |
| Religion: | The accused sometimes worship at the Praise The Lord Evangelical Centre at Blueberry Road, Portmore, St Catherine. |
| Previous Conviction: | Accused has no previous conviction recorded against him. |
| Source of Information: | Information contained in this report was obtained from the accused himself, citizens of his community and police records. |

## Bail

An accused person, once bailed, is obligated to attend court on each and every date until the matter is disposed of. The practice is that where an accused is absent, his counsel will indicate the reason to the Court, with the requisite supporting evidence if necessary (such as a doctor's certificate stating the person is unwell for a specific period). Such certificates should be placed on the case file and endorsed accordingly with the information received. If the accused is unrepresented, the surety or someone else should come with the information of his status. The particulars of such persons should also be endorsed on the case file.

Where an accused has been offered bail, but has not taken it up, same bail offer (SBO) should be endorsed on the case file on each occasion that the matter comes before the court. This should be indicated to the Court, especially if it is before a Judge of the Parish Court who did not offer the accused bail. The SBO is to be endorsed on the accused's prisoner card.

An accused person can be on bail in the matter before one court, but may be remanded in custody (RIC or RC) in another court. This should be clearly written on the case file to show that bail is extended in the instant matter, but the accused is remanded in custody on another matter.

The notation would then be as follows – 'BE in inst, RIC on another matter.'

Sometimes there are requests for variation of bail conditions. When granted, the variations are to be endorsed on the case file. The Judge of the Parish Court may also sign the information regarding the variation. The variation may sometimes be written on a new bail bond, and the accused and surety are to receive a copy. One copy is kept on the case file.

## Certificates

There are two types of certificates regarding the outcome of a trial (section 280(3) of the Judicature (Parish Courts) Act). The first is a certificate of conviction which is prepared and placed on a defendant's case file when a defendant has been found guilty of an offence. This certificate need not be done as a matter of course, but can be done on request.

The other certificate issued is a certificate of acquittal which is prepared when a defendant has been found not guilty. The certificate is often prepared as a matter of course as it may be necessary to retrieve property, reinstate job positions, and collect salaries that might have been in abeyance.

Multiple copies of the certificate should be prepared and each signed and sealed by the Clerk of the Courts or the deputy Clerk of the Courts. Importantly, these certificates are only prepared if the matter is tried and ends naturally or formally in a verdict. Sometimes a matter ends before a verdict is handed down such as when it adjourned *sine die* or no order is made. For such circumstances, letters regarding the case are prepared as necessary or as requested by the complainant, accused, or other interested parties.

## Defendant Not Appearing (DNA)

Where an accused is bailed but fails to attend court, the Court may order a bench warrant for his or her arrest. New files should be checked for bonds to ensure the date that the accused is to attend is actually the date the matter is before the Court. Check if the court sheet for the last court date (LCD) and/or whether the case file states that bail was extended until that date. The Court may also order that the bench warrant be stayed until a future date. However, if the warrant is to proceed immediately, the bail bonds will also be ordered to be escheated. As such, the surety must pay the amount which was pledged. The Judge of the Parish Court then signs the warrant and the proceedings are immediately in effect.

**Figure 23.2   Sample Bench Warrant**

# BENCH WARRANT

JAMAICA S.S.                    }

    Parish of                    }


To the Constables of ...... Kingston 20 ...... and to all other Her Majesty's Peace Officers with the parish of ...... Kingston ...................... and to every one of them whom it may concern. These are to will and require, and in Her Majesty's name to charge and command you upon sight hereof, to bring before me, one of Her Majesty's Parish Court Judges for the parish aforesaid at the Parish Court now holden at Corporate Area Parish Court (Criminal Division) in the Corporate Area the body of ...... John Doe ...... who stands indicted before me at this same Court for ...... Unlawful Wounding ...... if the Court be then and there sitting, or if not, before me or some other of Her Majesty's Justices of the Peace of the  same parish, to find sufficient sureties for his personal appearance at this Court to answer the said indictment, and all such other matters as on Her Majesty's behalf shall be objected,  and if he cannot be taken during this present Court, that then as soon after he shall be taken, you bring or cause him to be brought before me or some other of Her Majesty's Justices of the Peace of the said parish, to find sufficient sureties that is to say one surety in $100,000 Jamaican Dollars, for his personal appearance, at the next sitting of the Parish Court for the said parish, to answer as aforesaid, and further to be dealt with according to Law.


Hereof you are not to fail at your peril.


Dated in open Court at the Court House at aforesaid, this 3rd day of October in the year 20--


*Tom Strokes*
......................

Judge of the Parish Court

Where an accused is summoned to attend court and fails to attend, checks should be made that the summons to him was served personally or inmately.. This is done by checking the case file for returns of the summons. If there is none, then it would not be known if the accused received the summons. If there are returns, ensure that the court date is correct and the mode of service (whether personally or inmately) is endorsed on the back. If it was served personally, then the accused should be present. If it was served inmately (on someone at his place of abode to give it to accused), then the accused might not have received it. The position should be indicated to the Parish Court Judge. If a summons was served personally, but the accused did not attend court, then the Judge can order a warrant in disobedience of the summons. The execution of that warrant can be stayed until a future date or it can proceed immediately.

## Case and Cross Case

This is a situation where at least two persons are both the accused and complainants in a matter arising out of the same incident. Assault cases are the most common examples of case and cross case. A Clerk of the Courts must decide which is first in time and, therefore, which matter to begin with on the appropriate day.

## Fingerprint

There are many fingerprintable offences under the Fingerprint Act. Where the Court orders an accused's fingerprints be taken, the endorsement is to be made on the file. A Parish Court Judge will sign the order to take an accused's fingerprint and, the Clerk of the Courts should ensure that the date that the order is made is endorsed on the file. The fingerprint will then be taken by the assigned police officers.

Section 4 of the Fingerprint Act details that the fingerprint and photograph of anyone convicted of an offence specified in the First or Second Schedule should be recorded in the space provided on the fingerprint form.

Notably, per section 4A, if such a fingerprinted and photographed person is subsequently acquitted of the charge, the fingerprint form and photograph should be destroyed within three months from the date of acquittal. This is, however, subject to other provisions in the same Act. The person and counsel (if any) are to be apprised prior to such destruction.

## Pleas

Where an accused pleads guilty to a charge, the Court may decide to sentence the person immediately or subsequently. There may be a variety of reasons why the Court would consider making a decision about when to sentence an offender. These include an application by the attorney on the record, a need for social enquiry reports, or antecedents and the like. If there are multiple offences, the Clerk must examine the case file to ascertain if there are any offences on which it might be justified to offer no evidence. Situations in which this might be justified include if the Crown would be unable to proceed on the offence.

When an accused pleads not guilty, s/he is taking issue with the Crown's case and so will have his right to a trial. The accused can decide if s/he will represent himself at trial or secure the services of an attorney. The accused may request time from the Court to settle this representation.

## Photographs of Accused Persons

Section 33 of the Criminal Justice (Administration) Act prohibits the taking of photographs of persons who are before the court for any offence.

## Prisoner Card

Where an accused is in custody, there is a card for each offence that s/he may have before the courts. These cards are endorsed with the information about the matter on each occasion that it is before the court. Generally, the next court date should be endorsed. Specific examples of notations include if the accused has a bail offer or if the Judge of the Parish Court has ordered specific medical treatment of any kind. The card travels with the accused through the courts until the matter is disposed of.

## Social Enquiry Report (SER)

Where an accused pleads guilty or is found guilty, an SER may be ordered by the Judge of the Parish Court who will then instruct the probation officer assigned to the matter to carry out investigations in the community of the accused, speak to the accused himself, any complainants, victims, as well as family members, and other persons as necessary and submit a formal report to the Court on the sentencing date. However, if there is no probation officer present in court at the time of this instruction, then the Clerk of the Courts relays the Court's request afterwards for the SER.

## Witnesses

An unrepresented accused may have witnesses in a matter. The Parish Court Judge, after hearing the statement of the defence or otherwise, may form the view that there are persons whose evidence might be material to the accused's case. Pursuant to section 280 of the Judicature (Parish Courts) Act, the Judge may ask the accused if s/he wants any or all of such witnesses summoned. The accused person may also apply to the Judge to have witnesses summoned. The Judge should then adjourn the trial, taking all necessary steps, either by remanding the accused person, or by granting him or her bail in accordance with the Bail Act. To procure the witness(es), the Judge should take the same steps as would be taken to ensure witnesses for the prosecution attend court.

## Writs

If an accused who is in custody is not brought before the Court, a writ can be issued. This writ instructs the keeper of the gaol, where the accused is being held, to ensure that on the date stipulated in the writ the accused is brought before the Court. The writ is signed by the Judge of the Parish Court. The Judge of the Parish Court who ordered the writ does not have to be the same one who signs it. All that is required is that the Judge of the Parish Court has seen the specific order in the court sheet.

## Medical Examinations

Depending on the circumstances, the Judge of the Parish Court may order a medical examination of the accused. This examination can be done by a psychiatrist or a medical doctor. The report of the practitioner is submitted to the Court. In some instances, a prisoner medical journal is completed by the doctor and is brought to court with the findings of the examination.

## Death of Accused

If an accused dies while a matter is before the court, there is a procedure to follow. There must be formal evidence of his death presented to the satisfaction of the Judge of the Parish Court. In *Archbold 41st edition*, 192, notes 3–51, it is noted that formal evidence of the death of an accused should be given.

Figure 23.3    Sample Social Enquiry Report

**DEPARTMENT OF CORRECTIONAL SERVICES**
**COMMUNITY SERVICES**
**SOCIAL ENQUIRY REPORT**

**TO THE:**    St. Mary Parish Court              **ON:** APRIL 25, 20--

**BEFORE:**    His Hon. Mr. John Doe

---

**SURNAME:** Robe                    **CHRISTIAN NAME:** Jane

**ADDRESS:**    65 Reel Road, Kingston 22

**AGE:** 30          **D.O.B.:** 23/02/1990          **RELIGION:**    Unattached

**OFFENCE:**  Unlawful Wounding

**PREVIOUS:**  None Ascertained during Investigation

---

| FAMILY MEMBERS | HOW RELATED | AGE | ADDRESS | EMPLOYMENT |
|---|---|---|---|---|
| Cherry Plumber | Mother | 50 | 65 Reel Road, Kingston 22 | Domestic Helper |
| Lychee Robe | Father | 53 | United Kingdom | Unknown |
| Jane Robe | Subject | of | Report | |
| Ken Plumber | M/Brother | 25 | 65 Reel Road, Kingston 22 | Sales Representative |
| Guavina Plumber | M/Sister | 21 | 65 Reel Road, Kingston 22 | Vendor |
| Icy Minto | M/Aunt | 70 | 65 Reel Road, Kingston 22 | Retired |
| Raheemi Flamming | Daughter | 2 | 65 Reel Road, Kingston 22 | Infant |

## CIRCUMSTANCES OF OFFENCE

Reports are that Jane Robe used a pot to hit Cornio Flamming on his head and a knife to cut him several times all over his body during an altercation.  She was subsequently arrested and charged for the offence preferred against her. On appearing before the court, she pleaded guilty.

## HOME

Ms Robe lives at 65 Reel Road, Kingston 22, which is an informal settlement with her extended family. She occupies one room. Kitchen and bathroom facilities are detached. Basic amenities are attached to the premises.

## EDUCATION

Ms Robe stated that she attended the Dinnesh Primary and Dinnesh High School. She informed that she was suspended on two occasions because of fights. In 2005, she left the latter institution in Grade Eleven.

## EMPLOYMENT

After leaving school, she worked temporarily as a labourer at Sisco Trading Company. She spent two years with the company before she was made redundant. Her weekly wage was Two Hundred Dollars ($200.00). At the time of her arrest, she was employed as a cosmetologist at Cute Cut Salon at 7 Cute Cut Street, Kingston. Her weekly wage is Five Hundred ($500.00).

## HEALTH

She reportedly enjoyed satisfactory mental and physical health. There is no known family member who suffer from any mental illness.

## EARLY LIFE AND FAMILY BACKGROUND

Cherry Plumber, the mother of Jane Robe, informed that a visiting relationship between herself and Lychee Robe produced one child. That relationship ended five months after she gave birth to Jane. She further stated that her daughter's father migrated to the United Kingston, and she had total responsibility for her.

Ms Plumber revealed that Jane Robe knew her father for the first time when she was ten years old. He began to give financial support through his mother who also helps in giving the necessary guidance. Additional support, she said, was forthcoming from subject's maternal relatives, including Sky June-Plumber, the maternal grandmother who insisted that she attended church regularly up to age fifteen years. Ms Plumber further revealed that her common-law husband, Tele Phipps played the role of a father to her daughter and they shared a cordial relationship.

Ms Plumber stated that her daughter was obedient to her; however, she was summoned to her school on two occasions when she was involved in fights. She informed that in recent times her daughter left her premises and entered a visiting relationship with Cornio Flamming. The relationship has produced one child, Raheemi Flamming, who is now two years old.

## INTERVIEW AND PERSONALITY APPRAISAL

Jane Robe was co-operative and emotional when she related her version of what caused the incident. She stated that she and the complainant were in an intimate relationship for five years which produced one child, who is now two years old. She stated that previously when she left for work, the complainant would always encourage her to return as soon as possible.

On the day of the incident, the complainant asked her the actual time she would return. While she was at work, she reflected on the question the complainant asked and, as a result, decided to return home early. Upon her arrival at the complainant's home, she looked through his bedroom window and saw him in an intimate position on her bed with a young woman. She became angry and entered the room and a tussle developed between the complainant and herself. She punched him several times in the face, hit him with a pot, and used a knife to cut him all over his body. She has expressed remorse.

## INTERVIEW WITH COMPLAINANT (CORN FLAKES)

Mr Flamming stated he and Ms Robe had numerous quarrels during the years that they shared an intimate relationship. These arguments he said resulted from jealousy on her part. He said that she has never been physically abusive to him before, and he was very surprised at her behaviour.

He stated that on the day of the incident a young woman with whom he had grown up, visited his house and took up his cigarette and, as a result, a tussle ensued and they landed on the bed. It was at that point that the defendant approached him and became violent. He said that she used a pot and hit him twice on the head, used a bottle to hit him in his face, and proceeded to cut him with a knife. He spent one week at the Kingston Public Hospital and received two (2) stitches. It cost him One Thousand Dollars ($1,000.00) to see the ophthalmologist. Mr Flamming is asking for reimbursement of his medical expenses and compensation for his pain and suffering.

## COMMUNITY REPORT

Residents in the vicinity of 65 Reel Road, Kingston 22 informed that Jane is not a violent individual. They claim that she is very talkative but a hardworking individual. They further stated that Ms Robe reacted violently because of infidelity on the part of the complainant. They disagreed with her actions but are asking for leniency on her behalf.

## ASSESSMENT AND RECOMMENDATION

Ms Robe has pleaded guilty to the offence of unlawful wounding. Although her growth and development lacked the touch of her biological father, her extended family tried to steer her along a socially acceptable path. Generally, infidelity in our culture is frowned upon. This seemed to be the case which confronted Ms Robe, who acted without considering the consequences.

Community members have spoken positively about her behaviour prior to the committal of the incident and are asking for leniency on her behalf. Although the parties are young, they are parents and, at this stage, Ms Robe's development, given her upbringing and usual temperament, should have caused her to act in a more mature manner. It seemed that she was overcome by her emotion and, as a result, has now committed a very serious act. She now must face the consequence of her actions.

Ms Robe does not appear to be beyond redemption and with some social intervention can be diverted to learn to control her emotions and use non-violent methods to resolve problems.

The decision is however left to the court to dispose of this matter as it sees fit.

**Date of Report**: April 25, 20--

.................................

Roy Dogood
Probation Aftercare Officer
Corporate Area

.................................

May Gotting (Mrs.)
Senior Probation Aftercare Officer
Corporate Area

Usually, it is the investigating officer in the particular case, who would have become familiar with the accused by virtue of the case being before the Court, who identifies the accused's dead body, either at the morgue or at the deceased's funeral. The police officer should then give evidence of the accused's death in open court. The death certificate, burial order, or post-mortem of the now deceased accused is also to be submitted to the Court. After all of this has been done to the satisfaction of the Judge of the Parish Court, the court sheet is endorsed as follows:

> Sergeant Xavier Yelch, having given evidence that on (insert date) he identified the body of (insert accused name) in the (insert place where body was viewed) as being one and the same of the man he arrested on (insert date) on the charge of (insert charge). It is, therefore, ordered that the records be endorsed as aforesaid and declared now of no legal effect and that the file be closed unless and until the Court, on cause being shown otherwise orders.

The Clerk of the Courts can also copy this order onto the number one information to be signed by the Judge of the Parish Court. Obviously, the manner and method of proof is adjusted as the circumstances dictate, but death must be satisfactorily established regardless.

# Chapter 24

# Defence Counsel in Court

## Summary

Advice is offered throughout this book on the duties of the defence counsel. However, this chapter touches and concerns a few specific areas that are generally encountered in the Parish Court by defence counsel.

## Terms _____

> Amicus
>
> Defence Attorney in Court
>
> Fiats
>
> Watching Proceedings
>
> Habeas Corpus Applications
>
> _____

## Amicus

As a duty to the Court, it is not unusual for any defence counsel present to rise and indicate that s/he is appearing *amicus*. A defence counsel appears amicus when acting as a friend of the Court, and in that capacity, will either take instructions from an accused or seek to explain a particular point to an accused. The defence counsel may sometimes offer to appear amicus at sentencings, where an accused pleads guilty and the like.

## Defence Attorney in Court

Where there is more than one defence attorney present in court, the seniority rule operates. The most senior attorney's cases are called up before those of more junior counsel. The attorneys themselves make the decision about who is senior, Queen's Counsel being the most senior counsel followed by the attorneys according to their number of years at the bar. Of course, a Parish Court Judge may deal with matters on the court list in whatever order s/he desires, regardless of defence counsel seniority.

If a defence attorney is seeking an adjournment, ensure that the case file reflects this. When a defence attorney is absent, this is to be noted on the case file. Where defence attorney has communicated with the court (e.g. through letter, telephone, or another attorney) about absences and the like, these too should be indicated to the Court. The Clerk of the Courts does not hold for the defence counsel, but if s/he has made a particular indication through some communication channel, the Court needs to be aware of it so that it can make a proper determination about a matter.

## Fiat

The Director of Public Prosecutions can, with discretion, confer a *fiat* on any attorney to associate with the prosecution as regards a matter in the Courts.

## Watching Proceedings

Sometimes, an attorney-at-law has an interest in a case that is before the court and has been retained either by a complainant, family of a victim, or possibly even a third party. This attorney will usually indicate his/her position to the Court and to the Clerk of the Courts. However, that attorney has no *locus standi* and can take no part in the prosecution of the matter or give any formal instructions. Any advice, suggestions, or other assistance from an attorney who is watching proceedings may only be used as the Clerk of the Courts deems proper.

## *Habeas Corpus* Applications

These applications are made by the defence attorney, to the Court, pursuant to section 286 of the Judicature (Parish Courts) Act, to have the Judge of the Parish Court enquire into the circumstances under which an accused remanded in custody has not been charged. In *habeas corpus* applications, the attorney files four sets of the application at the court's office. These are duly stamped or sealed with the court seal, and the attorney is advised of the date when the Parish Court can accommodate the matter.

This date is endorsed on all the applications, one of which remains at the court's office. The application is listed in the court sheet of any available sitting court. Service is then effected on the sub-officer in charge of the facility where the suspect is being held and acknowledged by both the Court and an officer at the relevant police station.

Before the court date, the Clerk of the Courts should check with the facility where the suspect is being held so that the suspect can be brought before the Court. At the same time, a copy of the stamped and dated application is also sent to the facility by the attorney. So the checks by the Clerk of the Courts are really only additional efforts to ensure that the accused faces the Court on the specific date in the application.

Chapter 25

# Back Desk

## Summary

The back desk is a vital part of the court's organizational system as it is a key record repository.

It is where completed case files are held. When matters have been fully disposed of in the courts, the case files are sent to the back desk through the relevant channels of court administrative procedure. Notably,

1. It houses many of the official books used in the court system when they are finished.

2. Interested parties may make requests about disposed of matters that were before the courts.

3. The disposed of case files and the various official court books that are received from the courts on the court building are logged in a records book so that a proper record of all the items is kept.

## Individual Case File

This is usually filed chronologically and per the information numbers. If the case file is removed for some purpose, the slot remains until it is sent to the back desk for placement accordingly.

## Court Sheets

Court sheets from all the courts housed in the courthouse are sent to the back desk when they are finished.

## Applications for Results

Persons can make requests about the results of matters. To request the result of a matter, a form supplied by the court must be completed. There is no fee attached to the request. All requests are logged and list the nature of the request, the name of the applicant, the date, and other particulars.

Specifically, the staff at the back desk uses the information provided by the applicant to find the requisite court sheet and case file. The particular information requested on the matter is provided in letter form, usually in multiple copies. The letter, the case file, and the court sheet are perused together by the Clerk of the Courts to ensure that the correct information is being recorded. The letter is then signed by the Clerk and sealed with the court stamp.

The applicant signs to acknowledge receipt of the letter in the book in which the request was logged initially.

It is not unheard of for applications to be made many years after a matter has been disposed of and, as such, careful recordkeeping is critical. Court case information can be requested by accused persons, complainants, and organizations with an interest in the matter. The latter often includes employers of accused or complainants.

Where the records are not found for a matter, when the letter is generated, the court copy is usually kept with the application in a folder. The folder consists of all such requests for each year.

## Criminal Index

The criminal index details for each year, an alphabetical listing of the names of accused persons, the offences, the results of the case, and the specific sentence, if any. If necessary, the index can generate letters regarding the outcome of a matter. Therefore, the criminal index is important if no other record on a matter can be found.

## Warrants

Unexecuted warrants are filed in a folder according to the year in which they are returned.

Executed warrants are placed on the respective case file if it is at the back desk. Then the case file is sent to Return Court (for practical purposes, the matter is now 'new' again!). If the Return Court is not sitting, but there is another court sitting, the matter of the warrant can be dealt with there as well.

If the case file is still in the system, the warrant is sent to the Return Court assistant. The case file is located and the warrant placed thereon. The matter is then dealt with as noted above.